THIS DARK WORLD

THIS DARK WORLD

A MEMOIR OF SALVATION
FOUND AND LOST

CAROLYN S. BRIGGS

BLOOMSBURY

Published by Bloomsbury, New York and London
Distributed to the trade by Holtzbrinck Publishers

Library of Congress Cataloging in Publication Data

Briggs, Carolyn S., 1955–
This dark world : a memoir of salvation found and lost / Carolyn S. Briggs.
p. cm.
ISBN 1-58234-161-3
1. Briggs, Carolyn S., 1955- 2. Christian biography--United States.
3. Ex-church members--United States--Biography. I. Title.

BR1725.B495 A3 2002
280'.4--dc21
[B]
2001052440

Author's note: The names of some individuals and places have been changed.

First U.S. Edition 2002

10 9 8 7 6 5 4 3 2 1

Typeset by Hewer Text Ltd, Edinburgh
Printed and bound in the United States of America by
R.R. Donnelley & Sons, Harrisonburg, Virginia

For David who walks with me in light
and for my children shining there.

I took it up, and held it in my hand. I was a trembling, because I'd got to decide, forever, betwixt two things, and I knowed it. I studied it a minute, sort of holding my breath, and then says to myself,

"All right, then, I'll go to hell" – and tore it up.

– Mark Twain
The Adventures of Huckleberry Finn

This story is an accurate account of events, according to my memory. I have systematically changed the names of people and places. Some identifying characteristics have been altered to protect the privacy of those involved.

LOST

When I was in second grade, our family was nearly wiped out in a single night. We rented a farmhouse near the town dump. It was tall and white, a homestead as plain and windswept as the next on the Iowa landscape. The winter I was seven, Daddy stacked bales of hay around the foundation and tacked Visqueen over the windows. Even then, we were cold. We wore heavy sweaters and shoes and socks whenever we were up. Sometimes I tried to wear mittens, but Momma made me take them off. "You're not that cold," she said.

My little sister and I rode the school bus each day. We had learned to cover our mouths as we waited for the bus to come to keep the spit from freezing on our lips, cracking the corners of our mouths. We wore boots with artificial fur around the top and coats two sizes too big so that we could wear them another year. We weren't regular country kids because we didn't have a farm. We lived by the dump, and something always was smoldering on the hill behind our house. Old mattresses and recliners, pot scrapings and potato peels, bones gnawed clean. All of this burned and filled the valley with a lingering stench. When the bus pulled off the main highway and drove toward our house, the other kids teased us by plugging their noses. "Ooh," they'd squeal. "It smeeells!" "It smells like someone farted!" "It smells like some dead guy farted!" My sister and I laughed too and plugged our noses to prove that we also thought it was stinky. But it was clear that we weren't supposed to join in. The yellow Allendale School District bus plowed through the rancid haze; the door split

1

open and we were home. As we pulled off our coats, I only had one question.

"How are the pigs doing, Momma?"

My mother had agreed to try her hand at rescuing the runts of the litter from certain death. For every piglet she saved, our farmer landlord would take ten bucks off the rent. Momma was always fussing with these sucklings, the ones the sow refused to feed. I remember scrutinizing the piglets, examining them for blemishes and shortcomings, wondering what it was about them that their mother had shunned.

My mother nursed them with milk from baby bottles and kept them in the oven in a newspaper-lined box. Gentle heat wafted through the linoleum kitchen from the open oven door. I loved peeking in at the piglets and seeing their hairless little bodies squirm in comfort and warmth. I gave them unimaginative names like Pinky and Curly, and I wrote stories about our tiny pigs in my Big Chief tablet, in which they grew up to be wonderfully clever pigs, talking ones, and always very clean.

But most of the time the pigs didn't make it. When they died, Daddy loaded the box in the car and drove down the gravel road to the bridge over the Raccoon River. He unceremoniously dumped the little pigs over the railing. They made big splashing sounds and then disappeared for a minute. When the piglets made their way back to the surface, I always felt a strange elation – it was the nearest thing I'd seen to resurrection. I'd scream, "There's Pinky! I see him!" Momma didn't let us watch for long. I'd be upset for the next few days, and then we'd get a new Pinky, a new Wilbur, and I'd start all over.

It was late January and I sat at the kitchen table with my tablet in front of me, but all I could do was lay my head on my arm and watch the pigs out of the corner of my eye. Momma had a bad headache and wore her pink robe on top of her clothes.

She was a hardworking woman; our house was always spotless, the dishes done and the beds made. My mother never let down and never stopped working, but all day long she had moved very slowly, softly brushing my forehead with the back of her hand whenever she passed me. We were all sick with the flu; my brother and sister lay on opposite ends of the couch, alternately watching a soap opera and napping. They were only five and three and whined for Mother's attention. I was old enough to know she was sick, too. I watched her and I watched the pigs, but I didn't ask for anything. When Momma brought me graham crackers and milk, I slid them far away; just the thought of the cloying sweetness of a cracker packed in my molars and gums made me dizzy with nausea.

We made it through the day and rallied only when Daddy came home from work bringing a pot of soup Grandma had sent. Momma served bowls of the greasy chicken broth with the lumpy, formless noodles Grandma made. We laughed about Grandma's noodles. "Bless her," Momma said. "She doesn't know how to make soup, but she has a good heart." We didn't eat much. Momma cleaned the kitchen and washed the dishes, and Daddy said he was going to lie down and try to get rid of his headache.

That's when the story could have ended. We all fell asleep in that early evening, the Iowa sky graying into darkness while our little pigs died unattended. When my father's alarm clock sounded the next morning, we did not move. Not one of us. My parents were in their double bed, their bodies twined into each other, my father's work uniform buried in the folds of my mother's pink chenille robe. My sister held our baby brother on the couch, both motionless. I had made my way to my bed upstairs, the coldest part of the house. I was still wearing my shoes.

Grandma panicked when we didn't answer the phone that morning. She knew we were all sick. She knew we had to be there. She called Daddy at work and learned that he had not showed up that morning. She called our neighbor and pleaded with him to go look. He agreed, I'm sure a bit reluctantly, to drive down the narrow lane to our house. He saw our Plymouth parked in the driveway, but no one answered the door, though the television could be plainly heard and an alarm clock rang endlessly. When our neighbor axed down the door, he found us all unconscious. He tried to rouse us but failed. Mom and Dad couldn't speak, could barely open their eyes, their limbs rubber and useless. My brother and sister and I were red tinged, hearts laboring for oxygen, our blood swilling lazily through our arteries. The neighbor threw open the doors and windows and called the ambulance. Our chimney had been blocked by birds' nests, frozen and clogged completely by the recent ice storm, and we had been poisoned by carbon monoxide, hours away from certain death, but we had been saved.

We had been *saved*. Maybe that was when I began my search for the salvation that comes outside myself, the man with the ax, the redeemer who will bring me out of my slumber and wake me up. Prince Charming with his kiss. Jesus Christ with his passion, his thorn-wrapped heart. Save me, someone.

I was perceptive enough, even then, to doubt I could save myself. I spent the first sixteen years of my life being the short girl, the one who looked like a little kid, the one to whom grown-ups used baby talk even when I was in junior high. My grandmother called me a dwarf once, simply a joke, but in her remark, I heard a slip. I knew there had actually been a dwarf in our family, some relative of Grandma's from Missouri. I had seen pictures of him wearing tiny overalls and holding a pipe in his short, fat fingers. I was convinced that Grandma had let out the family secret.

And when a traveling salesman stopped at our house with a child-size accordion, it appeared my fate was sealed.

4

The salesman was from Duluth. He strapped the silver-and-red monstrosity over my shoulder, stood behind me, and put his large, doughy fingers on top of mine. He pressed my fingers onto the keys: Up and down the scale we went; "Mary had a little lamb . . . ," we went; "One little, two little, three little Indians . . . ," we went; and all the while he stretched the accordion apart and then pushed it back together. I could smell coffee and cigarettes on his breath and feel the scratchy lapel of his suit on my cheek. I felt swallowed whole, as if I had disappeared right inside the salesman. By the time we were done with our recital, he turned to Mother with great excitement.

"She's got real talent, ma'am," he said. "You don't see this kind of natural ability very often."

Mother politely asked for prices and terms while I stood with my arms at my side, looking down at the gleaming white keys and the rows of tiny silver buttons. It was cold and silent in the kitchen again, no *whoosh* of air and coffee, just me in my saddle shoes trying to keep from toppling over.

"And she might like to make it a career, you never know. Tiny little girl like that playing an accordion, well, that'd really be something," he was saying.

I pictured myself a thirty-year-old dwarf with an accordion strapped to my chest. Little children staring and mothers trying to turn them away while my sturdy little legs tapped out time, my hands flying up and down the keyboard. I would work for the circus, probably, and I would have a clever name: Tiny Tina or Midge the Midget.

Mother turned the salesman down. "I just don't think we can afford it," she said softly.

The salesman shook his head in regret.

"I hate to see you pass up this opportunity, ma'am. I really do. How about you, short stuff? Don't you want to play the accordion?"

"No," I whispered. "It's too heavy." Tears sprang to my eyes then. The burden of looking out for myself seemed almost too much to bear.

My parents rented apartments and houses for several years of my childhood, always in and around Allendale. Thirteen times we moved, and each time, my mother had the beds set up with fresh sheets and bedding, the kitchen and bathroom scrubbed, dishes and pots and towels stacked neatly on new shelf paper in each cupboard, all of this before she put us to bed in our new bedrooms. Mother would stay up as late as she had to in order to unpack the rest of the boxes. When we woke up the next morning, it was our home again, all the same pictures and drapes, the tablecloths and candles, and everything gleaming from polish and wax.

An orderly universe, that's what Mother demanded. All of her energy went into maintaining a tidy world for us to live in. Make no mistake about it, my mother loved her children ferociously, but she kept our complexities, our lusts, and our fears at bay. These went unacknowledged. By her hands and her sweat and her labor, she kept potential disasters manageable. Therefore, cleanliness was the first principle in our home. We all had to keep at it, scrubbing windowsills, sponging down mopboards, vacuuming, vacuuming, vacuuming. Mother's only other recognized foe was illness. She wanted us to be well; she worried about our health constantly. We took vitamins; we ate right. We went to the doctor a lot, every sniffle, every fever. Mother was a vigilant nurse, staying up all night with my brother and his earaches, bringing us tea and toast and new books from the library when we had the flu.

I suppose all children grow up in the present tense, with little allusion to the past or future, but in our house especially so. If I hadn't known better, I would have assumed my life was always going to be safely contained in my house and my elementary school, with regular trips to the library and the municipal swimming pool. There was no mention of puberty, other horizons, or life beyond Allendale. That's why I listened carefully when my aunts made prophecies about us, when my aunts alluded to a life other than the one Mother controlled. My mother may not have paid attention to her sisters' forecasts, but I did.

Especially when they talked about me and Lisa.

My little sister, Lisa, grew past me before I had even started school. For a year or two before, family pictures show that we were just about the same height: two little girls in pinafores with our arms around our little brother, Chris. He was half our height, with a wide, happy face, pale, and ears that stuck straight out. He wore suspenders and bow ties and looked frail from his constant battle with ear infections. Lisa and I looked hearty in comparison, well nurtured and neatly dressed. Lisa's hair was not just blond, it was platinum, white and naturally curly. And soon it became clear that she was going to be supermodel tall, graceful, head-turning.

"She's always going to get attention, Ellen," my aunts would tell my mom. "That one's going to be a handful. The men won't leave her alone, that's for sure."

Mother always looked surprised when her sisters issued these kinds of warnings about Lisa. I don't think she could picture us as anything but children. Parenthood wasn't that complicated as far as she was concerned; her job was to keep us fed and clean and safe. My mother wasn't the kind of mother who invited confidences or asked you questions about your day. She just asked if you had made your bed.

"And that one," Aunt Mary said, and nodded in my direction. I frowned at the shoe I was holding, so tiny, so impossible to get Barbie's permanently arched foot into. I held my breath. What? What would she say about me?

7

"She's going to be a late bloomer," Aunt Mary finished, and nodded as though she had made it so. "Wait and see."

Late bloomer, I mulled. That didn't sound like a good thing. But the other aunts weren't arguing, and one by one they glanced at me tenderly, kindly.

"When are the girls going to get braces?" Aunt Jill asked.

I clamped my teeth together and waited to see what Mom would say.

"Lisa is going to get them," Mom answered, and began to tear apart her sweet roll. "Not Carolyn; her teeth aren't so bad."

"Does she ever say anything about getting braces?" Aunt Jill asked softly, but I heard.

Every night I slept with the heel of my palm pressed against the top row of my teeth. I had heard somewhere that could work. I hoped to wake up with my teeth in perfect alignment after a few years of this self-treatment.

"It doesn't matter if she does," Mom said, sighing. "We can only afford them for Lisa."

I could hear Lisa playing outside, where she was climbing on the swing set with our cousins. She knew she was going to be the one to get braces; everyone agreed she needed them – her front teeth were wildly crooked, flared and serrated, a bit of a mess for a beautiful face like hers.

Lisa. The braces Lisa would get were only the first of many blessings I longed for as the firstborn. All my sense of justice in the universe was skewed by having Lisa for a sister. Everything that was meant for me ended up belonging to her. I had recently begun wearing her hand-me-downs. Our family portrait showed Lisa in the big-sister spot just because she was taller. Lisa standing in my place, smiling to beat the band, smiling as though she didn't know that was *my* place.

But Lisa was my little sister, and I loved her. She didn't tell on me when I did nasty little things to her, like the time I shoved her off a chair she was standing on. I had no particular malice in my heart at that moment, just opportunity. When she landed on her head, I felt bad and held her in my arms, begging her not to tell. Lisa did errands for me and talked to grown-ups I was too shy to approach. I'd tell her what to say or ask, and she always did. When I was too scared or nervous to sleep, Lisa let me come into her twin bed and then made no protest as I wrapped my arms and legs around her so I could calm myself. Nothing could happen to me as long as I was connected to Lisa. Lisa was too golden to be vulnerable to night terrors, but I knew I was marked.

Lisa was ten years old the day the orthodontist put braces on her teeth. We all drove to Iowa Falls for the procedure. My mom and dad went inside the office with her and told Chris and me to wait outside in the car. It was a long wait. I had brought books to read, so I was okay, but poor Chris had nothing to do but play with his plastic dinosaur figures. He kept up a running monologue as he played.

"I am Stegosaurus and I want some vegetables," he said as he moved the bright aqua dinosaur across the dashboard.

"He doesn't eat vegetables, Chris," I said without looking up from *Half Magic,* my favorite book, which I reread every summer.

"Yes, he does!" Chris protested. "He's not carnivorous. He's omnivorous. That means he eats vegetables." He was smug in his knowledge; everyone was impressed with a freckled little kid who said he was going to be a paleontologist.

"Veg-e-ta-tion," I said. "Not vegetables."

"Same thing," he shot back.

"Not either," I said, and kept reading. Chris wanted to keep it going, but it was suddenly too hot in the car and I was tired of waiting. I closed my book and sighed.

"When's Metal-Mouth getting out here?" Chris asked.

"Don't you dare call her that," I warned.

"When's Bucky the Beaver getting out here?" Chris then asked.

"Knock it off, Chris," I said. Pete Walden had called me that last week, and it still hurt. "It's dumb to call people names, you know that? Would you like someone to call you Big Ears?"

He clamped his hands over his ears and shook his head. He was very self-conscious about his ears, mostly because Mother used to tape them back while he slept – the same overnight theory I used with my overbite.

"*Tyrannosaurus rex* is looking for a nice tasty . . ." He shifted around his Tinkertoy can of figures and pulled a midnight blue horned dinosaur out. "Triceratops! That's what he's hungry for!" Chris clashed the dinosaurs together and made chewing, tearing, angry sounds. He lurched back and forth on the front bench seat of the Fairlane. He leaned against the horn and it blared long and loud.

Chris froze and looked at me with panic. "I didn't mean to!"

I looked at the dentist's big red door. If it didn't open in just another minute, we'd be all right. Then it opened. Dad came barreling out. He was scowling and shaking his head. We all got spanked occasionally; sometimes he'd whip off his belt at one sassy word. He jerked open the driver's-side door and slid inside like an athlete, one motion, all muscle and determination.

"Goddamn it, kids," he said. "What do you think you're doing?"

"I didn't mean to do it, Daddy," Chris said, scrambling down to the floorboard. "Sorry. Sorry."

"Why are you horsing around in here? Can't you just behave yourselves? Jesus Christ, your sister is in there having a hell of a time and you two are out here acting like you don't have a goddamned bit of sense," he said. He was swearing a lot, even for him. I could see he was more upset than an accident with the horn would warrant.

He shook a cigarette out of the pack and put it between his lips. He struck a match on the canvas ceiling and lit his Marlboro. He didn't look at me; he just turned his head toward the window. "She's almost done – they've got her rigged up with more wires than you've ever seen." He took a deep drag and held it for a minute. He let it out in a sudden exhalation.

"You two better be God-blessed nice to her, do you hear me? Her mouth's sore and she's feeling pretty bad. Jesus Christ, I hope you look out for her, Carolyn. People are going to give her a hard time, I'm afraid," he said, and looked at me in the rearview mirror.

I looked at his eyes in the mirror and nodded. "I will, I will, Dad, I promise. I'll take care of her, OK? Don't worry."

He nodded back, just once, and threw his cigarette out the window. "I'm going to go back in now. You two hold it down, OK? No more horsing around."

Chris and I were silent when he left. He put his dinosaurs away in the can. I kept my book closed and watched the big red door.

It was another half hour before the door opened. When Lisa appeared, I was so primed for compassion that I wept before I even saw her face. Her shoulders were hunched in her brown teddy bear coat. She had pulled her face backward into the hood; I could see only a fringe of light brown fur and an empty place in the middle. I waited for her to get closer. Oh, God, she was a monster. She was wearing a huge external headgear that attached to the wires on her teeth; an enormous, thick metal bar protruded from her lips like a coat hanger. Her face was red and mottled. When she sat down beside me, I could feel her arms and legs tremble. I put my arm around her and pulled her close.

"Lisa," I whispered. "Oh, darling, I love you." I had heard Cary Grant say that in a movie once, and I had always wanted to say it to someone. Part of me was thrilled with the drama of the afternoon. It was a break from the quiet unfolding of my days.

She didn't respond; she just stared straight ahead. My mom and dad sat in the front seat and didn't turn around.

My mother sighed.

Dad peeled away from stop signs, slamming the accelerator once we got out into the country. Chris clung to one of his dinosaurs and looked at the floor. Mother sighed again. Lisa cried quietly.

It was going to be a half-hour drive home.

I kept my arm firmly around Lisa and tried to think of something to say. I couldn't tell her she looked fine or that no one would make fun of her or that it would not last forever because we were ten and twelve and two years is forever.

Finally I did the only thing I could. I told her a story. In my mad and selfless state, I gave up my role as heroine and let Lisa be the star. I knew Chris was listening, so I put in lots of dinosaurs and used their correct names just as he did. Lisa was a ravishing princess with straight and beautiful teeth who rode a *Tyrannosaurus rex* bareback, vanquishing the orthodontists in the land – a shamelessly opportunistic tale, but I was already aware of the way words could seduce and the places they could take you. We drove back to Allendale and passed through twenty-five miles of little towns that Rand McNally would eventually stop naming. The story grew more and more elaborate. She stopped trembling and listened closer and closer – everything but the story had vanished for her. I loved feeling my sister slump into my shoulder, surrender.

CHEAT

I cheated regularly in Sunday school. Even though Mom and Dad weren't religious people, Mom thought it would be good for us to get some exposure to religion, so they dropped us off and went home to read the Sunday *Des Moines Register* in peace. My sister and brother and I had to endure the hour-and-a-half indoctrination, inaccurately called Children's Hour, on our own. I had never encountered hubris like that found in kids who have memorized entire books of the Bible in exchange for a week of Bible summer camp.

Knowing the right answers had become very important to me. Although grown-ups knew things I did not, I had found books to be the most reliable source for answering the kinds of questions I had. I ate with one on the table, I practiced piano with an open book in front of my memorized sheet music, I slept with another under my pillow. Sometimes I would finish reading a book and bring it to my face, just pressing it to my cheek out of love and gratitude. I had read my way through the children's shelves and was beginning the young adult shelves at the Allendale Public Library. (Here I was running into problems because Mrs. Hillsborough, the head librarian, was also a member of Allendale Baptist. She told me which books I could and could not check out, often pushing back my selections with a firm shake of her head.) I had made good headway at the school library as well, where my name appeared on the junior high honor roll. I was a smart kid, a bookworm, but I was out of my league on Sunday morning; there was no way I could compete with the righteous kids at

Allendale Baptist Church. My mom and dad knew nothing about the Bible – I couldn't ask for their help. And I wasn't willing to read the foreboding thing; I rebelled at the King James language every time. No, the only answer to maintain my self-image as a smart kid was to cheat. I had no choice.

It was agonizing to be dropped into the middle of the righteous elect. I knew and they knew that Lisa, Chris, and I were not of their kind. I especially dreaded making my way through the crowded foyer after Sunday school. The families stood intact before the heavy vestibule door, waiting to enter the holy of holies, eleven o'clock church. They began reading the newest issue of the *Baptist Bulletin* and reviewed the chart of numbers on the wall listing last Sunday's attendance and offering. These pillars of the church scanned the crowd and nodded at each other, thrusting forth hands for body-shaking handshakes. I was waist level, so what I remember best are the gloved hands that clutched patent-leather pocketbooks, the black Bibles that everyone carried, and the arms that encircled waists or wrapped around the shoulders of children on their way to the sanctuary. Those same children knew me from Children's Hour, but they didn't let on they knew me when they saw me upstairs in Big Church.

My seventh-grade Sunday school teacher was a farmwife named Mrs. Frommer. She was intimidating in her own right, red hair and black-rimmed glasses with a six-foot-one frame, every inch straining toward God. She intended to save us from hell and the Catholic boys, both threats to the Christian girl. The fattest and most righteous girl in class, Sarah Wilkins, filled out her quarterly *Far Out with Jesus* carefully, complete with notes and cross-references. She had memorized the entire book of I Peter last summer and earned a week at Clear Lake Bible Camp. She wore a gold cross around her neck and open Bible earrings. At the close of our lesson, she was the only one to pray out loud, and she always asked God to make her a soul winner. I copied from her open quarterly every chance I got. When Mrs. Frommer called on me, I would give her Sarah's answers. Sarah always reacted the same way, a quick look of surprise and suspicion, and sometimes she would move her quarterly away, but it was too late by then, I already had the right answers. The next Sunday I would choose the folding metal chair next to her and begin to fill out my quarterly whenever Sarah turned her head or was distracted with hymn singing or praying. Mrs. Frommer had no choice but to acknowledge that I had answered the questions correctly and very exhaustively.

"Do you want any more cross-references?" I'd ask. "I've got more."

"No, thank you, dear," Mrs. Frommer said, smiling indulgently. " 'Thy word have I hid in my heart,' is that it?"

"Yep," I answered. I don't know how to explain the perverse streak that somehow took root in my timid psyche. There was an audacity, a sassiness, that popped out from time to time. I liked that about myself, but I didn't know how to enlarge or predict it.

"Your flesh, dear. It's your carnal spirit, the one Jesus Christ came to save." That was what Mrs. Frommer would have said.

I suspected I needed saving, but I also knew I could never be a Mrs. Frommer or a Sarah. I didn't want to be, either.

After class, I steeled myself to walk the length of the foyer, right through that Red Sea of the Chosen People. I wanted to walk with dignity, but I never did. I half loped, and when I saw the large glass doors leading to the outside, I dashed the last few feet past the cheaply framed pictures of missionaries on the wall, every one of them looking haggard and uncomfortable. Outside in the parking lot, Mother waited in the red Fairlane convertible. My mom was stunning, her hair auburn and piled on her head. She was long legged and wore halter tops in those days. Draping her graceful freckled arms over the side of the door, she sat there with her head leaning back into the headrest, just smiling up into the sun. The deacons could never resist standing close to her car. Their job was to direct parking, but my mom kept them distracted. They called out things to get her attention, like "Nice day" or "Looks like rain," just so she would look at them. She smiled at them but rolled her eyes when she told Dad about them later. I said that one of the deacons looked just like the Neanderthal man in the encyclopedia, so we called him Link after that.

Before we stopped going to Sunday school entirely, I did have an encounter, a moment when I felt something my jaded self could not explain. The pastor of Allendale Baptist Church was a large man, so enormous that he couldn't even find a shirt to fit him in Allendale; his wife drove across three counties to the Big and Tall Men's Shop to buy his beautiful suits. And he did dress impeccably, in spotless, starched white shirts, emerald green and sapphire silk ties, and gray trousers that fell into delicate pleats along his tree trunk legs. His brown hair was combed neatly in waves across his forehead. The women in our church especially loved him; even my mother asked me casually if I had seen Pastor Jim lately. He preached children's sermons at vacation Bible school without any thumping of the pulpit or Bible. Something about his voice made me want to listen. Even if I was doing a crossword puzzle or connect-the-dots, my pen would hover over the page as something about Pastor Jim's cadence or tone caught my attention. Many times, I turned off the smart-ass commentator in my brain and just watched the show of Pastor Jim. He laughed easily and he wasn't afraid to cry, but when he did cry, it was just like Jesus on the cross; two or three tears would make their way down his cheek, and Pastor Jim just looked at us as if he were asking how come we had to go and be such sinners when he loved us so? Sometimes I'd cry with him, nodding my agreement.

It was July, and I had just finished seventh grade. I was too old to be at vacation Bible School anymore, but Mother had insisted that I go one more year. I had been enduring the two weeks of VBS by silently mocking the change purses we were making for all the poor native children of Colombia, South America (tanned buckskin with three-dimensional crosses etched into the hide), who most likely had no change, but no matter, Jesus was pleased with the willingness of our clumsy little fingers. I also coveted the day's treat: a good-size Snickerdoodle, a soft cookie with sugar and cinnamon on top. I politely turned down the warmish Kool-Aid that accompanied the cookie, feeling I was too sophisticated for a little kid's drink.

After Pastor Jim finished, it would be time to claim that cookie. I didn't feel like listening to any sermon. But Pastor Jim was crying again, and I had to see why.

"It's the Lamb of God, precious children. He's knocking on the door of your heart, gently, gently. Can you hear Him now? Listen! There it is, that soft little tap. Tap, tap, tap. Oh, so softly. Jesus is a gentleman, children. He's not going to go barging into your house without your invitation. Won't you let Him in, little children? Let Him in. . . ."

I did feel something. I couldn't deny it. There was something on the inside of me that hadn't been there five minutes ago. I didn't know if it was a tap on my heart or what. I didn't recognize it; I didn't know what to call it. I just knew I felt something tingling inside of me, as though I had to go to the bathroom, maybe. It was a sense of urgency like that.

"He loves you so, oh, how He loves you and me. . . . Take that chain off, pull open the door latch, it's Jesus! Look, children, it's Jesus! He's waiting for you! Oh, precious, precious Jesus, how we love You. How we throw open the doors of our lives and welcome You! Oh, sweet Savior. . . ."

When Pastor Jim asked us to raise our hands if we were

going to let Jesus into our hearts, I couldn't keep my hand down. It went up, all on its own, just thrust itself into the thick, still air of the church sanctuary. I remember looking curiously at my arm. It was straight and unwavering and reaching for something. I was not the kind of girl who liked to draw attention to myself, but this morning I didn't care who was watching. This was between Pastor Jim and me. When he began to lumber toward me, I felt close to swooning.

Pastor Jim laid his hands on my shoulders and prayed over me. I felt swallowed up and conscious of Pastor Jim's hands, large and warm, spread over my frame and soaking me in. Carolyn, all I knew of me, was absorbed into something, *Someone,* strong and capable and all-knowing. It felt right, this disappearance, like something I had been expecting. It was definitive, opposite of the ennui that cocooned me, and I was, more than anything else, relieved. There was something else, then. There was more to life than what appeared to be so.

I kept waiting to shake hands with Jesus or something. I squinched my eyes and tried to see His face, happy and welcoming, but I didn't see anything except bluish squiggles. Pastor Jim's hands began to feel sweaty on my blouse. His belt buckle grazed the back of my neck, sending a sudden shiver down my back and my legs. I shifted in my seat until he let up and moved to the next kid two rows up. I knew there was some protocol, that there were certain appropriate acts one did after being saved. I thought about falling on my knees or burying my face in my hands the way people did at the Billy Graham crusades Grandma watched on TV. I was pretty sure I should be crying, but I couldn't work up any tears. Finally I picked up the hymnal and started singing along with everyone else. "Oh, Lamb of God, I come. I come. Just as I am without one plea but that Thy blood was shed for me."

By the time we got to the fourth verse of "Just As I Am," I began to feel self-conscious. I tried to remember the euphoria I had felt moments ago, but I couldn't. I looked down at my lap. Back to my scabby knees and too short dress and ugly sandals. I was surprised that my encounter with the Almighty was such a flash in the pan. It should have lasted longer, shouldn't it have? Did that mean it didn't take? Did that mean that God/Pastor Jim weren't all that impressed with my signing on? I tried not to look around at the church kids, the good ones who had been saved when they were preschoolers or at least by first grade. They weren't going to buy my conversion, I knew that. The grown-ups at church would crow about it and pat me on the head, but not those kids. They knew an outsider when they saw one. But still, maybe now that Pastor Jim had singled me out the way he just had, maybe now they'd give me a chance.

On one side of me sat Sarah Wilkins. On the other was Ruth Ann Evans. Both from upstanding Baptist families, their fathers were deacons; their mothers were teachers in vacation Bible school. I debated – whom should I turn to to check my status? Sarah was definitely the holier of the two, but that might work against me if her standards were too high. Ruth Ann was prettier than Sarah, and that made her a little more worldly and open-minded when it came to newly repentant sinners. At least, that's what I hoped. I turned toward Ruth Ann and raised my eyes to meet hers.

She was torn, I could see that immediately. She didn't want me in the fold; it was clearly her domain, this world of the sanctified elect; but if God had wanted me, how could she protest? She smiled at me, but it was phony and cold, a slippery smile that dissolved immediately. I smiled back, a habit, a plea.

Let me do this, I smiled.

Of course not, she smiled back. *You do not belong here.*

Please, I smiled one last time.

Your mother's outside waiting in your convertible, she smiled for the last time. *Run on out there.*

Pastor Jim finished the invitation, and the last chord of the organ stretched out underneath his "Amen". The children and teachers began gathering their belongings. I leaned back in the pew to allow Ruth Ann and her friends to squeeze by me. No one met my eyes; they were embarrassed by my audacity. I had accepted an invitation that I should have recognized as only a polite gesture, not one of true intent. The miscue began to sink in to me. Idiot, I chided myself. Nobody was inviting you anywhere.

But then Pastor Jim called out.

"Shelly, Carolyn, Tim! Please come and see me a minute." He stood at the front of the auditorium, mopping his face with a big handkerchief. As I got closer, I saw the flourishing *J* embroidered on the corner. He nodded at the steps leading to the choir loft.

"Have a seat," he said, and then he began to sit down with us. He flipped his tie over his shoulder and hitched up his dress pants. He eased himself down on one of his haunches and then settled onto the other as his Old Spice wafted over us. I could see the pulse in his neck – I was that close.

"This has been quite a day in heaven," he began. He looked at us one by one, and I imagined his eyes lingered on me. "Do you know why?"

" 'Cause we asked Jesus into our heart?" Tim ventured. He was a scrawny little kid the church bus picked up from Allendale's only apartment building. He belonged here even less than I did. He didn't even have a dad.

Hearts, I corrected silently. *We all have our own heart, moron.* I panicked at my sinful response. Oh, it was true, then – I wasn't saved. I couldn't have Jesus living inside of me and still have thoughts like this. Jesus would never call anyone "moron".

"That's right, buddy," Pastor Jim said, and put his arm around Tim's thin shoulders. The wave of jealousy that filled me confirmed my suspicions. I was definitely still a sinner.

But Pastor Jim didn't know it, and he kept smiling at me as he did the others. He looked at us as though we were his kids or something, as though we were his *favorites*. "Today in heaven there is a celebration like nothing you've ever seen. There's a parade of angels, did you know that? The angels are beating the big bass drum, playing tiny little flutes, shiny bright horns, and they're marching down the golden streets celebrating the three new souls who will live in heaven forever and ever."

I laughed nervously. Tim and Shelly looked at me, trying to figure out the joke.

"It's amazing, I agree, Carolyn," Pastor Jim said, and closed his eyes in prayer. "Father, thank You for bringing these new lambs in Your kingdom. Thank You for being the Lamb without Blemish and for dying on the cross for our sins. Oh, Jesus, how we thank You for this day, this day of salvation. Amen and amen."

When I opened my eyes after the amens, I saw my mom standing at the back of the auditorium. She looked out of place in her short-shorts. The church moms wore below-the-knee skirts and stiff white blouses that buttoned all the way to the top. I wanted to rush her out before anyone saw her, but it was too late. Pastor Jim waved at her and said, "Two minutes, Ellen!"

"Take your time," she said easily. "It just got too hot out there in the parking lot."

"Oh, it's a scorcher, that's for sure," he said, and then turned back to us.

"Now, before you go, little brother and sisters," he began. Oh! He called me sister, but of course, he didn't know I was an impostor. "The Word of God says that you must give testimony about the new life you've found. You need to tell others how you have been born again! A brand-new life – how about that? I want you to tell at least one person today what happened to you, OK? Carolyn, you're lucky because your mother is right here. Go tell her, honey."

I couldn't even rejoice over the "honey" because I was suddenly filled with dread. Mom liked us going to Sunday school and vacation Bible school, but I knew she would be embarrassed if I told her about Jesus saving me from my sins – it was the kind of thing Mother would call nobody's business. Mother didn't like to talk about private things. As I walked across the auditorium, I let my fingers linger on the edge of each pew, my mind racing, trying to figure out how to please Pastor Jim and not embarrass myself or my mom with my announcement.

Pastor Jim just didn't understand what my family was like.

Our family wasn't like the families at Allendale Baptist. We didn't talk about *anything* personal and certainly not religious stuff. My mom cleaned, and my dad worked, and when they weren't cleaning or working, we played. We listened to Perry Como records and watched Dean Martin on television. We all laughed at Foster Brooks' drunk-guy impersonation. My dad had tattoos, and my mom got a suntan every summer. This was our only concession to spirituality: At supper my sister and brother and I prayed a long word in unison – God-isgreatGodisgoodandwethankHimforourfoodamen. And my dad didn't even close his eyes; I knew because I watched him.

How could I tell Pastor Jim that our family just liked to mess around, that's all? God was just a swear word my dad used sometimes. My folks played cards, Twenty-one and poker, with their friends on Friday nights. They got together with my mom's huge family of brothers and sisters to eat fried-chicken picnics on splintery tables by the Iowa River in Marshalltown. We had a badminton net in the backyard, and we played boys against girls. Sometimes our family would all load into the car on a Saturday night, my brother and sister and I in our pajamas already, pillows and blankets under our arms. Mom filled big brown grocery sacks with freshly popped popcorn. It was my job to salt the popcorn and pick out the flavor of Kool-Aid. Lisa stacked our aluminum glasses (the colors of the rainbow) and carried them out to the car. After many trips back and forth from the house to the car, we were set to go to the drive-in theater in Iowa Falls. We kids watched most of the first feature from the backseat, trying to see around Mom's and Dad's heads, spilling our drinks, whining for hot dogs from the concession stand, and complaining that it was still light outside and we were in our pajamas; but it wasn't serious complaining. We were hyped up, stimulated by the proximity of our parents and the glamour of Hollywood. It was too much fun to fall asleep, but invariably we did before the second movie began. I can imagine how relieved my parents must have been when we finally quieted down. We were safely asleep, our faces sticky upon our pillows, and Mom and Dad were alone in the darkness, watching John Wayne gallop across the Iowa sky. They must have held hands and kissed a little.

They did kiss. We saw it all the time. Dad chased Mom around the house, a great game for us kids. She squealed and protested; he laughed and called her silly names like Ellen Wild Horse, and we kids followed from room to room, laughing and shouting. "She went that way, Dad!" "Watch out, Mom! He's coming!" And then she'd collapse on the floor, hiding her head, tucking her elbows to keep him from tickling her, but he'd sit on her and tickle her all the same, and we took it all in.

How would Pastor Jim understand that we just didn't pay much attention to God? His family probably prayed morning, noon, and night. Just that morning, he had been talking about the family altar, the family Bible session, and all the church kids nodded as though they knew what he was talking about.

And there she was, my beautiful mother in the white short-shorts, waiting for me at the back of the church. Behind me,

Pastor Jim depending on me to give witness to the gospel. I wished I could stay somewhere between the two of them and never commit to either. I could walk back and forth for the rest of my life, toward the cross, away from the cross. I –

"Carolyn! C'mon, pokey! We have to get the other kids," Mother said, and reached toward me. She gripped my shoulder and propelled me toward the door. The foyer was crowded with kids and teachers and parents. I walked stiffly and nervously, and all I could think of was Mom's white short-shorts. But nobody seemed to notice; in fact, nobody noticed my mom at all. They looked on all sides of her, but nobody called her name. I knew she would like it if they did, and suddenly I felt bad. I took her hand then and squeezed it. Neither my mom nor I belonged here. I wanted to hold her and comfort her. I wanted to wipe her tears away, but she wasn't crying.

We drove home from vacation Bible school in the convertible, our family car. Mother reached into the glove compartment for a silk scarf to tie over her hair. I sat up front with her, and Lisa and our little brother, Chris, sat in the backseat. Chris ducked to keep out of the wind. Lisa sat up straighter so her hair whipped back in a long golden wave. I just watched my mom. She looked like Princess Grace in her sunglasses and scarf. I admired her with all my heart. There was no way I could tell her about my encounter with God that morning. I felt guilty and sad about that, and I knew Pastor Jim would remind me that Jesus wasn't ashamed of me, why was I ashamed of Him? I turned away from Mom and looked up toward heaven. I whispered, "Don't be mad, OK? I love you, Jesus, OK?" I scanned the sky and waited for a sign. A fist-shaped cloud scudded into view. After that, I closed my eyes and leaned my head back.

We ate bacon-and-tomato sandwiches for lunch. Momma shared her Pepsi with me and gave me a quarter to go to the swimming pool that afternoon. I didn't think about God again, not once, until the next Sunday. I was awarded a new Bible with my name written inside, a gift from my Sunday school teachers in honor of my conversion. It was black and gold. Red letters were used for all of Jesus' words. I wished Jesus would just come on down and talk to me; Pastor Jim said he talked to Him all the time. I prayed, Say something just to me. Then I opened the Bible and let my finger fall on a Scripture. I hoped for something lovely and special from gentle Jesus meek and mild, but my finger always landed on some dietary law or an arcane detail of how many cedars were felled in Lebanon to build the temple. I tried to open toward the back where the red letters were, but the Bible stubbornly opened in the middle.

I sighed. It didn't seem worth pursuing, this life of faith. I didn't have enough. My family had less. I was going to have to go it alone.

ROGUE

By the time the braces came off my sister's teeth, no one could deny that Lisa was going to stand out in our little town. Allendale, a small town of three thousand, boasted a sky blue water tower, a town square with a bakery and pharmacy (complete with the soda fountain, Green Rivers and cherry Cokes), two hardware stores, a shop or two that were constantly going out of business and opening under new ownership, and three taverns. Fields of corn grew right up to the city limits sign on all the highways leading in and out of town. The sky was hopelessly black at night outside of Allendale, barely penetrated at all by the single halogen light found in all farmyards. Our town was only a little cluster of lights where we lived briefly, keeping our best ties at the back of the closet, our good dresses waiting in the dry cleaner's bags, and all of us stretching our dying as thin as we could.

In small towns, in the middle of the country, just past the middle of the century, this is all that mattered: sports. Football, track, baseball, and basketball – the sole raison d'être. My dad had made his mark this way. He had been the star receiver of the Allendale High School football team twenty years before, and people still remembered that. A little gridiron or basketball court fame can go a long, long way in the Midwest. By the time Lisa was in eighth grade, she was tall, coordinated, and not afraid of taking chances. My father's legacy fell to her.

And then there was this: She looked pretty good in the girls' basketball uniform. She had long legs and huge breasts,

breasts as large as any found in the soft porn hidden under the local boys' mattresses. High school boys began to attend Allendale Junior High School's girls' practice just to see my sister run laps. They stood in a clump and watched her run down the court and back, quick stops, starts, running backward. They never took their eyes from her.

I was the one who was in high school – the one who should have been noticed, not my little sister. But the boys who were drawn to my junior high sister were certainly not noticing me. I watched their eyes move over me without a trace of interest.

I had begun thinking of myself as almost invisible, a wisp of a girl who never fully materialized for anyone. But I was wrong about that – there were places I definitely stood out, and gym class was one. Allendale High School gym class comprised all four classes: freshman, sophomore, junior, and senior. After my usual humiliating performance in basketball or field hockey, the physical education coach blew on his whistle twice and we were herded back into the locker room to shower and change.

With women on all sides of me in various stages of undress, I tried to not look at their bodies, even though they didn't seem to care who saw them. They wore lacy bras and bikini underpants. Their bodies looked like my mother's, so grown-up, so sure of themselves, so unapologetically womanly. Their breasts spilled out of their bras, and they complained about their fat asses, all the while I quickly and silently peeled off my blue gym suit and reached for my school clothes.

I had a little girl's body, straight, flat, nothing but hard bones and wrists and ankles. I was hoping my hair didn't stink of sweat; I was wondering if I had a barrette in my purse to pin it back; I was thinking a dozen different things, and I didn't notice that a few girls had stopped dressing and had gathered around me, watching me dress.

I looked up and saw three of my classmates, at least three. They were all seniors and they were all staring at me. They looked as if they had just seen a freak, Elephant Man in the locker room. They stared at me, and I stood there letting them stare at me.

Then another senior girl across the room spoke up.

"Stop doing that, Marlene. It's not nice," she said. "Leave her alone."

"I just can't believe it, that's all," Marlene said, and with one last head-to-toe sweep of me, she looked away. "Jesus Christ."

The locker room became silent, a *whoosh*ing in my ears, a steady thrum of my hands and fingers smoothing my clothes, pulling the gold-ribbed body stocking over my pitiful chest and arms. I straightened the cuffs and turtleneck and then buttoned my skirt. I buckled my belt and then folded the part that was too long, tucking it under. It was a performance, my dressing. I did it slowly and systematically and tried to keep my hands from betraying me with any tremor. My face did not reveal anything, certainly not the fierce hatred I felt at that moment for Marlene. I hated her for thinking she could comment on me as if I weren't even there. My face was hot, oh God, I was going to cry and I would not let her know how she had made me feel. Quickly, I began conjugating Spanish verbs in my head – *hablo, hablas, habla, hablamos, hablan* – but I couldn't stop hearing the disgust in Marlene's voice, and I sank, weeping, onto the bench, one shoe on and the other in my shaking hand. The bell rang and the silent girls filed out. I didn't move – I just studied my shoe, my children's size thirteen shoe. I slid my foot inside the shoe and tied it. I decided I would dress in the toilet stall from then on. I was mad at myself for assuming I could be just another girl in the locker room. Idiot, I accused myself. Fool.

The rest of the day I saw girls whisper and glance my way.

Sometimes they'd laugh, and it was sharp, staccato, the kind of laugh that escapes before your good sense holds it in. I acted as though I didn't hear it.

Finally, the bell rang after seventh period. School was out. I stood at my coat locker in the sophomore hall, holding a pile of books on my chest. My locker had the required combination padlock that stymied me daily. I could not get the hang of opening it, no matter how many times my locker mate demonstrated the part where you go left two times. Often I just waited for her to come and open it. She always sighed and opened our locker, telling me to hurry and get my stuff. I was waiting for her to come and hoping that she would appear any minute when a senior boy stopped in front of me.

"Hi," he said, and smiled. He was so close, I could smell his cologne and I could see the hair on the backs of his hands. I knew his name. He was a jock, and I had watched him play varsity basketball for the last two years. I remembered all the times I had called, "You can do it, Cal!" at the top of my lungs in the anonymity of the crowded bleachers. Now that implied intimacy; the idea that I had the right to urge him to do anything made me feel like an idiot.

"Hi," I said, waiting. I tried to smile; I twisted my lips upward briefly. Cal Dawson. Talking to me.

"Are you Lisa Gilbert's sister?"

"Yeah," I said slowly. Lisa was in eighth grade. She was in junior high.

"What's your name, anyway?" he asked.

"Carolyn," I said, and my voice cracked. "Carolyn," I said again.

"Carolyn, huh? How come I've never seen you before? 'Cause you're such a squirt?" he asked. He pulled a toothpick out of his pocket and started digging at his teeth. "You're really in tenth grade?"

"Yeah," I said. "Sophomore."

He screwed up his face, shook his head. "C'mon."

"It's true. I'm a sophomore, class of '73 . . . ," I said, trailing off self-consciously at the end.

"No way you're old enough to be in high school," Cal said skeptically. He pointed his toothpick toward me when he said the word *you're*. I couldn't help it, I jumped, and he laughed.

"OK," I said. "Think whatever you want." But then I smiled and made direct eye contact, because *Young Miss* said that gave a boy the message that you were interested.

"Did you get promoted and skip a few grades? You some kind of genius?" Cal finished with the toothpick and put it back in his pocket. He looked over my shoulder and then behind his.

I was trying to think of a clever way to answer him. I knew I could make him laugh again if I just had another minute to come up with something. I smiled, stalling.

"Listen, I got to ask you something," he blurted.

"What?" My mind was racing. Could this be happening?

"The guys and me," he said, and stopped. "The guys and me wondered if your sister's boobs are real." And then this quickly: "You should know, are they?"

"Lisa?" I asked stupidly.

"Yeah, Lisa, your sister," he said impatiently. He lowered his voice. "The one with the huge tits, you know. The size of watermelons, I swear to God. Are they real or not?"

I blushed, instantly and fiercely. I had never talked to a boy about a woman's body before. It wasn't nice, that's what, and it wasn't something he should be asking. And then this: Deeper and fiercer than indignation, I was filled with jealousy. Cal Dawson was interested in Lisa, not in me.

"You think I'm going to tell you that?" I asked, and glared at him.

"C'mon, Carolyn. Tell me, please," he wheedled. He squeezed my forearm, and I looked down at his hand, so strong and firm, his AHS ring gleaming under the fluorescent lights.

The whole scene was absurd, and I knew it. I was humiliated; we were talking about my baby sister. All he wanted from me was information. I was aware of all that, but I didn't want to make him mad. I still wanted him to like me. I didn't even have enough integrity to tell him to go to hell.

"Why should I tell you anything?" I asked, my voice shaking.

" 'Cause you think I'm cute?" he suggested, and lightly touched my nose. "Because I think you're kind of cute?"

I buckled.

"OK," I said, and kept my eyes on my feet. I made myself look up. I made myself make direct eye contact with him again. I cleared my throat and said clearly, "They're real, all right."

His eyes lit up, hard and happy. "Goddamn! I knew it." He turned around to leave. "Thanks a lot . . . Kelly," he said, and disappeared down the hall.

My locker mate had arrived and had seen me talking to Cal. She looked at me curiously. Seniors didn't come into the sophomore hall very often, especially ones like Cal Dawson. She opened the lock and stepped back for me to get my books and pull out my coat and put it on. I put my clammy hands inside my mittens, my heart pounding so hard that I could barely hear my locker mate's questions.

"Well?" she asked when I turned around.

"What?"

"Why was he talking to *you*?" she asked.

"He needed to know something," I mumbled. I should have handled it differently. I should have told him I'd tell him tomorrow or the next day. I could have kept him going for a while, I knew that. I could have prolonged the whole exchange if I'd played it right.

31

I walked past the old gym, where the junior high teams practiced. The ceiling lights encased in giant metal baskets and the decades-old orange varnish on the bleachers and floor made everything golden. The junior high girls' team was running a lay-up drill. I saw Lisa's head bobbing above the rest, her curly blond ponytail swinging from side to side. I didn't stay to watch.

I loved my dad. And the one consolation I had at Allendale High School was that it was the same school my dad had attended. Other than new windows, things had changed very little since my dad had been an AHS football jock who, according to my mother, looked like a young Paul Newman. Whenever Dad told stories of how he had tormented and back-talked teachers, I ate it up, admiring his nerve and courage in the same adult world that stymied me. My science teacher had been his science teacher, and he had stood up to her. As punishment for his attitude, she had drawn a circle on the blackboard and told him to stand facing it with his nose in the center. The circle was just high enough that my dad would have to stand on his tiptoes to reach the center of the circle with his nose. She stood there with the chalk still in her hand and waved for him to come to the blackboard and take the position. Dad didn't move.

"Peter," she said in her no-nonsense voice, "I'm waiting."

Dad began to rub his temples and stare at the board.

"Peter," she said again, "come up here right now."

"God, Mrs. Kilpatrick," he said weakly. "I'm getting a migraine, right now. Ohhh," he groaned. "I'm seeing black dots before my eyes. . . ."

He stood up quickly and knocked his books on the floor before stumbling out the door. Everybody laughed, and there was nothing Mrs. Kilpatrick could do about it.

I told the other kids the story about my dad and Mrs.

Kilpatrick. Some believed me, but most of them said I was lying. Mrs. Kilpatrick would have kicked my dad's ass, they said.

But she didn't and I knew it. I bent over my worksheet on distance and time, and I kept a running monologue: You didn't boss around my dad, Mrs. Kilpatrick. Peter Gilbert was not intimidated by your mean brown eyes and your outsize waddle. He took care of you, all right. Do you even know I'm his daughter, Mrs. Kilpatrick? Maybe you should watch out for me.

An empty threat – I did my homework and volunteered for extra credit.

Sometimes I imagined my dad walked with me down the mosaic hallways. I could almost see him leaning against a locker with one arm draped around a girl while he sweet-talked her into meeting him that night at the Old Tower, the make-out spot by the river. She'd probably say yes; what girl would say no to the receiver who had won last Friday's game with an eighty-yard touchdown? This same boy had taken a dare to lie between railroad tracks and let a train run over him. The train was getting closer and closer, the whistle warning the teenage punks to get back, stay away. Instead, my dad threw away his cigarette and sauntered over to the tracks. With one quick salute to his awestruck friends, he positioned himself in the very middle of the track and lay down. The train ran over him and his friends screamed with laughter and horror and waited. Dad emerged splattered with oil and cinders and made a big show of examining his letter jacket for damage. He was shaking, he admitted to me, and sorry he had done it, because it had scared the shit out of him to have that train thundering over his face for what seemed like eternity; but there was no way he was going to let on that he was afraid.

Later at home, I read his old yearbooks and the scrapbooks

of his newspaper clippings. I loved seeing his name – my name – in bold headlines. Sometimes I asked him about the broken collarbone he had suffered in a game, tracing it with my finger. I went to his softball games all through my childhood, yelled his name when he stood at bat, longed for the crack of the ball and our validation in one glorious launch into the outfield.

He called me "Squirt". My size amused him. I loved nothing more than making him laugh. It was hard to do because he was smart and cynical, but when I said just the right sarcastic thing, he burst out laughing and loved me with all his heart.

I wanted him to believe I was worthy of his attention, so I told him stories about my general success in the world outside our door. I made up boys for him, boys who liked me. I'd mention casually that Craig or Gary or Bill had a crush on me. Sometimes he'd growl that a particular boy was not good enough for me and tell me to stay away from that one. "All right, Daddy," I'd agree reluctantly. "But he thinks I'm very cute."

"I'm sure he does," Dad would say sternly, "but that doesn't make any difference. He's not the one for you." My dad, unlike anyone else I knew, thought I was a good catch.

That fall, not long after the locker room fiasco, I did something right. I won the American Legion essay contest, but I didn't know it until the *Allendale Index* made the announcement and published my winning entry. Mother and I had just walked into the house with armloads of groceries in brown paper sacks when my dad practically flew from his chair. He took the groceries from my arms and set them on the floor, and then he hugged me to his chest. "What an essay, Squirt," was all he said. "What an essay." I sat down right in the middle of the floor and read my essay from the newspaper, my words typeset: "Why Fly the Flag?" by Carolyn Gilbert. I was surrounded by bananas and Wonder bread and cans of kidney beans while my dad beamed at me on the other side of the paper.

I had lived an unremarkable life, a quiet life of losing at dodgeball and listening to boys whistle at my little sister while I walked by her side. Coming in first place, seeing my name in a headline as the *winner* – well, it was heady stuff. My dad's approval sent me over the top. I cried. Mother called from the kitchen for the rest of the groceries. Daddy hugged me one more time, and then I scrambled to put the cans and boxes back in the brown paper bags.

When the prize arrived, a gigantic seven-foot American flag, I opened the box and read the instructions for display. Included was a reminder of flag etiquette: "The flag must be burned if it touches the ground." I was nervous after that and didn't want to unfurl it for fear it would touch the kitchen floor. I left the flag in the box and kept reminding Dad that we needed to mount it on the front of the house. I liked to think about the huge flag dominating the neighborhood and somehow advertising me.

But my flag was never displayed; it never made its way out of the box. Other things were happening in our household.

When I began to discern the slightest shift in my parents' dynamic with each other, I panicked. They never argued, never made a scene, and certainly never told us there was anything amiss. But there was. I could read my mother's face; I could hear the shift in my father's tone when he spoke to her. Something bad was happening to their marriage, and I began to track their movements and habits closely. I worried silently and fiercely, my gut twisting as I strained for my father's headlights sweeping across the neighbor's house. I tiptoed to the bottom of the stairs and listened to their late night conversations. I heartened when my dad sat on the side of the bed and I heard a rustling sack. That meant he had brought her deep fat-fried shrimp and french fries from the Backdoor, the tavern downtown. He was thinking of you, Mom! I encouraged her silently. He loves you, see? If my dad just sat in his chair and watched Johnny Carson, I knew my mom was alone and sad in her bed, and I cried on the cold stairs. "Go in to her, Daddy," I whispered. "Please turn off the TV and go tell her you love her."

And sometimes he didn't come home at all. I'd watch for him from my bed, the curtains parted at the window so I could see the flash of headlights on the corrugated tin of the lumberyard behind our house. I kept my eyes trained on that sheet of metal and prayed for light. "Come home. Come home. How can I go to sleep if you don't come home?"

Mother did not let on in the morning; she told us that Daddy had left early for work, but I knew his side of the bed had been empty all night. When Mother was busy elsewhere in the house, I would sneak into her bedroom and open Daddy's underwear drawer. My entire universe was composed of that drawer, those boxer shorts and T-shirts and socks. If they were still lined up in neat stacks, then everything was okay, nothing had happened that was unfixable.

It became an obsession, that drawer. At school, I'd watch the clock's minute hand at the end of the day. I knew when it made the final jerk to the 11, the bell would ring and I could run home. Often, I didn't stop at my locker, I just carried the day's books home with me so I could get home faster. I ran the six blocks, ran across the main highway, and heard a semi's blaring horn well behind me. I went straight to my parents' bedroom and stood before their blond dresser. Except for the top drawer, each drawer alternated his and hers. The top drawer held my mother's costume jewelry, insurance policies, a scrapbook with black-and-white pictures anchored in place with gummed black corners, and an aqua book called *The Marital Relationship*. It was a book I read every chance I got. I knew the drawings of positions by heart and had mulled over them many times. I was curious, but more than that, those pictures made me ache with some nameless longing. I felt old and tired as I studied those positions, suspecting this mysterious union was another that was going to be denied to me, maybe eternally.

Even this book had no allure in the high pitch of my anxiety. I opened my father's drawer, the third one down, and it was empty.

My parents had been married sixteen years when they separated. My dad took a garage apartment across town; my mom became vacant and lost. I didn't know why or what had happened. That fall I was fifteen years old, and I hoped the way a child does, dumbly and simply, for a quick resolution to my parents' separation. Then a girl in my typing class told me that she had seen the announcement of my parents' divorce in the paper and she was very, very sorry. I nodded and typed, "Oh no oh noohnoohhh", in the middle of the day's typing exercises. I rolled the paper out and handed it in, and ignoring the confused teacher's questions, I left class with twenty minutes to go. Just walked out of school and across the playground to the old bell tower. I leaned against the brick wall and wept.

It was a dismal house without Dad. I had always been embarrassed about the house anyway, a one-and-a-half-story shingled with gray asphalt. When I read about a family living in a tar-paper shack, I decided that was what our house must look like: a sharecropper's shack right in the middle of town. But the inside of the house had been redecorated, paneled and carpeted with the finest avocado green carpet Royal Castle Furniture Store stocked. We had brand-new linoleum that looked like cobblestone and a lemon yellow stove in the kitchen, and all through the house, Mother had hung perfectly pleated beige curtains, so it was presentable enough and, of course, impeccably clean once you were inside; but few of my friends ever got that far. I had people drop me off a few houses down and vaguely nodded at the green Victorian mansion that stood there.

"You live there?" they'd ask.

"Yep," I would answer. "See you around." And then I'd walk slowly in the direction of the neighbor's house until I saw the car disappear.

Living in my real house with my depressed mother was my first taste of hell, the place I did not want to be, the place I would do anything to avoid. Mother lay on the couch, day and night. She lay there wan and wigless. Her three wigs were bright red poly-something or other, and for the last two years she had worn them from morning until night. No more. The wigs were all placed on the Styrofoam heads on Mother's dresser. Sometimes I would stand beside them and dig my fingernail into the Styrofoam, telling myself those vacant faces needed eyes, they needed mouths; but really all I wanted to do was inflict pain on the vain and helpless things.

My mother kept the television turned on, but she did not watch it. She stared at the ceiling and gave us orders in a weak voice. Lisa and I would look at each other and do as we were told. Chris watched television nonstop, eating endless pots of Kraft macaroni and cheese. He was eleven and filling the hole as best he could. He stopped talking about reptiles. He stopped trapping down by the river. He got fat. Our baby brother was definitely fat. Nobody said anything about that. Nobody said anything about a divorce. Nobody said anything.

I took a summer job. I went to work in the cornfields like most of the other working-class kids in town. We were cheap labor for the farmers whose fields needed roguing and detasseling. I had played in those fields my whole life, and even though I knew teenagers often worked there, I never thought I would be tough enough to do it. That summer, however, everything changed. My mother was depressed and not moving from the couch. My dad wasn't coming home. I decided that maybe I could take it; whatever punishment lay in the fields could not be more painful than what I was suffering at home.

Right away, I could see I was in for it.

The crew boss didn't like me. It was such a shock to have a grown-up take an instant dislike to me. Most simply didn't notice me, but it was an entirely different state of affairs when I could read an active dislike in someone's face. The crew boss had glanced at me and then looked away so quickly that I looked down at my clothes. Had I missed a button? Was the fly of my cutoffs open? Everything looked okay. I looked at him again, but he had turned to the back of the pickup and was filling his arms with spades.

He handed us our spades. I had never held a tool like this. The spade had a thick, blunt blade and a long handle with Iowa soil packed inside the grain.

"Now this spade ain't your boyfriend; you're not supposed to make it feel good," the crew boss said, holding the spade between his legs and eyeing us for a response.

Some of the girls around me giggled. I had been assigned to the New Castle crew, and these girls might as well have been from Paris as half a county away. I knew my daddy would kill this man for talking this way around me.

A girl whose boobs looked about to bust out of her shirt was putting zinc oxide on her nose. She looked up and said, "We know what to do. We were all on the same crew last year – all but her." She pointed at me with her white finger.

The crew boss eyed me. "You never rogued before?"

"No," I said.

"Well, girl. I guess you'll be needing a lesson on roguing. Watch me now," he said as he took my spade from my hands

39

and walked over to the first row. He put the tip of the spade into the ground and gave it a thrust with his foot. In one motion, he uprooted the renegade corn and flipped it into the furrow. "Easy, ain't it?" He looked tired at the backs of his eyes.

I had lived long enough to know that what was easy for other people was not necessarily easy for me. The other girls were rolling up their cutoffs even shorter, folding down their socks, and tying blue or red bandannas over their hair. I reached for my own hair and touched the bill of my father's baseball cap.

The crew boss – he told us we would call him Big Chief – started assigning rows. We all followed his wide behind as he took off across the field.

"These two are your rows." He looked me over. "How old are you, anyway?"

At fifteen, I still lacked five feet by an inch, my chest was flatter than the blacktop we'd taken out of town, and my face hadn't changed much since grade school – a kid's face with an overbite.

"Fifteen," I said, and pulled my lips over my teeth.

"You the runt of the litter?" he asked, hitching up his pants while he looked toward the end of the field. "Go ahead and try one." He toed a rogue at the mouth of my row and nodded me over.

I struggled with the stance. I made a swipe at the rogue and missed. I tried again, this time putting my foot on top of the blade, but it was wet with dew and my foot slid off.

"Looks to me like that spade's handling you," Big Chief said, and spat. He stood about a foot away. The girls with unassigned rows were in a clump behind him. I glanced over in time to see one roll her eyes at me. They were all chewing gum open mouthed.

"Give it another try. Show it who's boss."

I held the spade firmly and thrust it toward the stalk. I sliced the weed level at the ground.

"No sir. That is exactly what you do not want to do." Big Chief was more awake now. He looked meaner and happier. "Girls, lookee here. You can't be a-cutting these rogues above ground. That don't do shit. You gotta get your spade under it, you gotta go deep – get your spade under it for the root." He started roguing everything in sight, sent green pungent plants flying. The watching girls scattered, but I stayed where I was, feeling the dirt pelt my bare legs and arms.

"Now try again," Big Chief offered as he motioned me over to a rogue about ten feet down my row.

I placed a foot on top of the spade and stomped it into the field and prayed for it to go in deep. The New Castle girls had stopped talking. "Good God," I heard one of them mutter.

The spade was halfway in the ground. I levered until I thought it was well under the weed, tried to lift, shocked at the weight of the earth. I pulled it upward again and the weed came out, flying up with a blast of tiny clods.

Big Chief snagged the uprooted plant, held it up, turned it to the light. "Guess you got it this time. You need some muscle, girl. Your arms ain't but sticks. I've seen more meat on a Slim Jim."

That stuck – the name Jim. The girls on the crew lifted index fingers good-bye when I jumped out of the truck at Allendale High School and said "Jim" when they saw me again in the morning, but that was about it.

All that summer I would get up before it was light. The sun had just barely risen when I walked past the houses that were each a little country of their own. I walked the six blocks to the school on sidewalks that were as old as Allendale. The concrete buckled and parted every few feet. And even though it was six in the morning, I forced myself to take the kind of limping, zigzag steps needed to protect my mother's back.

I was determined to do a good job in the fields. I wanted Big Chief to like me. I knew I could make him laugh like as hard as my dad did when I got on a roll. "Big Chief," I'd drawl sweetly, "is your first name Hank R.?"

Instead, everything I did irritated him. Again and again he'd thrust a handful of rogues in my face and yell at me for missing them. I tried not to cry, but I couldn't help it. I'd tell him I was sorry.

"Sorry don't cut it," he always said, and then he would tell me that I had no business out being out in the fields with people who could do their jobs.

After a long week, I walked home on Friday, tired, worn out, happy because I would see Dad that night at his game. When I walked into the house, Mother looked up from the sofa and told me to get my clothes into the washing machine and take a shower before I sat down. It hurt to take a shower; the Dial soap stung the blisters and cuts on my hands. My legs were bruised, and I often found welts on them, white and shaped like continents, some sort of rash, I supposed, because they itched a lot. But I was earning money and hopefully earning my father's respect.

After I was clean, I made a bologna sandwich, slathering Miracle Whip on the spongy white bread while Lisa watched me.

"You get filthy out there," she said. "And your legs are scuzzy looking," she added. She popped the lid from a bottle of Seven-Up.

"I know," I said, and sat across the table from her. Her hair was gleaming, even more platinum than normal from the summer's sun. She was wearing a bright white blouse and denim shorts with pink daisies embroidered on the back pockets. Her nails were painted a pearly pink.

"Dad has a game tonight," I said. "Wanna go with me?"

"I can't," Lisa said, and stretched her long legs in front of her, turning them from side to side to see if there were any imperfections. "I have to meet some guys at the pool."

"They just want to look at your boobs," I said, and took a bite of sandwich.

"Whatever," Lisa answered. She wet the end of her finger and rubbed a spot her knee.

"Carolyn!" Mother called from the living room. "Come here, please."

Lisa and I exchanged a look, a barely acknowledged and amorphous empathy for each other, so brief that I couldn't tell later if it had happened or not; but our eyes had locked, and for a moment I didn't feel alone.

Mother lay on the brown-and-orange sofa. The curtains were drawn. She looked like a girl not much older than me. She wore her white shorts and a short-sleeved top. Her arms and legs were long and listless, beautiful, but so sad.

"Will you brush my hair?" my mother asked, handing me a brush.

"Brush it hard, Carolyn," she said, and I obliged. My mother's head in my lap and her hair falling between my thighs, my skinny legs trembled to be so close to her. Afterward she asked me to rub her feet, and I rejoiced again. Her feet in my lap this time. My mother's head and her feet, all mine. I held each toe in my fingers and squeezed and pulled and kneaded. Her feet were callused and large, not ladylike feet because she was a tall woman. I remembered the story of the sinful woman who broke a jar of perfume to pour upon Jesus' feet, so I went to find the Jergens lotion. I slathered her feet and rubbed them while I stared unseeing at the TV. Instead I prayed more sincerely than I ever had before: Be well, Mother. Be well.

I thought God had answered that prayer a week later when Mother stirred, got up from the couch, and went hunting for a wig. I was slightly uneasy – was she going on a date? But mostly I was happy that she would not be on the sofa staring at the ceiling while I was gone. I had plans to stay overnight with Anita, a girl I had chosen to befriend mostly because she was as short and shy as I was. But even after a school year together, we remained slightly awkward with each other, our time alone filled with long silences and false starts. Still, she was nice and her parents were so grateful to me for being their daughter's friend that they bought us frozen pizzas and pop and paid our way to movies every time I stayed over.

"So I'll see you tomorrow, Mom?" I asked while I closed the clasps on my overnight bag.

She sat at the vanity, clipping on earrings and peering closely at herself in the mirror. She was still wearing her slip, no dress yet, but I could see her good shoes had been pulled out in front of the closet.

"Sure, honey," she said. "Have fun."

"Are you going out with Aunt Mary?" I asked tentatively.

"Hmm," she murmured. She stopped rummaging in her drawer for another pair of earrings and looked at me. She looked like a different woman in her wig, but still so incredibly fragile. "Carolyn, stop fussing over me. You'll be late. I'll see you in the morning."

And later I would hear the whole story of her evening from so many willing witnesses that I would have to turn them away.

"I was there, you know," they'd start, and then I would know what was coming.

"Great," I'd say. Then I'd walk away. If I was feeling bold or pissed or just tired, I'd add under my breath, "Glad you could enjoy the show."

Sometimes I even forget I wasn't there. I can see it all, every minute.

He was in the dugout when she arrived. His team was up to bat, and Dad sat with Allendale's young-bloods, waiting their turn at bat. He was a handsome man in his late thirties with tanned and muscled arms, a buzz cut, and sideburns, masculine as hell. I'd seen women when my dad talked to them; they got goofy like girls my age, giggling, punching him in the arm when he purposefully called them the wrong name. But the men in our town also loved my dad. They remembered him in his youth and his days of football glory. They had heard the same stories I had; they knew about the railroad tracks and the way he stood up to his abusive stepdad. They knew my dad had been a marine, fighting a year in Korea while they tinkered on cars in their backyards. And now he was coaching their sons in Little League, working his ass off by taking a second job at Standard Oil on weekends, and still sweating the outfield, catching pop flies and fielding grounders.

It was these men who starting whooping when a woman on high heels began teetering her way across deep left field. "She's hurt," someone said. "My God," another said. "What's the matter with her? Who is that?"

"It's my wife," my dad muttered. "It's my goddamn wife." He jumped up and ran out to meet her. She had just brushed aside the shortstop's hand on her arm and was walking, faster now, toward my dad.

I can imagine the hard and excited faces of everyone who watched, the tiny gears turning behind their eyes, the greedy noting of details as the scene was filed and stored for the retelling. Even children must have stopped whining for Sno-Kones and Sugar Babies to watch the lady with the red hair who was crying in center field. She was wearing a black dress, short with spaghetti straps; that's the detail no one ever left out.

"Get home," my dad hissed.

"No, Peter," my mother answered. "I'm not going. I won't, not without you."

He put his arm around her and pulled her toward the

dugout to end the drama, to get her out and past the bleachers, to shove her in the aqua Plymouth and drive her back while she cried and screamed. He didn't care what it took; he was going to get her out of his life.

Mother pulled away from his grip and jerked back, falling into the mesh of the fence. The other players scooted out of the way, standing up and leaning back, trying to give my dad some space to work. Mother was crying, pleading, looking for something to say to make my dad love her. She saw a pair of cleats on the ground and picked one up, holding it high over her head.

"Peter!" she shouted, brandishing the shoe, waving it in the air. Some people in the crowd stood up to get a better view.

"Peter!" she yelled again.

"Goddamn it, let's go," my dad said, almost in tears himself.

Then my mother hit my dad, just whacked him with the cleat for all she was worth before stepping back. Blood instantly ran down my father's face from the three holes newly punctured in his head.

"Jeeezus," the other softball players said. They pulled at my mom now while my dad stood mopping his face with a white handkerchief. Dad sank down to the bench in the dugout, someone ran for ice, and my mother watched it all for a moment, as though she were trying to make sure everything was taken care of before she went. Then she walked past the stunned bleachers of townfolk and didn't look their way at all.

That's the way the story ended, more or less. Some people said my mom went home and cleaned out every one of the kitchen cupboards, a strange and not altogether unbelievable instinct on her part, but who would have seen her do so? And my father, it is said, got royally drunk at the Backdoor downtown and went home with some bimbo who worked at the bath oil plant. That seems likely as well. I was at a pajama party on the right side of town, and I had no idea what my blood was up to.

I would turn sixteen at the end of the summer. It was obvious my dad wasn't coming home, but I was beginning to feel the optimism that I always felt at the end of August. Every year for as long as I could remember, I had laid out my new first-day-of-school outfit with my new shoes, notebooks, pencils, and two gum erasers on my bed and stepped back, imagining where sixth or eighth or tenth grade might take me. Who would I be at the end of the school year? I always wanted to reinvent myself, but I didn't have the necessary vision.

I was relieved when I had only a week left of working in the fields. When the alarm went off at dawn, I lay in the half-light and wished I didn't have to get up. I could see Lisa sleeping like a fetus, curled in upon herself, chin buried in her chest. Last year in biology we had learned that the unborn child was covered with downy hair, and I imagined it then to be light blond hair like Lisa's. I felt a sudden surge of love for my little sister. She was just a baby, after all. I pulled the sheet over her shoulders and left.

ERIC

In books, things happen suddenly, overnight sometimes. Nothing happened quickly to me; everything so far had been delays, false starts, and postponements. Then the unforeseen happened. The summer my parents split for good and I battled Big Chief in the cornfields, I grew. In the space of a few months, I turned sixteen, grew almost five inches, got breasts, got my period, everything. My breasts weren't voluptuous and they were nothing like my sister's, but I filled out a real bra at last. I stood naked in front of a mirror as often as I could, just to make sure I wasn't dreaming. It was true, then. I was a normal girl, no matter what any of us had thought.

I had cool clothes to wear to school that fall, thanks to the money I had earned in the fields. That year I was a junior in high school, and I wore hip-hugger bell-bottoms and bright peasant tops with scoop necks that revealed my fading summer tan. My hair was sun streaked and my skin clear and healthy. I was so used to being the invisible girl that at first I assumed boys were smiling at someone behind or beside me. One afternoon after school, I was walking down State Street when a carload of boys honked and yelled, "Nice ass!" There was no one else on the street but me. I gloried in that bit of attention; it wasn't a nice thing to say, I knew that, but it meant I had been ushered into an arena where I had been denied access before. I looked at my reflection in Kramer's Department Store window and I smiled at myself. It turned out I wasn't a dwarf, no matter what Grandma had said. My overbite wasn't *that* bad. If round and kind of sticking out was

48

a good thing, then I did have a nice ass. Some boys, not all, certainly, but some boys were noticing me, flirting with me, saying that I had changed, what happened? Did I know how cute I was?

That fall I had my first real date, the homecoming dance, with a football player, no less. And we kissed a sloppy first kiss. His lips were soft and wet, and I wasn't so sure it was worth all the buildup, but still, it was a kiss and I had that monkey off my back forever. I dated Tony all fall. He was smart and shy. So was I, but we never talked about anything consequential. I spent a great deal of energy trying to figure out where to sit on the enormous front seat of his father's Buick. If I sat too close, I was giving him the signal that I was easy. If I sat too far away, I was sending a message that I was cold and not very interested. There was a spot between the two, and each time I got into the car I tried to find it. But finding the spot seemed terribly unimportant the night Tony and I left the dance where Renegade had played.

We walked out of the clubhouse at the golf course, and the cool air was an instant relief. It was eight-thirty, not late, but already pitch black in the Iowa countryside. Fog lapped at the edges of the golf course, and it looked like an inland sea, still and mysterious. Tony reached for my hand and I let him take it, but all I could think of was Renegade. No, all I could think of was Eric, the lead guitarist of Renegade. Eric and I were meant to be together, I had suddenly realized that night. Eric was the boy I had been hoping for.

I had seen Renegade play before at street fairs and once at a Sadie Hawkins dance in junior high, where the girls ask the boys, and I had found a very short boy willing to go with me. Everyone knew Renegade, a four-piece rock band: drums, bass, guitar, keyboards. Two of the boys were from Allendale, two from nearby New Castle. After the band hired an agent, they began to wear white bell-bottoms and purple silk shirts and were booked all over Iowa and even South Dakota. These boys, cute, cocky, neophyte Mick Jaggers, made an impact on our small towns – we could feel it – they were going to be famous someday. The girls, especially, were convinced. Most of the boys we went to school with were members of the FFA, Future Farmers of America. Those dull-eyed boys wore dark blue corduroy jackets with a cornstalk embroidered on the pocket and raised sheep for 4-H competitions. And when it came right down to it, even the elite of Allendale High School, the athletes, couldn't compete with Renegade. Making a hook shot in a big game was amazing and worthy of our attention, but it really didn't compare with a guitar solo on a darkened stage while a strobe light flashes and everyone holds their breath, waiting for the next lick. Some girls stood at the foot of the stage and waited for any flicker of attention from the band. They would dance alone with their eyes closed, but they were watching, they were ready, let me tell you. When Renegade won the Iowa State Fair Battle of the Bands two years in a row, even the adults had to admit the boys had something going for them.

But it was that night, that foggy night late in October, when I realized that the boy on stage with the shoulder-length blond hair, the one whose graceful fingers were fretting up and down the neck of the guitar without pause, this boy would love me if given a chance. I was relieved and excited at once. I tried to think of everything I knew about him. He drove a VW van and wore corduroy jackets, plaid pants, and platform shoes bought in big cities like Waterloo. He not only played the guitar, he played sax in the Allendale High School jazz band. But best of all, he wrote love songs for the girls he dated, and then Renegade played those songs in school gymnasiums across the state. My God, the immortality of having *your* song played all over the state of Iowa. I couldn't have imagined anything more exciting. As a bonus, he was the most reserved guy in the band. He didn't say a lot into the microphone when they were on stage, and that was a good thing; I didn't want anyone who didn't know how to be quiet. I liked quiet. It meant you were deep and soulful. I also liked soulful.

When I said good night to Tony that night and endured the sloppy kiss, I was hugging myself with joy. Soon I would be kissing Eric. I knew it was meant to be.

"You're a poet, I hear."

That was our first encounter. I was sitting on the brick wall outside of the high school while waiting for my friends to get out of class. I blinked the sun out of my eyes and saw Eric standing in front of me, his blond hair blowing, his Timberline cologne heady and delicious.

"Yeah," I said. "I guess. Sort of. I like to write, anyway."

"Didn't you write that daisies poem?" he asked, sitting down beside me. He put his saxophone case at his feet and pulled out a roll of wintergreen Life Savers. "Want one?"

"OK," I said. He was so close. Our legs were two inches apart at the most.

"That poem about the dead mother – that was yours, right?" he asked again, and smiled at me. "Someone told me it was."

"Yeah," I said again. He wore an enormous class ring, white gold, a sapphire stone. His hands, I had seen these hands move up and down the neck of a guitar with grace and fluidity, magic. Talk, I ordered myself. Don't blow this.

"My mom hated that poem," I said wryly. "She thinks it means I wish she was dead."

He laughed. "Do you?"

"No!" I said, and laughed with him. "It means I feel distant from her and that feels like death, that's all."

"It's really a heavy poem, Carolyn," he said, and looked at me squarely in the eye.

He knew my name. My God. He knew my name.

"Thanks," I said softly, and smiled. *Save me.*

"I cut it out of the paper, you know that?" He looked embarrassed. "It just meant something to me – I thought it was the coolest thing I'd seen in a long time."

The wind picked up. The clouds began to scud across the sky, and shadows became a strobe light. We were light and then we were dark and then we were light again. I felt plunked into a movie, suddenly the star of my own life, the curtains pulling back. The credits rolled over our faces, our awkward and shifting feet, our hands edging toward each other.

Falling in love was exactly the remedy I imagined it to be. I belonged to someone. Someone's name was linked with mine; it made perfect sense that I had become CarolynandEric. I was thrilled when he told me he loved me after three weeks. In another week I wore his class ring with nearly a skein of yarn wrapped around it to hold it on my finger. Eric was possessive and jealous of any attention I received from other boys, which surprisingly picked up once I was wearing his ring. Every afternoon I spent study hall at the same table with the same four boys, friends of Eric's who suddenly were intrigued by me. I flirted happily with them every day, answered their scribbled notes, fended off their suggestive remarks, laughed myself into stomach-grabbing, chair-lurching fits. I began to see myself the way those boys saw me, and I was surprised at this girl with a quick smile and a nice figure and funny things to say. I thought of Pastor Jim saying, "You must be born again." I felt that way. I was new inside and out, but it had nothing to do with God. Even the girls in my high school were looking at me differently.

I had girlfriends now, real ones. Just having Tony for a sort of boyfriend that fall had been enough to get me into their club. They were interested in my late-arriving romances, and they all thought Eric was perfect for me. He was a musician, I was a poet – they foresaw collaborations, they prophesied fame and fortune for both of us. Katherine, my new best friend, had a crush on the drummer of Renegade. We used to talk for hours about our double weddings to Eric and Dave, the drummer whose blond hair was bowl cut, perfectly styled, and shiny, no matter how late the gig or how windy the day. Eric said Dave didn't date, but that didn't dissuade Katherine. She knew how to get a man. Katherine, a gorgeous girl with a delicate nose and waist-long brown hair, had been dating for years. She promised to teach me everything I needed to know about the world of love.

"Are you Frenching? You should be Frenching by now, but for heaven's sake, don't let him feel you up. Not yet," she said as she painted her nails. "Got to keep him coming back for more."

No problem with that, I thought. Eric was very aggressive – who would have anticipated that? He was not exactly a billboard for testosterone. He was slight and narrow hipped and hated sports. Besides that, he was so quiet, almost shy, and sensitive of my feelings. But that hadn't kept his hand out of my pants or from fumbling with my bra clasp.

I must have been the most virginal virgin in Allendale High School. I didn't look like such a child anymore, but that didn't stop me from being unusually naive. One night Eric and I were alone in the dark kitchen at my house; there was no place for us to be together, not the living room where Mom and Chris were watching TV, certainly not the bedroom I shared with Lisa. We skulked around, making out in hallways, the kitchen, even the bathroom once or twice. That night he leaned against the refrigerator and pulled me toward him, his hands clenching my waist. I pulled back and smiled. I took off his glasses and let him kiss me. Then I pushed him away again.

"What's in your pocket, Eric?" I said, and began to slide my fingers into the front pocket of his Levi's. I stopped at something hard and cylindrical. "What's that?"

Eric laughed. "Life Savers."

"Oh," I said. And then I shoved the Life Savers with my thumb. "Maybe I want one," I said innocently. Eric laughed long and hard. It's not that I didn't know about erections, but I had certainly never seen one and I had no idea a penis could extend so far or get so hard. I just had no idea.

At first, it *was* innocent, a sweet courtship, full of games and presents. We bought toys at the dime store, silly ones like jacks or guns that shot Ping-Pong balls. Eric gave me nicknames, Scooter, Sugar, Sweetcakes. He brought me stuffed kittens and alligators, caramel apples, and an amber-colored pendant necklace that played "Somewhere, My Love". He held my hand and told me about travels with the band, movies he had seen, and how he had met real musicians and even shaken hands with Peter Cetera. I told him stories, too, my quiet, sad stories, the ones I had waited a lifetime to tell. Eric listened just the way I had always imagined someone would listen. And because there was really no good thing to say afterward, he just held me.

Eric had seen my dad a few times, but they had never talked. It was important to me that Eric know my dad and know about him. I was always looking for ways to bring him up in our conversation.

"My dad's an athlete," I said, picking up his softball glove in the garage. "He's really good at sports."

"Cool," Eric said. "We can go to one of his softball games when they start up again."

"Yeah," I whispered. "That'd be great. He's good, Eric. He always hits it way into the outfield." I was weepy then, missing my dad, wishing he were home again.

"Stop, Scooter," Eric said. "Don't cry. We'll make sure we spend a lot of time with your dad, okay? Maybe we can play catch or something."

The image of long-haired and slightly girlish Eric playing

ball with my dad, the flattop ex-marine, made me laugh. That wouldn't be happening. Eric brightened when I laughed and pulled me into his arms.

"You're not like other girls," he said, hugging me tightly. He kept talking, his lips in my hair, his breath hot on my neck. "I told my mom you were different from anyone I had ever met. Someday . . . ," he said, and trailed off. He signed his notes this way, ended our phone conversations the same way. "Someday," a lovely word, a quiet promise, just enough to keep me.

"You make me happy," I said. "You're all I need to be happy."

After a few months together, we grew bored of chasing each other around the house with suction-cup dart guns and took up drinking instead. I had never even tasted alcohol before, but I quickly learned how great it was to get trashed. For the first time in my life, I felt close to being a kid instead of a tired but vigilant adult. We didn't stay in the house anymore; we drove around and looked for deserted parking lots and dead-end streets. One evening late in spring we drove down the river road to the deserted Allendale Baptist Church Bible camp. It was Eric's idea. I had spent a few miserable weeks of my youth at that very camp, and I could vividly remember the heat and mosquitoes and the way we had tried to cool ourselves with paper fans donated from the funeral parlor: a forlorn-looking Jesus with His heart wrapped in thorns, holding up one finger. Even Jesus couldn't cut the humidity. I suddenly saw myself as a little girl, just to the side of the others, baking in a Quonset hut, waving my fan in front of my face, and counting the days until Saturday when I could go home again.

I sighed.

"What's the matter? Is this all right?" Eric asked.

"Sure," I said. "I kind of hate this place, that's all."

"We'll go somewhere else, then," Eric said, pulling into the caretaker's driveway. He put the van into reverse, but the tires only spun. He took it out of gear and tried to go forward. No luck. Reverse again. Nothing. We were stuck.

"I should have known the roads in the river camp would be muddy," Eric said. "Jeez. Why did I keep going?"

He shook his head in frustration and spun the van's wheels again. There was no way that van, a big boat with no traction, was going anywhere. The floodplain was all around us, and our back tires were rapidly disappearing in the sucking black mud.

I was about to suggest that we find some branches or something to put under the tires when the yard lights suddenly turned on. I'd forgotten we were in the caretaker's driveway. A large man moved toward us in long strides. It was George Kettleman, deacon of Allendale Baptist Church and caretaker of the Bible camp.

"What do you think you're doing?" he shouted, his red face bloated with fury. His eyes darted back and forth between Eric and me. I wanted to duck to the floorboard, but I made myself sit straight with my hands folded on my lap, my gaze just to his left. The look on his face was so fierce, so hate filled, that I feared for our lives. He's a deacon, I reminded myself. Deacons don't kill kids.

"Just turning around, sir," Eric said politely. "Then I got stuck. I'm sure sorry about this."

"You kids up here. You got no business here. This is private property. You've torn up my driveway, son," he said, narrowing his eyes. "Who do you think's going to pay for grating this driveway again?"

"I apologize, sir. I was just turning around," Eric said again.

The devil himself could not have looked as red and fierce as George Kettleman, I thought. I watched him stalk around the van, waving his arms, not using curse words, but managing to make his regular words sound as if they came straight from the pit.

"You kids. No business. Private. Destroying property," he muttered, glaring at us. It seemed like an eternity. He wanted to wring our necks, that's what, but he was a deacon and Pastor Jim wouldn't have let that go. Instead, he stood in front of us and just took us in, recording our height and weight, the symmetry of our faces, Eric's glasses and the mole on my cheek. He memorized us.

"For our God is a consuming fire" popped into my head. Oh, that was it. I'd been mistaken – George Kettleman wasn't the devil, he was the incarnation of the wrathful God, the one who sent people to hell for drinking beer and fooling around in a van.

"I'll get a chain and tow you out of there," he finally said. "I better never see your faces again. Do you understand me?"

Eric nodded. "Yes, sir. Do you need any help, sir?"

Kettleman glared at him. "Just stay in your van, hippie boy." He turned around and walked toward an outbuilding where three church buses were parked. "Hallelujah Express" one was called. "Glory Bound" and "Going Home" were the others. Kettleman disappeared between them.

"Sorry, Scooter," Eric said. He put his arms around me. "You're shaking!"

"So are you," I said.

"Goddamn it," Eric whispered. "I know I am."

Weeks later, we were still spooked about the whole thing. The last thing either of us wanted to do was go out in the country and park. Instead, we took Chris and Lisa bowling and fixed homemade pizza afterward. We made a scrapbook of all our ticket stubs and slips from fortune cookies. We went to a nursing home, and Eric played his acoustic guitar for the uninterested residents in the activity room. We were as wholesome as we could be for about a month, and then the make-out sessions started up again, steamier than ever, but always stopping short of going all the way.

Why did I make us stop? After a while, I started wondering about that. I had no code of behavior. I vaguely understood that I was supposed to be a good girl but what did that mean? Who defined good girls and bad girls? My Sunday school teacher? I thought of Mrs. Frommer and the way she fluttered her hands in the air when she talked about boys and the ways boys could lead good girls to hell.

"Let's do it next Sunday," I said one day after school. It was May and the weather had warmed up nicely. I thought maybe we could do it outside somewhere.

"Really?" Eric asked. "Are you sure?"

"I love you in so many ways; I want to love you with my body, too," I said, parroting something I had read somewhere. It sounded memorized, though, like a kid's line in a school play. I wanted this to be a grown-up moment, but I just didn't have the sophistication to pull it off.

"Wow," Eric said. He looked a little nervous. "Where would we do it?"

"Not in the van," I said quickly. "Outside somewhere?"

"Maybe the pasture?" he asked. His parents owned a large, undeveloped plot of land outside of Allendale. "It would be really pretty there, I think."

"OK," I said. "I'll bring a blanket. Can you get something for us to drink?"

"Of course, honey," he said. "I'll take care of that."

I fought the impulse to stick out my hand for a handshake to seal the deal. Sunday: you and me: 1:15 P.M.: Mission Deflower.

When Sunday came, I dressed carefully. I decided to wear my only summer dress, a long white muslin sprigged with lavender and yellow flowers. I brushed my now shoulder-length hair and pulled it back with a pale yellow ribbon. As a final touch, I sprayed my throat and breasts with Taboo, my mother's very grown-up perfume, a musk that left me breathless. I looked at myself in the mirror. I could see the little girl was almost swallowed up.

Eric's eyes lit up when he saw me. "Sugarcakes, you're gorgeous."

"Thanks," I said, blushing. "I guess I'm kind of dressed up."

"You look amazing," he said, and just stood there smiling at me.

"Thank you," I said. My voice sounded like a little girl's, high and sweet, as though I might break into a curtsy. I was suddenly nervous beyond belief.

"Are you ready?" he asked apologetically.

"Yeah, sure," I said, nodding to let him know how sure I was. "I'm ready." I picked up my grandmother's quilt, started to refold it, and then thought better of it. I didn't want him to think I was stalling. I grabbed his hand and pulled him out the door.

The pasture was filled with fruit trees, plum, apple, pear, and cherry. The fragrant blossoms were pink and white and gold, and petals fell on us like warm snow as we walked hand in hand. A stand of pine trees grew near the back fence, the sky a startling blue behind them. The fence was the only sign of a human hand; everything else was untainted. The fruit trees grew untended, wild and snarled, but taller than trees in backyards. It was like a perfume ad in the pages of *Seventeen*. It was the most romantic scene I could ever have imagined.

Eric and I sat on the quilt and pulled off our shoes. My new sandals were muddy from the hike through the pasture, and I picked up a stick to scrape off some of the mud. We sat politely cross-legged on the blanket and looked at each other. After a few minutes, I opened a can of Pepsi and poured out half and then nodded for Eric to fill it with vodka. I gulped the drink as fast as I could, waving away the bees that landed on the rim of the can. When I finished that drink, Eric made us another. Halfway into the next, we began to kiss. The kissing was different this time, though, hard and fierce and grown-up. This kissing meant business; it meant pulling up my dress, pulling off Eric's pants, and Eric crawling on top of me, groaning with excitement and desperation. All I had to do was spread my legs and let him figure out how to get inside. I felt a hard fumbling, knuckles and fingers, a pounding of something that would not fit, but there, it did.

My head was foggy, my limbs numb, and my stomach heaving so hard that I could hear the booze inside sloshing. I stared at the branches overhead and watched the bees; there were so many and they were loud, good God, they sounded like motor scooters winding their way around a dirt path. My head and back were chilled from the thawing earth. I felt no pain, nothing but a damp cold spreading down my legs and arms. When Eric gasped and rolled off me, I reached down to see how messy the whole thing had been and brought my fingers to my face. There was blood, but I had expected that. I held my hand to my nose and smelled semen, acrid and unpleasant. I made a face without thinking and looked quickly at Eric. He grimaced back and looked around for something to clean me up but couldn't find anything. Quickly, he unbuttoned his madras school shirt and laid it aside, then shrugged out of his T-shirt and handed it to me. I swabbed myself, clutched his Fruit of the Loom between my legs, and cried as discreetly as I could. I was ashamed and disappointed with the whole nonevent, but there was no sense in making Eric feel bad. When he pulled his pants back on and I smoothed down my long, white dress, I told myself the deal had been cinched. Eric was mine; he wasn't going anywhere now. I had given him something no other girl ever had, and I knew he would never forget it. I was cheered at that thought. I curled up next to him.

He stroked my hair and told me how wonderful it had been. I watched the bees. I didn't understand why we hadn't been stung yet.

When Eric took me home, my dad's car was in the driveway. Sometimes he dropped by when Mother was gone.

"Oh, God," Eric said. "Your dad's here. He's going to beat the shit out of me."

"No, he won't. Daddy won't beat the shit out of you," I said. I shook my head and smiled at him. "My dad's the greatest guy, Eric."

"Oh, God," Eric said again. "You're still drunk. We better just leave."

"No, sir," I said. "I never see my old dad. I'm going in there before he leaves again. I'm fine, Eric. Really." I couldn't find the door handle to the van; my head was swimming. I was worried there was blood on the back of my white dress.

"Carolyn," Eric pleaded, "please, let's go drive around for a while."

"It's all right, Eric," I said. "Scooter can handle this." Then I was out of the van, waving cheerily.

"Love you, boyfriend!"

"I love you," he mouthed silently behind the glass. He looked ghastly, sick with guilt and worry. And then he drove away.

I pushed open the door and smiled blearily at my dad.

"Pop!"

He took a long look at me and nodded. "Squirt," he said. He kept watching TV.

As I began to cross the room, I panicked. Oh, God, there was a way to tell a virgin by the way she walked. That's what everyone said. I must be walking differently; he'll know, he'll know. I stopped walking.

"It's a nice day out there, Daddy," I said slowly and carefully. "Bees all over the place, though."

"I'm trying to hear this, Squirt," Dad said, leaning toward the TV. I took advantage of his distraction and hurried past him to the bathroom. I undressed, ran a shower, looked at myself closely in the mirror. I did look different; something was new there in my eyes. Oh, God, Daddy must have noticed.

When I got out of the shower, I pulled my mom's terrycloth robe off the hook and wrapped myself up in it. I took one last look in the mirror at my betraying face and went out to find Dad.

The TV was still on, but he was gone. For the second time that day, I cried. I crawled into his chair and sat there for a while, trying to soak up the warmth he had left. I was still cold, and nothing, not the shower, not the robe, not even his chair, was helping me get warm again.

Renegade played every weekend, sometimes two or three hours away. When Eric returned home in the early morning hours, he would drive by the house where I lived with my mother and brother and sister. He drove by slowly, flashing his lights as a signal. Tiptoeing downstairs with my shoes in my hand, I felt like the most wicked girl on earth, and also the sexiest. We parked his van in the municipal swimming pool parking lot and then had sex by the amber, hazy glow of streetlights. Less than an hour later I was home with toilet paper stuffed in the crotch of my panties, my lips sore and bruised from kissing, my heart still pounding.

We stopped going to movies and concerts; now our dates were simple and uncomplicated: booze and sex. More than anything, getting drunk was a huge relief. For the first time in my life, I wasn't worried about anything. I didn't have to be vigilant and watchful, just waiting for the word or act that would hurt me. I was with Eric. He wasn't going to hurt me. All of my uncertainty, isolation, and disappointment had miraculously vanished. Being in love meant being relieved above all else. I luxuriated in the feeling of knowing there was someone who would be there for me; I never had to be alone and scared again.

Eric made my life worth living.

Having him in my life changed our sad, empty house, not only for me, but also for my brother and sister. Eric fixed the things that were broken, the window in the hallway and a leg of the kitchen table. Sometimes we'd go to the store and buy taco shells and ground beef, canned enchiladas and salsa. Lisa and Chris would be thrilled to see us walk in with groceries. They'd follow us to the kitchen and we'd all eat a big dinner in our little-used kitchen. My brother asked Eric questions about go-carts, and Lisa played her new records for him. When Christmas came, Eric took me shopping and we bought presents for everyone. I chose a flannel nightgown and a set of six water glasses for my mother, a stuffed dog and lip gloss for my sister, and an encyclopedia of snakes for eleven-year-old Chris, who had left paleontology behind and now insisted he would become a herpetologist. Eric reached inside his wallet and plunked the money down on the counter.

I didn't choose a gift for my father. He didn't come around and he didn't call. Allendale was not big enough to disappear in, but my father had managed to do exactly that. One morning my mother woke me up very early and told me that we had to have some money from my dad. She told me where he was living and gave me a note, which I was to place on the windshield of his car. It was six in the morning and I walked across town with a note I was afraid to read; I knew anything it said would hurt me.

I just clutched the note and put one foot in front of the other. Allendale became the moon, and I was barely breathing; any minute I thought I'd fall into a crater and disappear forever.

I found my dad's garage apartment and his car, a black-and-white Falcon, parked on the street. I hadn't seen my dad in months, but it never occurred to me that I might knock on the door or sit in the car and wait for him. It hurt that he could move on without us, but I didn't hate him for it. I was surprised that such a thing could happen, and that is what I remember feeling more than anything else: this voiceless surprise that never abated and never softened. I must have opened his underwear drawer dozens of times, and each time I was shocked that there was nothing there.

Later that day I told Eric about the mission my mother had given me. I tried not to cry as I told him how awful it had been to lift the wiper arm and put the note underneath it, all the while both hoping and fearing Dad would notice me through his window and run to see me. Eric listened and then silently pulled me into his arms and rocked me. I knew he understood.

My parents were doing their own thing now, but that was okay because I had Eric. I had less and less time for my girlfriends; no long phone conservations about boys and school or after-school get-togethers. I felt no compulsion to be a part of their world; I had a world now that supremely satisfied me. Katherine complained that I was shoving her out, and I couldn't argue – I was. If I had time to spend with someone, Eric was the only one I wanted. Girls couldn't give me what I needed: attention, compliments, the intoxicating feeling of being desired. Katherine wasn't happy with me; she wrote me notes and called me for a while, but eventually she stopped trying. I hardly noticed.

My junior and senior years of high school were spent watching my sister play high school basketball, studying at the kitchen table, and making love, in the van when it was cold or outside if it was warm. Eric's band gigs became a part of my life as much as they were a part of Eric's. If he was going to be gone for a weekend, I retreated into my books or took long walks. Sometimes I went with him and experienced the life of a groupie. I carried microphone stands and the lighter equipment like the monitors or guitar stands. The local girls would watch me go in and out of Renegade's bus, and I could see how much they wanted to be me. It was a new sensation, one of belonging, of having arrived. I let my glance flicker over the girls' faces with affected disinterest. Then I'd go back inside the bus and sit there for a while, just to let them know I could do anything I wanted in there. I never had to leave that big blue bus if I didn't want to.

Eric was going to give his all to the band; he made that clear. "This could mean everything for our future," he would say seriously. "I don't want us to worry about money – the band could really make it big, Carolyn. We've got what it takes."

I always agreed with him. Of course, of course. Renegade is heading for the big time, I'd say like everyone else. But as much as I wanted to believe it, I never could. My mother had raised me to be a realist. She told me once that it was a mistake to expect too much from life, and so far she had been exactly right. We were from Iowa, for God's sake. Nothing could come out of Allendale that mattered in any circle that counted. Renegade would fade; the boys would pack up the purple shirts and sell their expensive equipment and instruments. Someone would buy a used pickup with their share; someone else would get a girl pregnant and pay for her abortion. It made me sad that I could foresee all of this so clearly. I just plain wasn't able to dream big like Eric and the rest of the band. My dreams were of little houses with white curtains, books from the library on my night table. Eric picking an armful of lilacs that he would arrange in a crystal vase on our real oak table. I crept into this daydream every chance I got. I longed for a home like that.

"Maybe you could get a job at your dad's old plant," I said. "Just in case the band doesn't make it."

"We have to give Renegade a chance," he said. "Oh, Carolyn, I think it could happen if we work hard and if Dave and Joe put off college for a year. We just need to give it one year more after graduation. Just one year."

I had to let him believe it. It wouldn't matter in the long run, anyway. In the meantime, we had become comfortable and easy with each other. We both looked forward to drinking the flavor of the night: rum, cherry vodka, Mad Dog 20/20, sometimes cheap wine. Then came the sex, always predictable, unless I was putting on a show. And when I was drunk enough, I did exactly that.

"You fuck like a mink," Eric told me one night in his sister's bedroom. His parents were out of town, and Eric and I had the run of the house. His sister, Tina, was away at college. I liked her room. Dolls from all around the world stood on shelves and peered at us from behind glass cases. I welcomed their curious eyes watching me undress. I was aware that a mink probably knew more about doing it than I did, but I could fake it.

"I know," I whispered back. It was almost over; I could tell. Sure enough, he groaned a moment later and pulled out of me as he always did.

The front door opened. "Eric!" his mother shouted from the doorway. "Where are you? I need some help with these things."

We flew apart. I grabbed my jeans and shirt, my shoes, and ran into his sister's closet. "Goddamn. Goddamn. Goddamn," Eric said as he scrambled to put on his pants and shirt. I closed the bifold closet door, my heart racing, my belly and chest slick with semen.

"Eric! Get down here. What are you doing?"

"Coming, Mom!" he said loudly. "Coming!"

I was half crying and half laughing already, but when Eric said that, I yelped in hysterical laughter.

"Be quiet!" he whispered furiously, and rushed out of the room.

My hands were shaking too badly to get dressed. I kept picturing Eric's mom flinging open the closet door and discovering me naked in her daughter's closet. I stuffed my underwear behind Tina's winter coats and managed to get my jeans on, not zipping them for fear of noise. I pulled on my sweater, but there was no way to put on my shoes. I held them and waited until I heard Eric talking to his mother in the foyer. Their voices became more distant until I finally heard them coming from the kitchen. I opened the closet door and ran down the stairs two at a time. I pushed open the front door and ran as fast as I had ever run in my life. I held my jeans shut with one hand and clutched my shoes with the other.

I dashed across the highway and ran toward the deer park by the river. I was sure Eric's mom was behind me or soon would be, and I frantically looked for a place to hide. Oh, Donna would be so mad if she knew what we had been doing in her house. It didn't seem like such a lark anymore, all the drinking and my performance in the room of the dolls. I was scared now and could not deny how far I'd fallen.

As I was running, I saw the church spire of Allendale Baptist Church on my left and I began to cry, thinking of Pastor Jim. "Help me," I sobbed as I ran past the church. "Help me, Pastor Jim." I thought about turning around and running straight into the sanctuary, prostrating myself on the red carpet, begging for mercy from God. I couldn't do that, though, because I didn't believe in God.

I ran into the deer park instead and headed for the shed where equipment and feed for the deer were kept. I ran around to the back, zipped up my jeans, and thrust my sockless feet into my shoes. It was cold without my coat. A deer licked a block of salt and paused to look at me. Under his scrutiny I felt exposed as the shameful girl I really was, this godless girl who panted behind the shed, the bad girl who could not get her breath.

SHORN

My dad remarried that winter, and my mother remarried the following spring. My sister and brother and I weren't invited to either wedding, only learning of our father's marriage months after it had happened. My mother married Hal, a banker from the county seat, thirty miles away. Hal was nice to my mom and nice to us kids. He laughed a lot and teased us as though we were his best customers' children. I didn't mistake his joviality for interest or love, but I liked him being around. He brought sirloin steaks over and bags of potato chips, lots of pop. Mother was more relaxed; the anxious lines on her face softened. We liked our new stepfather fine.

Hal bought a new house in his town where we would all live together. Mom, Lisa, Chris, and I were moving out of our house in Allendale, the house where we had lived with my father. The broken-home pain had become a kind of background pain now, a wallpaper of regret. It was only when I watched Hal take apart the bed that had once belonged to my mother and father that my grief stormed its way to the surface. Hal sat cross-legged and awkward on their bedroom floor with a pair of pliers and a screwdriver, great drops of sweat rolling off his face. I didn't say anything, I just watched as he turned the screwdriver methodically. He knew how to use a ten-key adding machine, how to lock the combination safe at the bank, how to teach customer service skills to the young girls he hired. But I didn't know if he knew how to put things back together. I wanted to throw my arms around his neck and cry into his chest. I wanted him to put everything back the way it should be, and I knew that was asking too much.

Eric and I graduated from high school. He began practicing day and night with Renegade. Dave and Joe still insisted they were going to college that fall unless something big happened with the band that summer. In the meantime, I began to make my own plans for college. Hal generously offered to pay my tuition at a nearby community college. That was my best shot at further education, and I took it gratefully. I sat in my assigned adviser's office and told him I wanted to be a writer. He was rumpled and distracted, answering the phone, shouting at some other faculty member who passed his open door.

"Journalism?" he asked. "Write for a newspaper?"

Not really, I thought. But I didn't want to tell him about my poetry.

"OK," I agreed. "Journalism. I'll do that."

Just being on a college campus filled me with a strange stirring of hope, of possibility. I had been so sated by my relationship with Eric, his steady and reliable presence, that I rarely considered a life outside of the small one I had with him. The novel idea of being someone on my own and actually having a career occurred to me as I walked along the cracked sidewalks of the little city school. Could I get an apartment? What was an intern? Could I be one?

These half-formed ideas had little chance to take root. Two days later my life changed forever.

I didn't know a college physical included a standard pregnancy test, but it did. When the doctor's office called me a few days later, I took the call in my stepfather's unfinished basement.

"Miss Gilbert?"

"Yes?"

"You tested positive for pregnancy."

I stood staring up at the support beam in the basement. It was splintering. It was bowed. I hoped that the whole house would fall on me.

I didn't have anyone to talk to, no girlfriends, certainly no one in my family. There was only Eric, and he didn't disappoint me. Steady, wonderful Eric was shaken by the news, but he quickly rallied. He even bought me a small diamond ring that I couldn't wear, but it was a relief to know we were engaged.

"We'll have to tell our folks. We'll have to tell them we're getting married," he said as he held my hand.

"Do we have to tell them about the baby?" I asked. "Can't we just get married and tell them about the baby later?"

Eric was adamant that our parents know about the baby. I couldn't do it. I couldn't tell my mom and stepfather that I was pregnant. It was proof that I had been having sex, and suddenly it felt wicked, depraved, just plain wrong. My shame was deep and real. Every morning, all morning long and well into the afternoon, I hid in the bathroom, vomiting. I turned on the water and radio to disguise the sounds of my retching, and afterward I went out to lie in the sun, wearing a little bikini and sucking on orange Popsicles. The neighbor boys whistled at me, but I could find only a small pleasure in their attention. Instead of coming to terms with my sexuality at the age of seventeen, I closed it down. I was done with the experimenting. I had made my sole discovery. Nervously, I told my mother that Eric and I were going to get married soon. Eric, however, wrote his parents a letter telling them I was pregnant. After his mother received that letter, she called my mother to see what she thought of the mess the kids were in.

My mom and I were in the den watching television when she answered the phone. I heard her say cautiously, "Hello, Donna," and then she looked at me. I remember my mother's face, the face I loved so, confused and shocked and sad. She told Eric's mother that I had a lovely new engagement ring, anyway.

When she set down the phone, she sighed. I waited for her to say something. She had just found out her teenage daughter was pregnant, for God's sake. We sat in the den together and watched TV in silence. I counted the knots in the pine paneling; I tore at my fingernails and peeled back three too short. After a while, I sighed, too, and sank into the recliner, throwing the footrest back with a clunk.

"Donna said you should have bought baby clothes instead of an engagement ring," my mother finally said. I looked at my tiny diamond on my shaking ring finger and then back at my mom. Tell me what to do, I prayed. Tell me.

Maybe she wanted to. Maybe she was filled with pity and turmoil, just like me. Maybe my mother really did understand that I was afraid and ashamed and angry. But if she did understand, she didn't have a way to let me know. She just didn't know what else to say to me, so she folded the laundry and watched the rest of her soap.

Once the hard part of telling our parents was over, Eric warmed to the idea of a baby girl and a wife and even wrote a song about our new family. I sat in his parents' basement and listened to Eric play the ballad, watched his fingers, tried to be happy. But we were surrounded by the musty relics of his parents' miserable marriage. Boxes and boxes of slides no one wanted to watch, a player piano for the parties his mother had wanted to host that had never materialized; decades of disappointments all sorted and stored in the unfinished bomb shelter where the band practiced. Eric smiled at me as he sang, "I will always love you," but I knew he was singing it to make it so. I knew he was scared, too. I smiled up at my boyfriend and tried to remember how secure I was in his love, how I only wanted his arms around me forever and ever, but it was hard to do now that the future was decided. He smiled back at me, and I wondered what secret fears were behind his smile and what second guesses lurked there. When he turned away to put on a record, I wound up the metronome and listened to its steady tick. I tried to imagine that a life like this was exactly what I wanted.

My father called me a few weeks later. It was almost my birthday, and he said that he wanted to give me a present.

We drove silently to the park on the edge of town, the topsoil-heavy Iowa River brown and rich. I kept my eyes on the river while he stumbled through his announcement that he had been married a few months before. My mother had already told me this, and more besides.

"I heard something about you having a baby," I said morosely, still tracking the brown water slowly undulating to my left.

My dad stiffened. "Yeah, that's right," he said angrily. "I suppose your mother told you that."

I didn't answer.

"OK, Squirt. I'd better get you back home now."

I wanted to tell him about my pregnancy, how scared I was, how disappointed in myself I was, how much I needed him to love me no matter what. I looked at his profile, the broken capillaries on his cheek, his sad and downcast eyes. I knew that my own baby, my secret sin, was the thing that made me more like my father than my straight hair or knobby knees. All the years I had worshiped my father had brought me to this hard place. He wasn't godlike, not at all. He was an aging athlete, and he had blown it by knocking up some woman in the middle of his life. And I was just as pathetic, pregnant at seventeen and about to make vows for life, a promise I had no way of keeping. I didn't feel like confessing anything to him. I gripped my new clock radio and the wrapping paper and sat silently as he drove me back home.

Not long afterward, I sat under a tent at the Iowa State Fair and watched Eric and the rest of the band set up for that night's Battle of the Bands. It was so hot that August, I felt continually suffocated, unable to breathe deeply enough to think clearly about anything. I was infinitely sad – everything was ending for me; I knew this instinctively. Just as things had started happening, the late machinery of the gods had seized and would not budge again. Some girl with lanky brown hair wearing a printed smock of red-and-gold geometric shapes made her way across the worn earth to me.

"Hi," she said.

"Hi," I answered, and kept watching Dave put a microphone stand together. His arm was bulging from the effort, and I couldn't help wondering what those muscles would feel like if I were to stroke them with my finger. I figured the girl was thinking the same thing and wanted to ask me about the guys in the band. It happened a lot. They were all lookers. Well, all but Eric, who was slight and sort of acne scarred, but a certain kind of forgiving girl always went after him wherever they played.

"I used to be like you," she said.

I turned toward her then, already offended, but curious.

"What does that mean?"

"I used to be lost, just like you are."

I turned toward her then, for the first time. She was holding a large Bible. I looked away and watched the prize sheep in various states of being shaved in the neighboring tent.

"I'm not lost," I said quietly, and kept watching the sheep.

"You need the Lord," she persisted. "He can fill you up. He can give you peace. He can save you from your sins."

Good Lord. It was a Jesus freak. They didn't come to Allendale, but I'd heard about them. I looked at the band

and tried to find someone who would rescue me, tell me I was needed to hold something, to carry the end of an amplifier or monitor, string some cords. No one would meet my eyes – instead they were smiling, wickedly aware of my predicament, enjoying my discomfort the way only adolescents can.

"It says right here in Romans that all men have sinned and fallen short of the glory of God," the girl continued, dogged and focused.

"Yes, I know. 'I am the way, the truth, and the life. No man cometh to the Father but by Me,'" I quoted back to her. I had memorized my share of Scripture trying to get Pastor Jim's attention.

"Do you know Jesus Christ as your personal Savior?" she asked, incredulous and chagrined that she hadn't been able to spot me as a believer.

"I sure do," I answered, and blew a bubble. I felt a sudden surge of confidence in her flustered response.

"Oh, praise God," she said mechanically, still unsure. After all, I had looked so lost, but how could she question me now?

"Praise Jesus," I answered, and smiled, stretching out "Jeeesus" the way I'd heard Pastor Jim do it a hundred times. The band kept smiling to themselves while I claimed to know God. I was pissed at them and at the girl. I felt singled out, the chosen victim, the one who was obviously blemished and stained. The girl and I sat next to each other for a few minutes – I'm sure she realized that I was lying, but there was nothing she could do outside of calling me a liar. She finally closed her Bible and tucked her hair behind her ears. She looked as though she were going to say something and then changed her mind. I didn't say anything to her, either; we just looked at each other like friends who had quarreled over some boy we both liked. She walked away with the Bible under her arm. I watched her disappear into the gathering groupies, and I felt even sadder than before. The band cracked up once she left the tent, and I laughed with them, but my laughter was uneasy, false, threaded with the bleats and bellows of the animals in the surrounding tents.

We would have a real wedding, thanks to Eric's mother. I had planned on getting married in the dress I lost my virginity in, an irony I knew I would enjoy and Eric would find touching, but Donna said I should have a real wedding dress. We went shopping in Des Moines and found a dotted swiss pinafore with a long veil, a dress that had been custom-made for someone who had changed her mind (about the dress? or marriage?) at the last minute. It looked like a child's first Communion dress; it was girlish, improbably small. Because I had been throwing up for weeks, I weighed around ninety pounds and the dress fit me perfectly. Donna got a deal and I was pleased; I couldn't help it, I loved the idea of performing, of playing bride. Next, she bought me a blue garter and a delicate necklace to wear with the dress, and white pumps. She ordered flowers and cake and packed her good crystal and silver to bring to the church basement for our reception.

It was a hurry-up affair, a "close your eyes and be happy even though they're just kids and she must be pregnant" kind of wedding. Our grandmothers wore hats and watched all the long-haired young people take their marks for the prescribed ritual up front. Eric and I both had hair that reached the middle of our backs; the band, who served as groomsmen and musicians, wore suits and had their long hair in great elaborate ponytails and braids, all festooned with lace and confetti. Eric played his guitar and sang to me as my dad led me down the aisle.

> Come down to me,
> I want to hold you.
> Come down to me,
> I want to show you how our life can be. . . .

I had requested a new song for the wedding, but this was the first time I had heard it. Eric had written it just days before our wedding, and he sang softly, sounding just like James Taylor, as my father in his cowboy boots and I in my dotted swiss approached the altar. My bridesmaids, Lisa and Katherine, waited tearfully for me, wearing lavender dresses and carrying yellow roses. Eric kept singing, but his song was not the reassuring anthem I had thought it would be. His words struck me as banal and meaningless. I couldn't stop thinking about Lisa and Katherine and their sentimental tears. This isn't perfect, I wanted to tell them. Don't think this is something it's not.

All through the ceremony, the vows, the lighting of the unity candle, Eric singing for me yet again, I fought the nagging disappointment, the sorrow, for God's sake, the sorrow I felt on my wedding day. I didn't know what it was I mourned, what I could possibly want that I did not have, but something was undeniably missing. My mother wore a brocade lavender mother-of-the-bride dress, and she sat beside my stepfather on the second row. My father sat behind them. I saw them all when we turned toward the guests and the pastor announced Eric and I were man and wife. My father was stoic; he didn't smile. My mother's smile was brief and forced. My stepfather nodded his approval at the deal being sealed. Handshakes all around.

After cake and champagne, Eric and I left Allendale for Pleasure Island in Des Moines for a weekend honeymoon. It was off-season and the brand-new theme park with two roller coasters, a log flume ride, and a spinning silo would not be open, but we would be able to see the park outside our motel windows. The guys in the band had decorated our car with shaving cream and something else that would eventually take the finish off it, but we didn't know that then as we drove through the night, peering out of the one clear spot on the coated window. Halfway to Des Moines, sardines began to fry on the engine block and the car filled with the oily and acrid smell of burning fish. I gulped and asked Eric to pull over. He left the highway, turned onto a gravel road, and stopped the car. I didn't trust myself to speak, I just shook my head no at him, don't follow me, and then I opened the car door. Moments later I knelt on the stubs of cornstalks, the razor sharp remains of harvest. My knees were bleeding. I lost the cake, the three swallows of champagne. This isn't perfect, I told myself. Don't think this is something it's not. And then I cried.

Our first home was a trailer, a ten-by-forty-two-foot trailer recently transported to a mobile home park called Grand Estates just outside of Des Moines. The trailer had been a vacation home for Eric's family for several years, but Donna had decided it was the housing solution for Eric and me. This aging trailer was yanked out of its lakeside lot in southern Iowa and towed upstate. I washed the paneling and scrubbed the cupboards and pink appliances, but the whole trailer smelled faintly of fish and algae. I put away our wedding gifts, the green-and-black plates we had bought at Woolworth's and the scrapbooks I had kept of my courtship with Eric. I spread one of my grandma's quilts on our bed. The bed had belonged to Eric's sister, the very one we had been messing around in after school and the weekends his parents were out of town. I knew the sags and the poking buttons of this mattress by heart. I lay in bed at night and ran my hand over the surface, searching for something familiar.

Everything was different now. Eric was working at the plant his father used to own, assembling hog confinement units. Three nights a week he went to the farmhouse Renegade rented and practiced until close to midnight. I was alone in a way I had never been before. I didn't want to go to school, even though I was still registered at the community college. It seemed a useless gesture to sit in a classroom and take notes about Western civilization. I wasn't going to be a scholar, I was going to be a mother. As far as I could see, there was no way to be both. So I stayed home alone every day. I watched *The Price Is Right* and ate Cheetos, the only food I could keep down. After another month of weight loss, my doctor prescribed antinausea medicine and I was finally able to eat.

Most of the time I didn't bother getting dressed. I wore baby-doll pajamas my mother had bought me at Penney's when I was still a girl. I pulled up the top and looked at the grapefruit-size lump in my stomach. My hips were narrow, my breasts only a bit fuller, and then that lump there. It felt hard and serious, and I respected it for that, but I was also a little freaked out. I remembered the term *symbiosis* from high school biology, and it seemed to me that was exactly what was happening. Something had hitched on to me and was making itself quite at home.

No, I argued with myself. It's not something; it's a baby, our baby. Allison or Matthew Anders, that's who it was. I made baby blankets, cross-stitched bunnies and dogs, and appliquéd quilt squares. I sorted through the sacks of used baby clothes Donna gathered and delivered regularly. I held up the tiny T-shirts and jumpers and imagined threading a baby's arms and legs into them. I kept telling myself I was going to be a mother, but I didn't believe it until I felt the baby kicking.

I was being nudged from the *inside*. It wasn't so much the fluttering that I had read about; it was a definite poke. Insistent, like someone saying, "Hey." I kept hearing it, at first the faintest of greetings, but yes, there it was again. "Hey!"

"Hello," I said back, and put my hand on my stomach, only this time I was cradling someone, a face this time, not a lump on my belly, but a little being with a face and arms and legs, and my God, I was going to be a mother, I really was.

I continued to travel with Renegade, just as I had done when we were dating. I was married and done with being a groupie; I was the lead guitarist's wife now. Because we had never made any public announcement, no one outside of our families ever mentioned the baby. I had lost so much weight the first months of my pregnancy that by the time I was in my seventh month I was beginning to look healthy, like a normal-size girl. We didn't have money for maternity clothes, so I wore my jeans with one and then two buttons undone underneath one of Eric's flannel shirts. This was my wardrobe for the entire pregnancy. One night in a town not far from Allendale, I was listening to the band wind up their final set when a friend of my sister's approached me.

"When's the kid due?" she asked.

I was eight months pregnant, but I thought no one could tell.

"What kid?" I asked. I could feel my face burning in the dark.

"Your baby," she answered, her face moonlike and surprised, floating there before me.

Your face looks like the moon, I wanted to say. I felt otherworldly, a liar from another planet, as I slowly spoke. "I don't know what you're talking about."

She was dumbfounded. She was silent. She turned away and my hand flew up to my stomach to stroke it, to tell the baby, Hush, never mind. I know you're there. I love you.

I listened to the band play "Color My World", a slow dance. I pushed back the curtains and saw the couples reach for each other, saw their bodies meld together, saw the hands of the boys running down the backs of the girls, their hands rippling like water at the shore, almost home, almost safe.

SALVATION

Concentrate on the baby, I told myself. Forget high school. Forget what anyone thinks of you. Just think about having this baby. I read everything I could get my hands on about pregnancy, childbirth, and baby care. Some of it was outdated and silly, but I read indiscriminately. The baby on my copy of Dr. Spock's baby manual looked like an Ivory soap baby, an oily curl on its head and a pink-lipped smile, the way babies looked when I was a baby, but I read that book thoroughly and I believed everything Dr. Spock said. He spoke with an authority that silenced me and made me pick up a highlighter in respect. When Katherine called me one afternoon, I was reading about anesthesia for childbirth. One month from now, I will be suffering great pain, I thought, answering the phone.

"It's me – Katherine! Oh, Carolyn! How's everything?"

I had spoken with Katherine a handful of times since the wedding, but I hadn't seen her and I hadn't mentioned that I was expecting a baby. She was a coed now at Iowa State, going through rush week, attending drinking parties, and certainly meeting people who were not from Allendale. I didn't know why she kept calling me. She probably wanted me to confess about the baby. I suspected there were rumors.

"It's fine," I said. "I like being married. Our trailer is nice," I added. I knew I would have to tell her soon; the baby was just about due, for God's sake.

"Carolyn? Something's going on up here."

"What?" I asked, and stopped flaking the toenail polish on my big toe. She sounded very dramatic.

"We're having Bible studies in our dorm! Carolyn, I've accepted Christ into my heart and I'm so happy!"

Christ? Christ? Who used the word *Christ* unless they were swearing? Nobody I knew anymore. It wasn't cool, for one thing. Katherine was beautiful and popular; religious people were always real losers. Sarah Wilkins wasn't exactly a far-out chick. And Noah Forrest, the Holy Roller guy in high school. He wore high-water pants and horn-rimmed glasses and looked like a Kewpie doll, his heart-shaped lips always parting over the words *God* or *Jesus.*

"Cool," I said because I had to say something.

"More than cool. Carolyn, I'm so happy. You and Eric have to come up here as soon as you can. Tonight! Tomorrow! You're not going to believe what's going on."

"Sure," I said. "Sure, we'll come up – maybe in a month or so." After the baby came, we would be able to go. By then the three of us would have our own little world and we would be an entity unto ourselves. There would be no intrusion from others, even a God who frequented college dorms, even a God who sat cross-legged on a futon and listened to prayers about final exams.

But I wished she hadn't called, all the same. I was tired of change. I had barely come to terms with being married; I was soon to be an eighteen-year-old mother, and now my friend was trying to convert me to a religion I had no use for. I tried to explain my exasperation to Eric that night over dinner.

"Katherine has become a Jesus freak," I said as I ladled a big portion of tuna and noodles, the only entrée I knew how to make. It was the third time that week I had served it.

He sighed and poked at the tuna with his fork. "A Jesus freak? How'd that happen?"

"Someone is having Bible studies in her dorm," I said gloomily. "Good God, Eric, can you imagine? Katherine? She's not a loser like the rest of those creepy Christians. Why would she do this?"

"It's probably just a phase," Eric said. "That's what happens to kids when they start college, they try on new identities."

"She's not a kid. She's our age," I reminded him. "She's not an idiot, either. I just don't get it."

"Forget it," Eric said as he buttered a piece of bread.

"Aren't you going to eat your tuna and noodles?" I asked.

"Yeah, it's just that I'm a little full from lunch."

"Your peanut-butter sandwich made you too full for dinner?"

"Some lady in the brooder department brought over a carrot cake. I ate a couple of pieces at break."

We stared at each other. "Oh," I finally said. "I see." I let my face fall a little, my hand drop to my swollen belly.

Eric looked chagrined and began to eat his dinner. He managed to get most of the noodles down before I showed him mercy and took away his plate.

The baby was born the day before Easter. She was amazingly tiny and red faced, with dark brown fuzz on her head. Her gray eyes squinched shut against the silver nitrate drops squeezed to keep her from catching VD as she left my body. I wanted to tell the nurse Allison didn't need anything in her eyes, that Eric and I were virgins who had been only with each other, but I doubted she would believe me, the teenage mother, the mother with the bell-bottomed jeans and waist-length hair parted in the middle. Eric was sent to the waiting room, where he read a science-fiction novel and waited obediently. I was given a room in the ward because we had no insurance, and there I held Allison Leigh at my side. I had no desire to nurse her; my breasts had grown only in the last two years and I wanted my breasts for myself. But I instantly loved the little baby who seemed to belong to the nurses more than to me.

I was so thrilled with the baby, the little girl who loved me, who needed me, who depended on me for everything, that I almost forgot I had ever known a life outside of being her mother. And then Katherine called again. She had received our birth announcement and she was thrilled, thrilled for us both. Could she come and see the baby? Could she bring some friends and come down next Monday afternoon?

I thought quickly. Eric would be working, but I would be home. I was always home. I didn't have a driver's license or a car and no place to go even if I did. I was Allison's mother. She consumed me; everything about her was significant and exciting. I spent hours writing in her baby book, careful to note everything that happened in her early months, what she wore when I took her to the doctor, what he said about her, the expression on his face.

Eric's job in the hog confinement plant came to a close. His father had used his influence to get Eric the job, but influence or not, it was still a seasonal job and the season was over. He needed a job closer to home, anyway. Again, his parents came to our rescue.

Eric's parents, Donna and Richard, looked out for us a lot in those early days. We were young and clueless, and they were in love with their brand-new grandbaby Allison. There was no way they were going to let us starve. Richard's latest project was an assignment to construct an elaborate pirate's cove at Pleasure Island, the very same theme park/hotel where Eric and I had spent our honeymoon. Richard's first order of business was to hire his son, who was the only novice in a crew of experienced carpenters.

Eric packed a peanut-butter sandwich and a carton of yogurt in a beat-up cooler every morning and spent each weekday sawing boards and pounding nails. The other men on the construction site grumbled at Eric's ineptness, convinced that he made their jobs harder. They called him Little Dick, and even Richard was often impatient and demanding. Eric's hands chafed and he suffered from windburn and sunburn as well as constant abrasions and punctures. When my husband came home at night, he was exhausted; his only pleasures were feeding Allison her evening bottle and watching an hour or two of television with me before he fell asleep. I woke him up long enough to get him from the couch to our bedroom. There, he slathered Cornhusker lotion on his cracked hands, slipped on a pair of disposable gloves, and crawled into bed.

In spite of the aloofness and resentment from the other carpenters and the strenuous labor, Eric went to work each morning and worked until dark. I watched him leave each winter morning as I stood at the window, running hot water over Allison's bottle. He ducked his head against the wind and clutched his thermos, his hands lost inside heavy rawhide mittens. He grimaced as he scraped the ice from the car. He looked so miserable, it scared me.

I rocked Allison and watched the news about Watergate. My God, I thought, our president is going to be impeached. This, on the heels of the endless war in Vietnam, depressed me. The world was so unstable. The Soviet Union. China. I did not want my baby growing up in a world of riot.

I rarely saw anyone those days; my mother lived an hour away and didn't drive out of town, and besides that, she had her hands full with my sister, Lisa, still in high school, smoking pot and skipping school. I hadn't met any of my neighbors at all; there didn't seem to be any other stay-at-home moms. Every day the trailer court was vacated; only the dogs chained at the backs of the trailers and Allison and I heard the freight trains roar through every three hours.

So Katherine wanted to come back into my life. She was waiting for an answer.

"All right," I said. "Come next Monday."

"Really?" she asked. "We can come and see you?"

"Of course," I said. "We love visitors. Bring anyone you like."

84

I hung up the phone and turned to Allison. "Company's coming, Ally." She pulled her icy teething ring out of her mouth and looked at me with a serious, perplexed expression.

"Yeah, I don't know what I'm thinking, either," I said, wiping her face.

I baked an apple pie for their visit. I was having company, and grown-ups baked pie for company, didn't they? My first attempt at domesticity, the pie could have been Lucy Ricardo's. The filling was viscous with lumpy cornstarch, and the slices of apple were too thick and undercooked. The crust was a tasteless plaster, white and doughy in places and burnt in others. I sprinkled sugar on top and sliced it into eight pieces. I poured glasses of Coke and waited for my guests.

Katherine brought two girls and a boy. The girls were tall with long, brown hair, the kind who dressed plainly and talked plainly and smiled at any pause or lag in the conversation. The boy's name was Sam. He played football for Iowa State and he had black, wavy hair, broad arms, and thick wrists, eyes as direct and piercing as I could take.

"Carolyn," he began, "I'd like to show you something far-out. You got a Bible around here?"

A Bible? Oh, for God's sake. Why hadn't I been prepared for this? They were witnessing to me. They were here to win my soul for Jesus. Shit.

The girls all looked at Sam as though their heads had been pulled with a string, then the string jerked them back my way. Marionette smiles painted cheerily on their faces. And there I was, the real girl, trying to not be dazzled by their bright eyes.

I started to say no, but then I heard myself saying, "I might have my old Sunday school Bible around here."

The four of them smiled wider, eerily in unison, like someone turning up the volume of goodness and harmony, and it spooked me enough that I fled in relief to the bedroom to dig through a box on the floor of my closet. I found the old King James. The cover was torn, the margins filled with doodles, the inscription still flourishing: "Presented to Carolyn Sue Gilbert from Allendale First Baptist Church". I brought it back to the living room and handed it to Sam.

"Thanks, sis," he said, and began flipping through the pages. I looked at Katherine to see if she thought it was strange he had called me sis, but she just beamed back. We all waited for Sam to find the passage.

" 'If I speak with the tongues of men and angels and have not love, I am a clanging gong,' " he read. "Wow, did you hear that?"

My stomach clenched. I felt like prey who had been cornered by these four happy hunters. I wasn't going to fall for it. Not any of it. I reached for the Bible and took it out of Sam's hands.

"Yeah, I remember that one," I said. "Do you want some more pie?"

" 'The greatest of these is love,' " one of the girls said quietly as she looked at her hands in her lap. "Carolyn, did you ever think –"

"Sure," Sam interrupted her. "I'll take another piece of pie. You're a great cook, sis."

And then a series of looks between them, secret and guarded, but apparently perfectly understood because they all slid their plates over for more pie, surely the worst they had ever tasted.

After that I tried to put it all out of my mind, but like it or not, God had made His presence known and I had to deal with Him. Suddenly, I couldn't carelessly brush God away, like crumbs on the table after breakfast. I didn't want to think about God – why should I? God was for people in the Allendale Baptist Church, for all those stuck-up people with pious smiles and phony handshakes in the light-flooded foyer.

I was too smart and too savvy for God, wasn't I? But there He was, like a toothache, sending little reminders during the course of the day.

The hound of heaven, I later learned, was after me.

I would change Allison's diaper and be struck by the luminous little eyes trained on me. I felt like a fraud sometimes. How was I going to give her certainty and order? I had none of my own to offer, and that plagued me. I loved her so – how could I not give her a centered and moral universe? What did I know about values and principles? I had fooled around before I was married. I was practically a teenage alcoholic. I was pregnant when I was seventeen years old, for God's sake. I could tell a lie effortlessly, and my language was as crude as any of the carpenters Eric worked with.

I had hoped for a security in marriage that I hadn't been able to find anywhere else, but it hadn't happened yet. Eric and I had lit a unity candle at our wedding, afterward blowing out our separate ends. That unity candle was now on our coffee table, a fat waxen lump, the wick swallowed in its milky depths. I had truly expected Eric to take up the sword for me for life, and instead I saw him swatting at his own issues, parrying, retreating, pushing back his glasses, and heading back at it, always slightly dazed and sweating.

If Eric wasn't going to save me, who was?

When I flipped through channels on the television, I'd linger on the religious stations for a moment or two. I was moved when I heard Jimmy Swaggart preaching with such confidence and clarity and simplicity. He closed his eyes and whispered "Jesus" and I felt the chills in my own body. His wife was smart and sassy looking, with her red hair styled and sprayed, and yet she too said "Jesus" in a way that you'd say a lover's name. And I watched *The PTL Club*, mesmerized by Tammy Faye's made-up eyes that constantly filled with sooty tears. They all talked about God as if they were in love. There seemed to be a mysterious passion running between God and man that was unlike anything I had experienced in the church. It was like a drug, almost. A drug that would alter reality, but in a good way, a way no one could object to.

My reality was a trailer on the north edge of Des Moines. It was so narrow that if I lay on the living room floor with my arms outstretched over my head, I could reach the opposite wall with my toes. My daughter slept in a borrowed bassinet beneath hand-me-down nursery curtains that were too long and safety-pinned to fit the very small window. My husband slept with gloves on his bleeding hands. I watched him play the guitar on weekends and saw his stiff, cracked fingers trying to fret as they had always done. I sat in seedy bars where his band played Santana or Cream or Chicago for greasy-haired boys and girls with wide, empty faces and wondered how much longer he would keep his dream for Renegade alive. Eric was not going to become a famous musician, and I had no plans for the future but more babies.

Katherine sent me little notes about the Lord. The Lord was so beautiful. He broke her heart with His amazing love. One Saturday morning she called me while she was still in bed, her open Bible on her chest and her heart, it seemed, overflowing.

"Oh, Carolyn," she said, "I don't know how to explain it. The Lord's so good, so incredibly good. I was reading this morning about the sinful woman, the one the crowd was about to stone. They dragged Jesus over there and said, 'You know we should stone her. The law says so. You said we should obey the law, so here, take a stone.'"

I was holding Allison on my lap, and she yanked the phone from my ear. I scrambled to put it back; there was something about Katherine's voice, sultry and innocent, a languorous passion.

"But He didn't take the stone, Carolyn. He bent down and

wrote in the sand with a stick, just drew little designs, I think, the Bible doesn't say. But after a while, He stood up and that's when He said, 'You who are without sin, you throw the first stone.' And nobody could, nobody could! They all walked away, and the woman's life was spared, all because of Jesus." She sighed softly. "He's so beautiful."

I sighed myself. Too much. This religious stuff was just over the top. I felt as if I were sitting in the Allendale Baptist Church basement and I were going to have to go back into that foyer where I didn't belong. It embarrassed me the way I was drawn and then repelled again and again. I wiped Allison's mouth of gummy teething biscuit and told Katherine that I had to go give Allison a bath.

"I think," Katherine said dreamily, as if she hadn't even heard me, "that this must be the way a bride feels."

Eric walked into the kitchen then with his oily hair plastered across his forehead. His face was broken out and his jeans were unbuttoned. I watched him pour his bowl of Uncle Sam's cereal, the natural laxative.

"You feel that good?" I responded. I hung up after a flurry of promises to read the Bible, to pray, to ask for light. Katherine reminded me that God would provide the light of understanding. And despite the tinny core of me, that thread of disdain for almost everyone and everything, I couldn't keep myself from praying for that very thing. Quickly, before I could change my mind, I asked God for light.

That night Eric and I made love, and I remembered how Katherine had sounded almost hot when she was talking about God. I longed for that kind of passion in my marriage. What had begun as a forbidden act when we were sixteen had changed now that we were eighteen into, oddly enough, something that seemed obligatory, like Sunday dinner at his mom's. I was always tense, listening for Allison, afraid she'd wake up and need me. We hardly ever drank these days, and that certainly cut down on the variety in our technique. But between Allison's presence ten feet down the hall and Eric's exhaustion, we weren't doing much more than sleeping in our purple shag-carpeted bedroom, anyway. Eric and I got along, though, and we both worshiped Allison. Our day-to-day lives were seamless, really. We were gentle and kind to each other. We discussed the minutiae of our days over big plates of Kraft zesty spaghetti (my new entrée of choice) at our kitchen table. I kept telling him about Katherine, what she was saying and how I responded to her. When I let Eric read some of Katherine's letters, he began to ask questions about the Bible.

"Does Katherine believe that story about Jonah being swallowed by a whale?" he asked. We were pushing the baby in her stroller on our evening walk.

"Probably," I said. The trailer court was nice in the evening. People were home from work and barbecuing pork chops on Hitachis on the cement slabs our trailers were anchored to. Little kids rode Big Wheels. Everyone waved when we walked by.

"Well, I read one time that a whale has a throat the size of an orange. There's no way a whale could swallow a human being," Eric said matter-of-factly.

"Got me." I shrugged. "There's lots of wacko stuff in the Bible."

"What about dinosaurs? Were they in the Garden of Eden?"

"I have no idea," I said. "I don't think Baptists believe in dinosaurs."

"Well, does it mention dinosaurs in the Bible?" Eric pushed his glasses up on the bridge of his nose, his thin blond hair blowing back from his face.

"Eric, I don't know. I just went to Sunday school when I was a kid," I snapped, and then, because I felt bad, I added, "Katherine says there's a Bible that's easier to understand.

Maybe we should get one." And then I added to myself, We're supposed to pray for light.

We found an edition of *The Way*, a large paperback paraphrase of the Bible, at Walgreen's. It cost $11.95. I pulled it off the rack and thumbed through it. "Genesis, Exodus, Leviticus, Numbers, Deut-eh-ron-no-mee . . ." The Sunday school song I had learned to memorize the books of the Bible, still there, still ready on the tip of my tongue when I needed it.

"Do you think we'd really read it?" I asked, hoping Eric had changed his mind and we wouldn't have to spend the money.

Eric was holding Allison, who was trying to get out of his arms. She had a great trick: She would stiffen her entire body and hold it ramrod straight while she thrust her body downward, sliding like butter through our arms. She had begun her descent, and Eric was distracted.

"Yeah, sure," Eric said. "I will, anyway. Let's just get it – that's why we came here, isn't it?"

He was right, but still it was a lot of money, and I wasn't wild about plunking that Bible down on the counter for the checkout girl to see. It was embarrassing.

"Come on, honey," Eric pleaded. "I can't hold on to Ally much longer. She wants down in the worst way."

"Let me have her," I said. "You pay for it and we'll wait for you in the car."

I hurried out of the store with Allison on my hip, my purse and her diaper bag on the other, back into the muggy evening. Old-timers say you can cut the humidity in Iowa with a knife. I felt as though I needed a machete as I crossed the asphalt parking lot and unlocked the door to the car.

I put Allison in the car seat and gave her a bottle of cold apple juice from the diaper bag. The sun was disappearing from view, a lazy, murky slide of orange and crimson. A family made their way into the store, a mother and a father with a little girl on his shoulders. The father was singing; I could just barely hear him. When he passed our car, he sang a little breathlessly, "It's not easy being the color of the leaves." His wife walked with hunched shoulders, holding her arms folded in front of her as if the summer evening were cold. She wore white pumps with a denim skirt, such bad fashion sense that I winced. Only the little girl appeared to be optimistic about things; the words of her father's song floated around her, but she batted them away and giggled. Finally, Eric walked out of the store with a Bible in a blue plastic bag. He looked tired after his long workday, but he was smiling as he got closer. I had a sudden impulse to lock the door, to keep the light from coming in, to keep everything the same.

That night we watched a little TV, as we always did. The new Bible was still inside the Walgreen's bag on the kitchen table. I walked past it several times that evening while I did laundry in the stackable unit inside the hallway closet. I just let the shopping bag and Bible lie there. I liked things to be tidy, everything straightened up by the end of the day, but tonight I was content to let our purchase remain untouched.

"After Allison goes to bed, we should read some of the Bible together," Eric suggested. "We could take it to bed with us."

"Sure," I said. "Why not? A ménage à trois."

Eric looked at me blankly. He didn't read the same library books I did.

"Just a joke," I said.

"Don't you want to read the Bible?" Eric asked. "I thought we were both interested. Now you've been acting all weird about it."

"I do want to read it," I said, and my voice cracked. I cleared my throat. "I just don't want to get all carried away or anything."

"Don't worry, honey," Eric said, pulling me into his arms. "I think this will be good for us."

So it began. Something had been set into motion that would propel us forward like mites into a turbine. Irresistible grace, John Calvin named it, this notion that if God wants you, He shall have you.

But I didn't know that yet. I read innocently enough, taking turns with my carpenter husband, my Eric, who alternately broke and hardened my heart. We slept in the back room of the trailer, the railroad tracks just a few feet from our window. The top of our dresser held a twenty-gallon fish tank with a school of neon tetras. The carpet was purple, the curtains were purple, the bedspread was purple. On top of this bedspread, a stuffed lamb Eric had given me the Christmas before. Mount Sinai in Polk County.

When we finally got into bed that first night, Eric brought extra pillows from the sofa. He propped up our pillows and pulled back the sheets. I was wearing my pink baby-doll pajamas and he was wearing only his Jockey shorts. We lay side by side with the fat green Bible between us. Eric was the first to pick it up.

"I guess we should start at the beginning," he said.

"Katherine says to start with the New Testament," I said, chewing on my fingernail. "She says we'll get lost in the Old."

"Where's the New Testament start?" Eric asked, and began flipping through the pages. There were black-and-white pictures of jubilant hippies interspersed throughout the text. They were pointing toward heaven with their eyes closed, or getting baptized in rivers, smiling as though they'd lost all good sense.

Or as if they had found something they didn't expect to find.

I reached over and turned the page to the New Testament.

"It starts with Matthew," I said. "We might as well read there."

"The genealogy of Jesus Christ, the son of David . . . ," Eric began. It felt odd, this whole experiment. Why were we doing this again? I decided to try the Lamaze natural childbirth breathing exercises. Relax, I told myself. Just listen, don't prejudge, just listen. You asked God for light, didn't you? Just see if it comes.

I felt better then. I wasn't a kook; I was a smart, capable girl. I didn't have to accept any of this if I didn't want to, but I should know what I was rejecting, right? Eric read the Bible for half an hour that first night. I listened to the ancient words in our little purple bedroom while I did my breathing, *in and out, in and out, cleansing breath*. I was nearly asleep when Eric's voice became scratchy and faint. Jesus was saying something about God's kingdom and who it belonged to, who it was that would inherit the earth. It's fine with me, I remember thinking, whoever gets the earth, it's fine with me.

The next night was my turn to read, so I just picked up where Eric had left off, the Sermon on the Mount. I felt alert and eager, a rare condition for me, especially at the end of the day, but there was something about hearing Jesus talk. It seemed apparent that religion wasn't the issue; the Gospels we were reading had nothing to do with dry and worthless religion. In fact, Jesus was bummed out by religion; he blistered the uptight religious types all the time. Jesus, it turned out, was this really cool guy who didn't take shit from the Establishment. I liked that. The contemporary language of the paraphrase was very appealing, nothing like the King James I had read in Sunday school. I smiled as I read, paused a moment, and smiled at Eric.

"Pretty neat, huh?" I asked.

"Yeah," he said. "Far-out, all right."

Under the covers, his foot brushed mine, pressed into it. I pressed back. Then I began to read again.

Our lives continued as before. The days were getting warmer and warmer. Eric wore short-sleeved shirts with his Dickies and work boots. Allison and I met him at the door and exclaimed over his new "owies", the scrapes and cuts, blackened fingernails where he had whacked himself with a hammer. He kissed our foreheads and asked what we had done all day. There was never much to report; it was an orderly life of grocery shopping and paying bills, planting petunias in a tractor tire in the yard, recording Allison's height and weight. Ordinary stuff.

But each night we dealt with the cosmos.

We kept reading the Bible, the by now well-thumbed green Bible. Afterward we shut off the light in the bedroom and lay side by side, holding hands. The Bible, like the birth of Allison to a lesser degree, was beginning to create a genuine bond between Eric and me. All of the other ties between us, infatuation, gratitude, initiation into love and sex, were fading. And even our mutual love for our red-haired daughter would not have kept us together forever.

When Eric read the Scriptures with tears in his eyes, my heart melted. He never seemed as manly as he did when he cried over the Word of God. I liked his insights, I liked the way he thoughtfully examined a Scripture and wondered about the connotation of a word. He seemed smart and holy and in control. I had always harbored a strange eroticism for the holy – Pastor Jim had done it for me, all right – and now I saw how I was drawn to my husband when he drew near to God.

We had made it through Matthew, Mark, and Luke. We were reading John now, and the Jesus he wrote of was the most appealing yet. Jesus *loved* people like no one I had ever known. He was nonjudgmental, patient, kind, passionate. Jesus was authentic and nothing like the hypocrites who claimed his name: the hateful deacon George Kettlemen, the white-gloved matrons of Allendale Baptist who ignored my mother in her white shorts, all of the church-bred kids who made me feel that I just wasn't good enough for salvation. Jesus liked people on the fringe. He sought them out wherever He went. He wasn't holding me at arm's length, not at all, instead I felt Him close to me, wooing me, pleading with me to believe.

Later, I would tell others the way the Word of God had eroded my hard heart; the ebb and flow just kept at it until I was malleable and I could accept truth at last. At the time, I didn't know whether to be relieved or alarmed, but there I was, lying under a white sheet in the purple bedroom with my heart close to bursting.

Eric held the Bible with Band-Aid-covered hands. He had recently lost another fingernail. That night he had tried to play the guitar and stopped after a few minutes. He looked so sad staring down at the guitar that I went to him and kneaded his shoulders. I asked him if he wanted to go to bed with me and read the Book of John. He had been reading aloud for almost ten minutes, and his voice had just become stronger.

" 'For my Father's will is that everyone who looks to the Son and believes in Him shall have eternal life and I will raise him up on the last day.' "

He stopped.

Our eyes met. His were filled with tears.

"Carolyn, this is –"

"True," I finished his sentence.

" 'I am the bread of life. He who comes to me will never go hungry, and he who believes in me will never be thirsty.' "

We read a few more Scriptures, both of us side by side, interrupting each other, pointing to another and another, flipping pages back to the other Gospels to compare the accounts of Jesus' death and Resurrection. In a split second, we crossed to the other side. There was no turning back now. Eric flung aside the bedspread and pulled me out of bed. He held me close. We cried. It was the first moment of absolute magic I had ever lived. There was a God. There was. There was.

QUITTING THE WORLD

"Katherine," I wrote. "We have met Christ. We're born again. We're His." I etched a cross under my name.

She called me, overjoyed to the point of near hysteria. She couldn't believe it. She knew God could do it, but oh, how happy she was. At the end of our conversation we were both crying.

"Praise God," she whispered as she said good-bye. "He is so good."

Meanwhile, the changes began. It could only be the instinct of a hatchling, this turning toward the light. Our born-again experience was a solitary one. We had Katherine with her notes and weekly call from Iowa State, but that was the extent of our nurture. Our remarkable transformation was not schooled; it was an inner reality that began manifesting itself in ways that floored us.

Born again.

Talk about mind-blowing, talk about a trip. I had been swept clean of everything familiar. I looked inside and tried to find any of my demons. Where was my chronic depression? I couldn't find it. Where was my malcontent nature, my resentment of my lot in life, my hunger for excitement, the rebellion I had harbored since I was a kid? It was all gone. Instead, I felt joyful and at peace. Joy? I was not prepared for joy at all.

My language cleaned up overnight. It wasn't a conscious decision to not say "shit" or "damn" when presented with the opportunity. I simply lost the words from my vocabulary – and found new expressions on the tip of my tongue: "Praise the Lord." "Bless Jesus." "God bless you."

I had never even said "God bless you" for a sneeze before. Suddenly I was blessing the sackers in the grocery store who handed me my groceries. This aberration was my first proof that this time salvation had worked for me. I was a new creature, just as the Bible said. Jesus was now living His life through me. I had become only a vessel. In fact, Carolyn Gilbert was dead: "Your flesh has been crucified with Christ. It is no longer I who live, but Christ who lives through me" (Galatians 2:20). When I spoke, I strained to hear Christ speaking. Every time I looked at my hands, I was conscious that they were Christ's. Every part of my body: His. He was continuing His earthly ministry using my body. It was sobering. It was also thrilling.

Nothing in my isolated life had prepared me for the feeling of being immersed in something bigger than myself. Destiny had always seemed an idea too noble for the likes of me, but as I realized that the Creator had chosen me before the foundations of the world were laid, I was overwhelmed with a sense of purpose. My life was going to count. I was going to be used by God! What could possibly compare to a calling like that?

It was strange to find myself caring deeply about other people. Strangers. The world at large. I felt compassion and interest for people I used to pass by without noticing. I began to offer up prayer for people in passing cars. I took the initiative to start conversations in waiting rooms or while standing in a checkout line, something that was totally against the grain of a shy small-town girl like me. Again and again, I asked strangers their names, told them mine, and then tried to steer the conversation that followed to spiritual matters. "I'll pray for you," I promised when we parted.

Eric and I read the Bible separately during the day, but we read at least one chapter together every night in bed. We no longer spoke about anything but the baby and God. I stopped fretting over our lackluster partnership, the unity I had longed to experience. There was something better now: We were sleeping with God, a holy ménage à trois. We both loved God, and His love was all we needed.

Replete. That's the word. I was satisfied at long last. I had love and security and the promise of a rich future. Nothing scared me anymore.

Not even when a tornado came ripping through Grand Estates Mobile Home Park.

The killer storms come with the spring in Iowa. When the last crust of snow has melted and the long barren trees sprout hard brown knobs, something happens in the sky. Fronts clash, warm air rises, and heavy clouds smother the earth. Everything becomes still and dark, the color of yellow underneath it all like a sick pallor. We know that look. We've grown up standing on our front porches, scanning the sky, just watching because the air feels ripe for tornadoes.

I could remember so many times of waiting out these storms in basements, a crackling radio tracking the path of the tornado. We would sit in the northwest corner of the basement in folding chairs. I'd never stay in mine; instead I'd stand in the corner, pressing my back against the crumbly cement block. I would watch my parents' faces by candlelight and startle at every crack of limb or thump above us. We wouldn't go upstairs until the town whistle blew the all-clear sign. Even then, I'd be the last one up, unwilling to leave the musty sanctuary of the basement.

But now I was grown-up and I lived in a mobile home. I had no basement, no shelter, no hiding place from the storm. Already that spring we had endured two tornado scares. Each time we had driven to Donna and Richard's house and sat in their basement for hours at a time. I entertained Allison with one of Eric's old hand puppets and a Candy Land game that was missing most of its cards. When we drove back to our trailer, we had to avoid downed power lines and tree branches littered across the highway.

When a tornado warning was issued one evening about two months after our conversion, I felt alarm, out of habit, I suppose. Emergency sirens blasted throughout Polk County. The Des Moines metro area should take immediate shelter.

Eric turned up the TV and listened closely.

"Do you want to go over to Mom's?" he asked.

And suddenly I knew we'd be all right exactly where we were. A wave of peace enveloped me, warm and reassuring.

"I don't think so," I said. "God will take care of us, won't He?"

"Yeah." He smiled and nodded slowly. "Yes, I'm sure He will. God is bigger than any storm."

Allison was crawling by then. She had disappeared down the hallway, and I went chasing after her. If I take such good care of my kid, I thought, then how much more will God take care of His kids?

I found her, my little overalled darling, pink and white, smiling to herself and letting me in on it. "Isn't that right, Ally? God's not going to let anything happen to us, is He?"

Eric was popping popcorn in the kitchen. I heard him filling glasses with ice and Pepsi. I smiled as I put Allison into her pajamas. We were going to have an amazing life on planet Earth now that we knew God as our Father. It was darker than ever outside; the wind had picked up, but there was no fear in my heart at all. I couldn't believe it, this absence of fear. Why was I so calm when a wicked spring storm was beginning to kick up? We should have been on our way to a storm shelter with Allison. I shouldn't have been waltzing around her bedroom. Eric shouldn't have been popping popcorn. But we were choosing to live by faith and not our human understanding, something Scripture continually urged us to do. My own wisdom hadn't got me very far in life; it didn't seem like such a sacrifice to put it aside in favor of trusting God.

"Do not lean on thy own understanding," the Scripture

said. "In all thy ways, acknowledge Him and He will direct your path."

OK. Yes. I believe.

I laid Allison in her crib, pulled her quilt up to her chin, and stroked her face.

"We'll be fine, Ally. I promise," I whispered, and left her there alone.

Eric and I sat at the kitchen table and ate the popcorn. We left the curtains drawn and watched the trees bend in the wind. The rain slashed against the aluminum siding. The hail began suddenly; the thunderous pelting made me jump. I wondered why Donna and Richard hadn't called, so I checked the phone. There was no dial tone – the phone was down. The lights flickered once, came back on, and then went out again with a loud pop. Eric reached into the kitchen drawer for our emergency candles and lit two. We carried them into the bathroom, brushed our teeth, washed our faces, and then headed for bed with the candles and the Bible.

"God," Eric prayed, "please give us a Scripture that will comfort our hearts right now. Please let us know that You will take care of us tonight, that we don't need to be afraid of anything at all."

He opened the Bible to the Book of Psalms.

"Just read what's there," I urged. "What does it say?" I bent over the page with him to see the verse at the top of the column.

" 'I will smash your babies against the rocks,' " Eric read slowly.

Well.

I scanned the rest of the psalm, something about Babylon, retribution, God's wrath, clearly not intended as a message for us. We sat in shocked silence for a few minutes, and then we looked at each other. We laughed nervously.

"Maybe . . ." I hesitated. "Maybe God just wanted us to laugh at that. Maybe it's His idea of a little joke."

"Maybe. But I think we have to be careful to not treat the Bible like a fortune cookie, too," Eric pointed out. "We should read everything in it and not just pick and choose."

"I know," I said. "You're right. Let's just pray, OK? It's too dark to read, anyway. Let's just ask God to watch over us."

So that's what we did. Eric asked God to put one angel at each corner of our trailer and hold it down. I fell asleep imagining four heavenly beings, radiant and statuesque, their confident faces turned toward heaven as they anchored our little family to earth.

We slept through the tornado that night. Although it destroyed a town five miles away, it skirted the edges of Grand Estates, jumping the way such storms do back and forth, uprooting trees and splintering outbuildings, blowing over a trailer not far away. Ours had shifted from its foundation, but for some reason, the inspector said, it had stayed anchored.

"For some reason," Eric repeated to me later.

We laughed at that. There were no random events for us, not then, and we never imagined there could be again.

Katherine wanted us to start coming to Ames for Bible studies. Wanted us to come and break bread. "What's that?" I asked.

"Have dinner together. How about every Friday? We always have some saints over for spaghetti on Fridays," she explained, obviously delighted to use a word like "saint".

A few weeks later, Eric and I put Allison in the car seat for the thirty-minute drive to Ames. We latched our seat belts and then Eric prayed aloud, asking God to watch over us. I added my prayers, asking God to please surround us with His angels as we traveled. It would become a ritual whenever we left the house. It made perfect sense to us – just as bowing our heads in fast-food restaurants did. We prayed before every meal, wherever we were. God was with us, and we didn't want to ignore His presence, not for anything.

Once we arrived in Ames, we felt as though we had entered the portico to heaven. Katherine lived in a two-bedroom apartment with four other girls. The apartment was filled with posters of Scripture passages and pictures of Christ, and there were Bibles everywhere. It looked like a tie-dyed convent. Chastity with peace symbols. Doves carrying psychedelic crosses. Jesus on the wall, even in the bathroom.

"Welcome," they all said, beaming, one by one. "Praise God."

Eric, a married brother, was one of the few people with testosterone who had ever entered the apartment. He was fussed over and waited on, asked again and again if he wanted anything. Whenever he spoke, the women were quiet and almost reverential. I looked at Eric with different eyes during those suppers. I tried to see him the way the sisters did. I knew already that the Scriptures taught the superiority of the male and his ability to discern truth in ways that women could not.

"Brother, what do you think Paul meant when he said it was better not to marry?"

"Brother Eric, how about another cup of tea?"

"Bro – do you think we should get rid of our television?"

It was intoxicating to be in that apartment and the others that we visited that year we drove back and forth to Ames. After I learned about the catacombs in Rome and the way believers fled there for their secret meetings and protection from persecution, I decided that the series of odd apartments in Ames were catacomblike. They were nestled away in basements and attics or in strange old houses that had rickety outdoor stairs leading to a third-floor apartment, apartments that were by the railroad tracks, rattling every hour with the passing train, the whistle sounding while we sang and looked at one another in amusement and joy. Just like the train, we were all passing through. Passing through this earth on our way to heaven. I was overwhelmed with joy that everything around me was temporary, that nothing mattered, not really.

"It's gonna burn," we said to one another often when someone expressed anxiety about a car or bicycle or any other material possession. We reminded one another that everything on this earth would perish one day when God sent the purging fire at the end of time. Everything we saw would go up in flames, so why care about it now? The only thing that mattered was our eternal soul. There was a freedom in not accumulating possessions. Such liberty would enhance all of our lives. In the Bible, in the Book of Acts, the believers shared all things in common. If anyone had a need, then the believers would meet that need. We gave each other money, clothing, food, furniture. It was a generosity I had never encountered before.

And being a part of the giving was as joyful as receiving. When we heard that one of the sisters had been praying for a pair of Earth shoes because her chiropractor believed the low-slung heel would help her chronic back problems, we went to the mall and paid for a pair. Neither Eric nor I would have bought a pair of such expensive shoes for ourselves, but the prospect of buying a pair for God's child was delightful. We beamed as we shelled out the forty bucks and gave the clerk our sister's phone number.

"Please don't tell her who bought the shoes," we said. "Even if she pleads with you to tell her. We just want her to thank God, not us."

"What exactly do you want me to say?" the clerk asked, wary, half smiling, half looking over our shoulders for a security officer.

"Could you just say that God has answered her prayers for a pair of shoes?" I asked shyly. I was learning to talk to strangers about the Lord more and more boldly. I pushed my hair behind my ears and looked him in the eye. "Because that's what happened – God laid it upon our hearts to buy the shoes for her, but it's Him who's doing it. After all, it's His money."

Eric and I laughed together at that. God spending His money at His whim. We were just conduits, but what fun.

"OK, fine. I'll call her." The clerk finished ringing up the sale and nodded at us. "Thank you . . . and God," he added, rolling his eyes upward, "for the business."

We smiled at that. "God bless you," we said in unison, and wound our way around the shoe displays, the stacks of polish and socks, the customers who paused in their selection to stare at us: two long-haired hippie teenagers with beatific smiles sailing out of the mall to their tiny red Saab in the parking lot. We drove back home, rehearsing over and over our sister's joy when she would get the phone call, the way she would praise God for taking care of her every need, her every desire.

"Redeem the time, little children, for the night is coming when no man can work," counseled the Scripture. We wanted everything to count for God. All our efforts, all our desires, they mattered only if they were directed toward Him.

Renegade had nothing to do with God. Already we could tell the arts were not going to be a big deal in Christianity. Nobody listened to anything but Christian music; not one of the Christian homes in Ames displayed any art but pictures of a handsome and muscular Jesus. Sometimes he was quite American looking and striking. The picture of Christ in Katherine's bedroom was a dead ringer for Robert Redford. Film was considered a complete waste of time, of course, unless it was a Christian film.

Eric came to his own conclusion. Renegade wasn't going to bring anyone into the Kingdom. No amount of worldly success counted beside that.

"I need to use my talent for God," Eric said. "I'm going to have to quit the band."

I agreed, of course. It was the only thing he could do.

Still, it was not going to be easy. I told him I would come with him, so I packed Allison's diaper bag and we drove across the prairie to the farmhouse where the band practiced. I stayed in the kitchen with Allison while Eric went into the living room, where the band practiced. I listened as the guys did the first couple of numbers in the set. Eric was praying for the right moment to break the news, I knew that. The guys were going to be upset; two of them had even put off college for a year while they waited for the big break, the gig that would get them the exposure they needed for a recording contract.

Not long ago, Eric had been the biggest cheerleader for the band, and now here he was quitting. This wasn't going to be easy at all.

I slid Allison over to my hip and starting washing some of the dirty dishes that were stacked on the counter alongside the sink. "You are never more Christ-like than when you are being a servant," I told Allison. I picked up beer bottles by the dozens and put them in a black trash bag. I dug silverware out of TV dinner trays and threw away snack-cake wrappers and peanut shells. It was a mess, but I was grateful to have something to do. After the band stopped playing, I prayed even harder for Eric to have the right words.

Someone hit the snare drum. I heard Dave's voice, and it was angry. Now Eric, conciliatory. I took a deep breath and walked into the living room. Eric had tears in his eyes. The band sat with their eyes downcast; the drummer began to thump the bass drum. The organist picked up and played a funeral dirge on his B-3.

"I know you're upset. I know I'd feel the same way if someone else was quitting. I love this band. I love you guys,"

Eric said. He was talking loudly to keep from crying; I knew that, but the band seemed to take it as a challenge.

"So Jesus doesn't want you to be in our band anymore?" Dave asked. "We're going to drag your sorry ass to hell, something like that?"

"I'm a new man. I've been saved," Eric said. "I want to serve God. As stupid as that sounds to you, it's the truth."

"So what about the gigs we have the rest of the month?" the drummer asked dully. "You just ditching us?"

"Get Wilkins. He knows all the chords," Eric said, naming one of the roadies who traveled with the band. "He'd love to play, you know that."

So it ended badly. The briefest of handshakes, a couple of weak jokes, and we were out the door. I held Eric's hand tightly as we walked across the farmyard. It smelled of manure, the smell of money, farmers said. We drove over gravel roads past the fields of knee-high corn. When Eric looked at me, he was weeping with joy this time. He had suffered for God's sake. We were part of the Kingdom, true heirs now. Allison cooed from her car seat. It was all the harmony we needed.

Two beggars huddle against a stairway. Only a few coins lie at the bottom of the cigar box in front of them. They don't have enough to buy even one sandwich, and night is falling. One decides that he will find a better location, a place where a tenderhearted and generous tourist might pass. After he walks a block or two, he finds a bakery with a sign in the window: FREE BREAD. He is incredulous but pushes the door open. "One of our wholesale customers didn't pick up his order today. We don't want to throw it out. Help yourself," says the owner of the bakery. He waves his hand toward a table overflowing with bread: dark pumpernickel, marbled rye, round rich-looking loaves with raisins and pecans, stacks of baguettes in brown wrappers. The beggar picks up several loaves and tears into one while standing in front of the bounty. He chews and swallows and reaches for another loaf, feeling relief, utter relief, that his hunger will abate and he will survive. He has hope again. Suddenly, he remembers his starving friend and runs down the street to give him the good news: free bread, all he can eat, there for the taking.

The born-again Christian's mission: to tell the other beggars that there is free bread – salvation is available and no one need perish. While some accused us of pushing our belief system in a way that was insensitive and brutish, we always thought of it as one beggar talking to another beggar. How selfish we would be if we didn't let others know the good news.

I began buying tracts (pamphlets explaining God's plan of salvation for the sinner) at the Christian bookstore, enclosing them with birthday cards to my relatives. I tucked some inside the bills I paid as well, reasoning that someone had to open that mail and probably that someone was lost and needed the Word of God. Years of electric, phone, and water bills were accompanied by literature with titles like *Where Will You Go When You Die?* I wasn't wild about the leering devils and flames on the front of some of the tracts. I preferred a more subtle approach, but I knew from the Bible that some would be teetering on the very brink of hell itself before they would see the light. I trusted God to get the right tract into the hand of the person who needed it the most. People were perishing without Christ; that was the simple truth.

I was shocked when I recognized how introspectively I had been living. I had been so wrapped up in myself for the first eighteen years of my life that I had been blind to the needs of others. I hadn't lived for anyone but myself. I was ashamed of my selfishness, and I wanted to make up for it. I asked God for forgiveness whenever I delved into self-pity or envy or anger. I wanted none of it. From now on, JOY: Jesus, Others, Yourself. That was the order of priority. I printed "JOY" on pieces of paper and stuck them up throughout the trailer. There was JOY on the refrigerator, JOY on the bathroom mirror, JOY over our bed.

One of the first people I wanted to witness to was Lisa, poor lost Lisa. I had always been jealous of her, resenting her natural gifts and beauty, and I knew now that none of those things mattered. She didn't have Jesus, and that was what she needed. I was the one now who had wealth and good fortune. I called Mom and asked her if Lisa could come stay with us on weekends.

"She could help me with the baby," I said by way of explanation. "Besides, I miss her."

"She's so rebellious," my beleaguered mother said, sighing. "She skipped school two days last week. I found her pot and flushed it down the toilet last night."

"I'm sorry, Momma," I said. "Maybe I can talk to her."

"I'm not getting anywhere with her, that's for sure," Mom said. "We can bring her down Friday after school if you're sure you want her."

I wanted her, all right. More important, God wanted her.

That Friday Lisa crawled out of the backseat of my step-father's car with a canvas bag of record albums and her new earphones. She was frowning at something Mother was saying, but when she saw me and the baby standing on the front stoop, her face lit up.

"Ally!" she said happily. "Oh, precious Baby Ally." Lisa took Ally out of my arms and waved over her shoulder at Mom and Hal as she disappeared inside the trailer.

I walked over to the car and hugged them both. Hal was jovial as usual and thumped my back while I hugged him. Mother sort of melted into my arms and whispered, "She's wearing me down."

"Come in, why don't you?" I asked, keeping my arm around her waist.

"No, we're going to run on home," Mother said. "It's just been too much lately."

I hated Mother being discouraged, especially now that she was discovering faith all on her own. She was reading the Bible and beginning to speak of spiritual things. It would be a quiet but real conversion for her.

"That bad, huh?" I asked, and stroked her arm. Her face was as lovely as ever, but her eyes were troubled and sad. I wanted to rub her feet, comb her hair, give her the strength to keep going.

"That bad," she answered. She waved toward Hal. "Hal does his best, but she's not his daughter. She's not going to listen to him."

Hal looked up from the sapling he was examining.

"Well, honey, we just have to be patient," he said, making it sound like a reasonable option.

"Humph," Mother breathed. "She's tapped me out."

"Just pray for her, Mom," I said. "God can do amazing things."

"I know, sweetheart. Thank you," Momma said, and hugged me. "I'm proud of *you*, that's for sure."

I stood in the driveway and waved at them as they pulled away from the trailer. My mom is proud of me, I thought. After all this time, I've done something she thinks is laudatory.

Our aunts had been right: Lisa had grown into a knockout, with long, wavy blond hair and intelligent green eyes. She had those spectacular breasts and slim hips and fashion-model legs. For all her rebellion, she was generous and loving. I watched her care for Allison with such compassion that I marveled. How could an unbeliever demonstrate such Christ-like love?

How I wanted my sister to be saved. After Mom and Hal left, I began to witness in earnest.

110

"Lisa, listen to this Scripture," I said, and began to read, " 'Today if you hear His voice –' "

"Carolyn, I'm not interested," she answered, reaching for her headphones.

"Please, listen. The Bible says, 'All have sinned and fall short of the glory –' "

"Carolyn," she said again. "*Please.*"

"Please what? Please let you go to hell? Please let you reject the Savior Who died for you?"

"Please let me listen to my music," she said simply. Her face was pale and smooth, red splotches on her cheeks, her beautiful mouth parted over perfect teeth. She looked like one of the dolls in Eric's sister's bedroom.

"You need to hear this, Lisa," I said, flipping to verse two on the road of salvation. I had highlighted the twelve Scriptures that could lead a sinner to God. I wasn't about to stop on the first Scripture.

Lisa didn't put on the headphones; she kept them around her neck and played with the cord. She closed her eyes and let me read the other eleven Scriptures. When I finished, she opened her eyes.

"May I listen to my music now?" she asked. She looked exasperated but kind. I didn't know exactly how to deal with her. The devil was plainly preventing her from hearing the truth. The Word of God was a sword, I knew that, it could pierce the heart and reveal God. That's exactly what had happened to Eric and me. It was all so mysterious and unpredictable, this seduction of God.

"OK," I said, feeling impotent and foolish. "I just wanted you to hear those Scriptures, that's all."

"I heard them," she said, adjusting the headphones on her ears. "Thanks."

"Sure," I said. "You're welcome." I stood there for a few minutes, watching her. She smiled at me and moved her head a little back and forth to what she could hear and I couldn't.

That night Eric and I prayed for Lisa. We asked God to bind Satan, to keep him from snatching the good seed from her heart.

Before the weekend was up, I was reading the Bible to Lisa through the locked bathroom door. I was determined to save her and to bring her to heaven. I was convinced that it wouldn't happen without my diligence, my persistence, my determination to snatch her out of the devil's hands. How often I felt unequal to the task, but I kept preaching to my little sister because I wanted her to have the life I had found. I wanted her to see rebellion as a dead-end road. I wanted her to know that her beauty could not save her.

I see myself, an earnest skinny girl, reading the ancient Scriptures through the hollow-core door in a mobile home. This nineteen-year-old girl believes that all the cosmos is pausing while she does the work of the Almighty. I was tireless.

We found an organization that supplied Bibles at a discount price. We began ordering Bibles by the hundreds from the New York Bible Society. Despite my failure with Lisa, I still believed salvation came from the Word of God. People just needed to read it as Eric and I had and then they would be saved just as we had been. We began to leave Bibles with the tip at restaurants. We opened unlocked car doors at the mall and slipped Bibles inside. Instead of a ride, hitchhikers found themselves running up to pick up the Bible we tossed with our shouted "God bless you!" It wasn't enough just to distribute the Bible. We were inspired by believers who spurned material possessions – we wanted to do so with equal ardor. We started leaving little piles of money in inconspicuous places: several dollar bills anchored by a pile of quarters. I felt exhilarated when we walked away quickly after planting the money.

Someone would think that God had done it! It would be proof that God loved them. And so we went, good little elves, doing the work behind the scenes for the Cobbler.

Eric wore a cross made out of wood and hung it from a rawhide leather string. One day he came home from work and gave me a bracelet band that looked just like the POW-MIA bracelets we used to wear during the Vietnam War. They said "JESUS CHRIST – AD 33". My dad once asked me what I was wearing. I thrust my arm up in his face so he could read it. He looked embarrassed, cleared his throat, and asked me if I had any aspirin in the house.

Right from the start, I didn't want to push my new faith on my father. I was scared of losing the tentative new start to our relationship. His new daughter and his granddaughter, Allison, were three months apart in age, and Daddy loved that. We got together and watched the girls play. I wanted to keep him in my life. I wanted never to be without him again.

"But what about eternity?" one of the believers in Ames asked me when I said as much about my father. "He'll spend eternity in hell and he will hold out his hands toward you in heaven and plead, 'Oh, Carolyn, if only you had told me about Jesus. . . .'"

My heart sank at that scenario. My own dad, with tears running down his cheeks, in hell, and it would be my fault. I must have looked stricken because Sam intervened.

"God knows Carolyn's heart. He will give her the desires of her heart," he intoned, putting his arm around my shoulders. He did this casually and often, but each time my heart would race. A college football player's arm around me.

So Daddy's reaction to the Jesus Christ MIA bracelet didn't surprise me. I knew where he was coming from. I got him the aspirin and handed them to him without speaking. It was awkward and I struggled, suspecting he was unhappy having a daughter who was a zealot. I loved my father, aging quietly and steadily, a man with severe arthritis, a man who had been disappointed in love and career. And now his oldest daughter had become a Jesus freak.

But, Daddy, I wished I could say. Jesus doesn't turn people into freaks. He turns freaks into people.

I never said this. I just patted his hand when he came over. I longed for him to come to the light, but the beggar in me was silent. Daddy didn't want the bread, I knew that. He would just as soon starve. This knowledge was something I carried within me all the time. My earthly father and my heavenly Father were at odds, and how I loved them both.

RAPTURE

I had been a believer for two years before I even turned twenty. For the next decade, I studied the Bible and prayed several times a day. I felt fortunate, blessed beyond all measure to know the truth, to be able to devote myself to the cause of Christ. Some of the texts I needed to study were difficult, beyond my capabilities, but that didn't stop me from poring over them and trying to learn "the whole counsel of God".

Our home was littered with study guides and prayer journals. Christian books of every description, missionary biographies, studies of eschatology: the end times. I especially loved those.

My favorites were the apocalyptic books by Hal Lindsey, especially *The Late Great Planet Earth*. I read it late into the night, shivering with pleasure at the description of the rapture, an event that would begin with the sound of a trumpet. All the dead in Christ would exit their graves, and the believers who were still living would be caught in the air and changed in the twinkling of an eye to be like Him.

According to Hal Lindsey, the rapture could happen at any moment. Everything that had to be fulfilled according to ancient prophecy had fallen into place. Because the Jews had rejected their Messiah, God had punished them with the Diaspora. The poor Israelites had had no homeland for centuries until 1948, when the nation of Israel was reestablished. Now the countdown for the rapture could begin! When Hal Lindsey explained the contemporary Middle East situation from prophetic biblical texts, it made sense to me, and I found it hard to believe that other people couldn't read the newspaper and see how close Armageddon was.

Saturday afternoon we headed north on I-35 to Ames for a Bible study in the Union at Iowa State. I was looking forward to the intensive teaching session coming up. I loved getting the *meat* of the Word from one of the earnest brothers on campus. I took notes in a spiral notebook as I listened to the teaching. If the teaching brother referred incidentally to another Scripture reference, I jotted it down to look up later. And it wasn't just me; all of the saints, the college students, and the few hippiesque outsiders who came to these studies were eager to see what the Word of God had to say. We revered it. It was the real thing in a world of counterfeit.

When a brother said, "Let's turn to the book of Galatians," everyone turned to Galatians. No one looked in the table of contents for the tiny epistle; they knew where to find Galatians. So after an avalanche of page turning, we were all there together, reading and digesting God's Word *together*. You could hear the sighs of satisfaction during these discourses. Once in a while, a zealot would say "Praise God," aloud, and others would agree quietly. Or someone would begin singing, "Father, we adore you, lay our lives before you." The energy and concentration were unlike anything I had encountered in high school or Allendale Baptist Church. It was electric.

I liked taking Allison to Ames. She was one of the few babies in the group, and everyone fussed over her. I dressed her in a red-and-black flannel shirt and railroad engineer overalls with little work boots we had found at a consignment shop.

"It's no wonder people think she's a boy," I said to Eric. He laughed and squinted in the sun. The traffic was bad – it was game day for the Cyclones.

"She'll probably get hair before she starts school, don't you think?" he asked, and put on his signal to change lanes.

116

"If she doesn't, I'll tape some pink bows on her bald head," I promised. As I turned my head to check on Allison in the backseat, a horn screeched, an insistent blast coming from nowhere and everywhere.

The rapture. Good grief. It was the rapture. Here we go. We're out of here. I can't believe it. I can't. The rapture.

But we weren't going anywhere, and traffic continued as before.

'What was that?" I asked. My legs were trembling, and I could feel perspiration racing down the sides of my chest.

"That semi – guy hit his air horn 'cause he thought I was cutting him off," Eric said. "Loud, wasn't it?"

"Oh, boy." I laughed shakily. "Scared me." I didn't want to tell him about the dream I kept having. In my dream, the trumpet, God's trumpet, really did sound to announce the rapture of the church. I began to jump in the air, willing myself to rise, but my feet stayed firmly on the ground. I watched the other believers be gathered into the arms of Jesus while I remained earthbound. I woke from the dream puzzled and unhappy. I knew I was saved; I knew that I would be caught up the way the other believers would.

Even so, I was scared sometimes that I could be left behind.

I dug in Allison's diaper bag for the plastic bag with her teething biscuits. I pulled out a piece of zwieback. I ate it slowly, trying to distract myself, but I couldn't stop thinking about the rapture.

"Eric?"

"Yes?" he asked. He tapped my knee like a cymbal.

"What do you think people will say after the rapture? I mean, all the people who are left on earth?"

"They are going to be majorly freaked out," Eric chuckled. "It's going to blow their minds."

"How will people explain all of us being gone? Nuclear war?"

"Maybe an alien invasion?" he said. "Or biological warfare, instant vaporization, that kind of thing?"

"I'm so worried about Lisa. And my dad. What about your folks? They'll all be so sad we're gone," I said, trying to imagine their devastation when we vanished. I pictured my dad picking up my Bible and thumbing through it, looking for answers to explain what had happened.

Eric was thinking the same thing. "God can use this to bring them to Himself. They'll remember what we said about God and the Second Coming. God will show them mercy, Carolyn."

"Yes, mercy," I repeated. "God is merciful." After some miles, I felt better. I wasn't going to be left behind. I knew too much to not be God's own.

I remember sharing that experience of being primed, of being ready to go at any minute, with Katherine and some of the other believers. They laughed and nodded their heads and told us that the same thing had happened to them many times. They told us that we needed to see a film called *I Wish We'd All Been Ready* – a Christian movie about the rapture.

"It's so real in the movie. Wow, when it happens, well, you just feel goose bumps," Katherine said. "They show it all the time, just check the *Register* for religious news; you'll find a church showing it."

We had gathered in a circle on a bare hardwood floor in a nearly empty apartment. The evangelist on campus lived there with his wife and twin daughters. There was a bed and a table and chairs. The baby girls slept with their parents. The family used a few discarded and mismatched sofa cushions for seating on the floor. A single picture of Christ hung on the wall.

"Yep, brothers and sisters," Steve, the evangelist, said. "We are not long for this world." He began humming the Seals and

Croft song "We May Never Pass This Way Again", and we all laughed. I looked around the room at Katherine and the college kids, Stephen and his smiling, virginal wife, Mary, the baby girls (including Allison), and I marveled at everything that had happened in the last year. I could barely remember what it was like to struggle, to be anxious, to be worried about anything. Just like the hymn we often sang, I leaned into His everlasting arms. He enveloped me.

Not long afterward, Eric and I found a Des Moines church showing *I Wish We'd All Been Ready*. To our surprise, we learned the movie had actually been filmed in Des Moines. This made the chilling scenes of everyday life giving way to the end times scenario even more gripping. We saw how those stubborn nonbelievers were indeed left behind. We saw how it happened in a split second, how a cake mixer was left churning a cake in a bowl for hours, how alarm clocks droned for days with no one to turn them off, and how an electric razor buzzed on the side of the sink. All true Christians were evacuated from the world. A few stalwart converts would be made during the next seven years – the great tribulation – but they would be persecuted and martyred all the way until Armageddon, the true end of the world. Sitting in the clammy church basement, we watched as the world quickly became a hostile place for those who refused the Mark of the Beast. There was nowhere to run, though the blond and leggy star ran for her life along the dam out at Red Rock – the same place we had picnicked a week before. It was heady stuff: knowing what would happen in the future. We knew what was going to happen, no mystery, no question about it. Our exultation was tempered only by the horrible suffering we knew our family and unsaved friends were going to suffer. They would have to take the Mark of the Beast to buy even a loaf of bread. How would they be able to survive without it? But taking it would mean they were doomed forever. It was a conundrum – how could we rejoice when our salvation meant there were others who would lose everything, including their mortal souls? Trust God, we were told. It was a matter of faith. A matter of turning off that insistent voice that demanded understanding. Man was a finite being and therefore unable to fathom the affairs of the infinite One, God. Faith was all that was required of me. I was called to believe, to take God's hand and stroll away with Him, swinging His hand like a child and exclaiming, "How I love You". There wasn't anything I could do but pray for the unbelievers. That and buy a bumper sticker for our car. It read: "WARNING! In case of rapture, this car will be unmanned!"

We didn't have a church to attend in Des Moines. We met in Ames with the believers at Iowa State, who warned us about "liberal" churches, which, they said, were nothing more than country clubs.

"You won't find Jesus in those empty places," they warned. "Be careful. Pray hard about it. There are false prophets everywhere."

But Eric and I weren't afraid. We were innocent of duplicity, hypocrisy, and anything else that would confuse the issue of simply being followers of Jesus Christ. There was a small white church near our trailer park, and we had noted the time of the Sunday morning service.

Our hair was long; sometimes we used headbands to keep it in place. Eric wore tinted octagonal glasses. I wore Allison in a Snugli; she was tucked inside the blue canvas with her face pressed against my breast. When we pushed open the church's door, we were overwhelmed by the smell of furniture polish and old books. Two old ladies stood in the foyer. They smiled uncertainly at us. We smiled back: sisters!

"Welcome," one said. She stretched out her thumb and

index finger, a crumpled Kleenex clutched under the rest of her fingers.

"Hello." The other nodded. "Please come in."

We smiled and nodded back, murmuring, "Thank you," waiting for some exchange we were familiar with, fervent praise to God, perhaps a Scripture bestowed like a kiss on the cheek, the happy question of how we had come to the light. But none of these things were forthcoming. The two women drew back, a gentle *swoosh*ing of powder and mints, Aqua Net hair spray, and we were alone in the dark foyer.

Maybe two dozen people were scattered throughout the pews, some middle-aged, others elderly, but there was no one who looked even close to thirty. We hesitated as we stood beside the pews, waiting for the outstretched arms, the friendly questions, the eager light that always came into the eyes of an old saint when encountering a new child of God. Instead, we received a few additional nods, some faint smiles; others didn't turn around at all, even when Allison began to babble noisily. The heads in front of me stayed fixed to the front of the sanctuary, where a six-foot cross stood, an odd geometry of mahogany and oak rectangles. The service began and we followed suit with those around us, flipped to the pages of the hymn being sung, listened attentively to the sermon, the first we ever remembered wanting to hear in a real church.

The pastor wore a satin robe with a clerical collar. He was balding and red faced, and his expression was one of continual and chronic surprise. "Good morning!" he said, as though he couldn't believe it was indeed morning again. "Turn to hymn number 202," he said, aghast that there was such a thing as hymn 202. "The Women's Missionary Society will meet this Wednesday night at seven o'clock in the church basement," he said, and paused, as though we must be as astounded by this news as he was.

He began his sermon, which turned out to be the lengthy treatise of the church holy days and the detailed sacraments that accompanied each one. Never once did he mention the Word, nor did he urge us to repent and be saved. We continued to listen closely, our hands trembling on our Bibles, ready to turn to any passage he mentioned. This, we had learned, was the way we grew: feeding upon the milk of the Word like newborn babes. Eric and I didn't know how to listen to God's Word without a pen in our hands, without our brains recording, filing, making connections to other passages. That morning we continued to sit uneasily and listened with our hands still on our laps. When the pastor finished speaking, he sank into a chair and did not look up again, even as we sang the closing hymn: "Rock of Ages."

We shook his hand afterward, and he barely managed to squeeze back.

"God bless you, sir," Eric said. "It was great to meet with the saints today."

"Are you passing through?" the pastor asked, his mouth a small O, his eyes round and startled. "Are you visiting the community?"

"No." I smiled. "We live in Grand Estates Mobile Home Park," I answered, pointing out the stained-glass window on our right. The pastor didn't follow my outstretched arm; instead he looked pointedly at my feet. I glanced down at my dusty, naked toes and wished that I had bought a pair of panty hose.

"Well, you must come again," the pastor said. "We certainly could use some young people in the congregation." While he said this, he was looking at Allison, issuing the invitation to her alone. She squirmed under his scrutiny and began to whimper, arching her back, stretching in the hot canvas carrier. We smiled, murmured our thanks, and left quickly.

"Guess we'll keep looking," I said as I unhooked Allison from the straps crisscrossing my shoulders and back.

"Amen," Eric said. It was the first amen I had heard all day.

We kept praying for a church in Des Moines. We prayed expectantly, as the Word admonished. We knew God would provide. And He did, a month later.

Eric was waiting to get his tires changed. He was bored, staring out the plate-glass window, when he saw a big guy in a running suit approaching the door. Once inside, the man walked past Eric, stopped, and turned around.

"Hey," Phil said.

"Hello," Eric answered, alert for something just like this. A chance meeting – it fit perfectly with our understanding of God's work behind the scenes, angels unaware and all that.

"Getting new tires, huh?" Phil asked, sizing Eric up, his eyes keen. There was something about Phil, Eric said later. He looked like a prophet, a seer.

"Yep," Eric answered, laughing. "It's long overdue, too. I trust the Lord, but I'm not going to test His watch care by driving with bald tires."

"I knew it," Phil exclaimed. "I knew you were a believer. And I'll tell you what else I know – you're looking for a church."

"Brother, that is exactly what I'm looking for," Eric said, nodding and smiling. "My wife and I are brand-new Christians, and we've been praying about finding a group of believers in Des Moines."

"Praise God," Phil said, nodding. He radiated a joy that Eric recognized instantly. Phil was a true brother, a true man of faith. "Praise the precious name of Jesus," Phil said quietly.

They began to exchange testimonies (how and when they got saved), Scriptures, even songs. They ended up spending the whole afternoon together in the waiting room of the Goodyear dealer. When they called each other "brother" and threw their arms around each other, the other waiting customers carefully focused on issues of *Sports Illustrated* and *Hot Rod*. Eric was overjoyed when Phil told him that he was forming a Christian band and there was an opening for someone who could play guitar and keyboards.

"I play both," Eric said.

"Are you interested?" he asked.

"Am I interested?" Eric repeated. "You bet I'm interested. Tell me when to show up and I'm there."

"Praise Jesus," Phil said.

"Yes, sir," Eric answered. Phil laughed, and Eric laughed with him. Phil shook Eric's hand again.

"Brother, you've got to come to my church Sunday morning. The Lord's brought us together for a lot of reasons. Praise God – He doeth all things well," Phil said. "You'll dig the music at this place, bro. Meet you there at nine-thirty?"

I wore a dress the next Sunday, the first I'd worn in years. I brushed my hair carefully. I couldn't shake the feeling that I had an audience with God. I wanted to be lovely. The church was large, with stained-glass windows, lots of light, hundreds of people streaming in and out the medieval-looking doors. Eric waved at a man who was surrounded by a group of people our age. He led me over to Phil, who parted the crowd around him with his hand outstretched toward us. His hair was long and dark, his face open and warm in spite of his intense dark eyes: All-knowing, I thought instantly. When I shook hands with Phil, his large size and his immediate affection for Allison and for me were overwhelming.

We all walked into the large evangelical church, where Phil was an intern. Immediately, I saw the two good-looking co-pastors, Steve and Terry, who stood behind the pulpit. One was very blond, and the other had dark hair, thick eyebrows, a

Mediterranean fire in his eyes. Jesus, was my first thought when I looked at him. They both wore expensive shirts and ties, and their hair was carefully styled. A choir stood behind them, and Steve and Terry were singing an upbeat melody as the choir sang backup.

> This could be the day
> that we go home to Heaven.
> This could be the day
> we all sit at His feet.

Behind Steve and Terry, the choir beamed with joy at the possibility of going to heaven this day. Steve and Terry also radiated this exuberance, and those of us in the pews caught the contagion of goodwill and excitement. I felt goose bumps on my legs. I turned to look at Eric – he was positively glowing. He loved music, loved to sing, and I could see that he was transported. Phil clamped his hand on Eric's shoulder and leaned over to smile at me. Phil seemed like an apostle to me, a man who would never compromise, a man who would die rather than deny Christ.

Nondenominational and evangelical, the Church on the Way would be our home for the next two years. The Word of God was taught every Sunday and was the basis for all doctrine: the inerrant Word of God, God-breathed, God-inspired, absolutely true in a literal sense – man is lost, destined for hell unless he has a Savior, and that Savior has been provided in Jesus Christ, the perfect Son of God born of a virgin Who died for our sins and rose again on the third day. One must accept this Christ as one's personal Savior or spend all eternity separated from Him and all that is good. "I am the way, the truth, and the life," Christ had said. The only way to heaven. The only truth, the only eternal life.

At first we were content at the Way, especially since we

also attended Wednesday night Bible studies with Phil in the church's basement. Steve and Terry, the co-pastors, liked having all the pseudohippies in their midst. We were radical and zealous, and these really very traditional pastors thought we would bring fresh air to the congregation. And that was true; we were not content to "talk the talk" about God the way a lot of evangelicals did – we intended to "walk the walk". It was obvious we made some people uncomfortable with our dress and music and the long hair most of us wore hanging straight down our backs. Our insistence on obeying the Word completely, no compromise, no watering-down of any commandment, was occasionally threatening to the righteous suburbanites who made up the congregation of the Church on the Way.

On Sunday mornings, I was surrounded at the young women's Bible study by Junior Auxiliary ladies with their periwinkle and sage suits, their single strand of pearls, their Gucci handbags. I saw their furtive glances at my smock and denim skirt, the handcrafted leather cover on my Bible, the white socks and sandals on my feet. Sunday after Sunday, we engaged in an odd bit of Christian civility: Smile like crazy and exchange some God talk, but don't get into anything too deep. I was disappointed in this lack of authenticity, but I soldiered on. I hoped they could tell that I had *died to the world*. That's what Christ has called us to, ladies, I said silently. Repent of your designer handbag and live for God with your whole heart.

"Make a way in the wilderness!" we wanted to say, echoing John the Baptist.

Oh, we knew most of those in the Church on the Way believed, truly believed, in God, but these believers didn't seem to be consumed by Him, not the way we intended to be. It seemed to us that these established Christians wanted to have God as a part of their lives, but not necessarily to the exclusion of building up their portfolios and buying a time-share on the

Gulf coast. We, on the other hand, were sold out to God and content to be penniless if that was His will for us. We drove battered cars and rented or bought houses on the south side of Des Moines, where they were the cheapest and most plentiful. We were innocents, really, and always quite stunned when the Establishment was not swept away by our zeal.

After a while, even Steve and Terry began to question some of our radical ideas. Every once in a while, they called the "hippies" into Steve's office, ostensibly to keep in touch with us, our needs and concerns, but actually more for an opportunity to check our excess, to determine if we were interacting with others with tact and love. Did we have to preach our hyper-Calvinism with such zeal? Didn't we see that our emphasis on the sovereignty of God and predestination called into question the whole idea of free will? They didn't want discord among the brethren, they said. Couldn't we compromise some of the finer issues of doctrine and let the body grow into their own truth?

"How can we, Eric?" I asked on the way home from one of these sessions. "We want to serve God with whole hearts. God hates compromise."

" 'I will spew the lukewarm from my mouth,' " Eric quoted.

"Are we in the right place?" I wondered. "Is this really where God wants us?"

"We have to pray about it, Carolyn," Eric said. "More than ever. Allison is getting bigger; she needs to be surrounded by a godly church, one that will make her spiritual growth a priority."

I tried to picture the designer-clothing ladies teaching my daughter about the infinite God, the maker of worlds. I saw them smiling at her and gingerly patting her head, mouthing empty platitudes, complimenting her on her good manners.

"Oh, Eric, you're so right," I said, turning to look at Allison.

She was alert and watching us. We owed her the true church. We owed her a church body sold out to God. It was the first of many times that we would use our child's welfare as an excuse to do what we wanted to do anyway. It was much easier to defend our radical Christianity as our child's birthright than it was to face the pride that rode us hard away from mediocrity of belief. We shunned traditional Christianity because we were too good for it, too pure, too devoted to orthodoxy to pay lip service to *phileo,* a fancy word for compromise.

Our prayers were answered. Not long after the conversation with Steve and Terry, Phil and some others came up with a plan that scared us to death but also thrilled us.

We could start our own church. With the New Testament Book of Acts as our pattern, we began our own New Testament church under Phil's leadership. No organs or hymnals, our new church had lots of guitars and lyrics on the overhead projector. We borrowed Zeppelin's "Stairway to Heaven" to sing a hundred-year-old hymn about resisting sin in the morning, in the afternoon, and in the evening. Fountain of Joy Chapel would meet in church basements, abandoned sanctuaries, office buildings, schools, the YWCA, anywhere we could rent space to hold our guitars and amplifiers, our overflowing preschool classes and nurseries of babies. Our children grew up singing this, pointing their fingers at their own little chests and the chests of the child next to them:

> You are the Church
> I am the Church
> We are the Church of the living God.

When people asked, we would tell them that we were part of a New Testament church. Our group consisted of about forty families who were devoted to the Scriptures, our final authority on everything. We were Elder ruled. The Elders were the shepherds of the church and held all authority. Women could not be Elders. We were not allowed to teach men the Word of God, although we had Bible studies where we taught one another. I was recruited for a ladies' study right away. On Monday mornings for an entire year, I studied *You Can Be the Wife of a Happy Husband*, a book that was based solely on the holy Scriptures.

Ten of us sat, sometimes knelt, in a circle in someone's dining room or living room. We took turns having the study in our houses; whoever hosted was also the moderator of the discussion, unless that woman was a baby Christian, like me. If she was not schooled in the Word, she had to let one of the older sisters in the Lord lead the question and answers. That was fine with me; I was very conscious of how much I didn't know. I looked up to my new teachers with the same reverence I'd had for Pastor Jim. I felt swallowed up again, and I liked that very much.

We ate desserts, healthy ones sweetened with honey and laced with wheat germ. We drank mugs of herbal tea. A praise-and-worship tape played in the background – John Michael Talbot, the monk who loved God, admonished us to seek after Him like a deer panteth after the brook. We sang with him sometimes and never stumbled over a word like "panteth", never once. For someone like me, who had lived such an isolated girlhood and adolescence, I was in heaven, *at peace*. Everything tranquil, everything blending into the next element – the strange desserts, the music, the quiet and holy laughter. You were so safe, you could lie down and sleep. You could just melt into the arms of any of the welcoming sisters and they would hold you close, no questions asked.

Even our discussions were muted, simple statements, nods and amens.

"As wives, our desire is for our husband, that's the thing," said Camille. She was a graceful, long-limbed beauty with perfect olive skin and just the barest sheen of lip gloss. I wondered if she was thinking of her husband, Phil. I was.

"God knew how it would be between a man and woman," Rebekah agreed. "The way we would be drawn to them." There was a murmur around the room, knowing glances as the women blushed prettily at each other.

I had already begun to notice a frank appreciation for marital sexuality in our group. God forbid you to have sex before you were married, but afterward, it was anything goes, swing from the macramé plant hangers in your humble little apartment and have naked picnics on your living room sofa. It puzzled me a bit. God was the Lover Who animated me, not my husband. Why weren't the other wives giving their all to God? They were distracted by their husbands, I decided. Not me, I had the hots for Jesus.

Elijah's Chariot: Eric's new band. Elijah was one of God's prophets who never compromised, who stood his ground against idolaters and those who would compromise. As a reward, God took him to heaven in a fiery chariot. Elijah had escaped death with this chariot, and that was the same message the band wanted to bring: Escape death, come to God. The band consisted of two couples: Phil and his wife, Camille; another couple who dimpled on cue, smiling, smiling; and one single guy: Mark. Mark was very good looking, tall, with a nicely trimmed brown beard and a holy, sculptured face with fiery dark eyes.

"Hello, little sis," he said, opening his arms for me. I hugged him and then stepped back quickly. He bent down to pick up his guitar and looked up at me with a gentle, knowing expression. He strummed it once, a chord I recognized.

"Don't you play anything?"

"Just Mommy," I said, hauling Allison onto my hip.

"Your husband's pretty good," he said. "We've been praying for a keyboardist for a long time. *Jehovah Jireh*."

I didn't really know what he meant. I smiled dumbly. "The Lord will provide," he prompted.

"Yes, He does. Praise God," I said on cue. Once, the jargon had seemed as impenetrable as a secret code, but now I was learning it. What a heady feeling of belonging. How intoxicating to be us against them: those who loved God and those who refused to.

"I'm praying for you, little sis," Mark said, closing his eyes as his hands moved up and down the frets of his guitar.

I stood there watching him play the guitar, and I suddenly remembered watching Eric on stage. I would stand or sit on the sidelines and watch the band, the kids dancing, and their reaction to Renegade. Sometimes I would accept an offer to dance, and I would move around the youth center floor with a stranger's arms embracing me, a stranger's cold belt buckle pressed into my stomach, and all the while Eric looked for me out there in the darkness. I felt a familiar flash of betrayal as I watched Mark, a formless, nameless desire for something other than what belonged to me.

I didn't understand how Mark could still be single. I liked the way he treated the sisters so tenderly. Mark noticed if a sister was down or struggling with something. He offered to pray right on the spot. I had seen him many times with his head bowed and his face furrowed with intensity, praying for a sister. When he was finished, he smiled this slow, liquid smile just for her, nobody else but her. Every time I had ever talked to him, he'd made me feel as though I were an objet d'art, something he would cradle in his hands if given the chance. Something precious he would stroke and smooth and exclaim over.

It occurred to me that Katherine would probably love Mark. She was looking for a godly husband. Mark would be knocked out by Katherine, that was for sure. She was beautiful in those days; salvation agreed with her. If I'd been a

131

man, I would have noticed her deep gray eyes, her long hair woven into an intricate French braid, and her soft and sweet lips, turned up in perpetual sincerity.

I would have to introduce them someday, if it were God's will. And it wasn't necessarily God's will.

The couples in the band, Mark, and those couples associated with Elijah's Chariot's ministry were our first friends in the church. We called ourselves the core group of the infant Fountain of Joy Church. Phil was the leader of the band, as he was obviously the leader in everything.

"Hey, you two. What's God done in your life since I saw you last?" he'd ask. We were accountable to each other, Phil said. That meant we had to be honest, vulnerable, and transparent in our dealings.

"I'm struggling, bro," Eric would often answer, anxious to be real. "It's hard to get enough time in the Word."

"You gotta do it, brother. Everything else is going to burn," Phil would say with such authority that I shivered. Yes, he was right, of course, he was right. The Lord was coming soon, and He was going to bring judgment to the world. Nothing would be left after His wrath was spent.

Phil was a large man, just a little overweight. He wore running shoes and a jogging suit all the time, even when we met to worship. He looked soft, but he wasn't. He was fierce about his (and our) allegiance to God and uncompromising in his pursuit of the Kingdom. Eric and I believed Phil was another John the Baptist, making a path through the wilderness. We quoted him to each other. When we entered a room, his face was the first we looked for. We adored him.

"I love Jesus Christ," he said at the beginnings of our meetings. "Do you?"

We murmured our assents, nodded our heads.

"Do you really?" Phil leaned forward and looked at us,

132

every one of us, pausing to make sure our eyes met his. "You love Jesus Christ, Scott?"

"Yes, Phil, I do," Scott answered eagerly, his bald head gleaming, his accountant hands poised.

"What about the house you're trying to buy, Scott? You and Debbie sure God wants you to buy such a nice house when there're brothers and sisters living in apartments?"

It was silent in the room. These kinds of confrontations weren't unusual, but they were always uncomfortable. We weren't used to "telling it like it is," no matter what our generation's reputation.

"Is that laying aside your life for the Kingdom?" Phil asked softly. His face was intense, burning with compassion for Scott and Debbie as they struggled with discipleship.

Phil sighed and tears filled his eyes. "I know, I know. It's so hard to seek His Kingdom and His righteousness first, but we know that if we do, all things shall be added unto us."

One of the guys in the band left the audience and picked up Phil's guitar from the stand. He began to play "Seek Ye First," a song based on the Scripture Phil mentioned, an admonition to not get our eyes on the world or what the world offers. It was as though the Holy Spirit had entered the room. We all felt it – the air was charged with His presence – it broke my heart. I was filled with a familiar paradox of grief and comfort. I was so unworthy of this; there was no way I deserved the new life I had found in Christ. I used to be a sinner! I was one of those who nailed Him to the cross, all of my disregard for God, my mocking of holy things, my flagrant drinking and sex before I was married – all of it proof that I had turned my back on Him. Yet He died for me because He loved me. I would never take that for granted, never. And even as I realized anew my former depravity, God filled me to the utmost with joy and reassurance. My hands started to shake. I felt the curious tightening in my chest and the light-headedness I always felt in the presence of the Lord.

Scott and Debbie were now surrounded by the saints. Arms and hands reached out to them. Someone began to sing along with the guitar. We joined in. Phil fell to his knees, a fluid, smooth motion defying his size. We all followed.

I looked around the room, watched brothers throw their arms around other brothers, saw the women reaching for each other, dipping their faces into the hollows of each other's necks. Hands were raised, palms opened and waved back and forth. The Holy Spirit filled the room, and it felt like waves in a warm ocean lapping against us, infusing us, a liquid love, energized, alive, the love of the Father. Times like these I could not stop smiling and crying and marveling that I was home from a treacherous journey. I was safe. I was loved. Everyone my eyes fell upon was someone who would die for me. Someone who would lay down their life for me. As I would for them.

"Praise you, Jesus!" It slipped from my lips before I could temper my passion. Others echoed, and once again I felt as though I were afloat on a sea, an otherworldly sea. My baby at my feet, my sisters and my brothers surrounding me, God weaving us together with His presence as we stood back on our feet, smiling at each other.

Scott embraced Phil and stepped in front of the podium. He opened his mouth and tried to say something but stopped. He shook his head and then tried again. Again, he swallowed and smiled back at us – we were cheering him on with our attention, with our love. Finally, he wiped his eyes with the back of his hand and then leaned close to the microphone to speak.

"Brothers and sisters," he began, his voice quavering. "The Lord's convicted me tonight – He's made it clear that Deb and I were operating in the flesh. Just like Cain, sin was crouching at the door, ready to devour us. I don't know why I didn't see that. It's my responsibility, and I let you all down, especially my wife. I'd had the feeling for a while that we needed to slow down on this decision and look at it a little harder. We want the Lord's will and nothing else."

After he spoke, Phil shook his hand and grasped his shoulder at the same time.

"Proud of you, bro. Praise God for your example to the church. Praise God, church, because you've borne witness to Scott and Debbie denying their flesh by not giving in to the lust of things, possessions, money. Those are tools of the enemy, and they're designed to consume you and ultimately destroy all of your testimony in Christ." He stopped speaking, walked to the center of the room, looked up toward heaven, and said, "Make us faithful warriors, O God."

We echoed, "Make us faithful warriors."

And so for many years afterward, that became my daily prayer. I wanted to fight sin wherever I found it, and I was never so naive that I believed it wasn't crouching at my door, desiring me, just as it had desired Cain.

ANOINTED

There were so many babies in our midst. Someone was always announcing a pregnancy at the same time someone else was giving birth. Most of these births took place at home after months of careful planning. When I observed the way my sisters organized their impending home births, I felt awed. They stacked towels, washcloths, and sheets that would be baked in a brown paper bag for an hour once labor began. They happily arranged rubber gloves, syringes, a pair of sharp scissors for cutting the umbilicus. And right beside these frightening accessories would be homey wicker baskets of herbal tea, hard candies for labor, little snacks of fruit and nuts for the coaching father. The whole idea of giving birth at home made me very nervous, but I admired the sisters for their bravery and their single-minded pursuit of pure and untainted families.

The family was the thing. Next to God, and in very close succession, was the family. My parents were establishing new lives with their new mates. Lisa had finally moved out of Mother's house and was living alone in a windowless apartment above the bowling alley in Allendale. My little brother was safely enrolled in a Christian day school, playing basketball and steadily losing the weight he had gained during our parents' separation and divorce. I loved them all, but now I had my own family and a new beginning.

Eric and I had been believers for a year and a half. Because our conversion had happened at the same time Allison was born, I often thought of myself in terms of a spiritual infant, then toddler, now becoming more and more independent, capable of expressing myself to others. She was growing up, and so were we. I genuinely liked having a child – I liked the routine of caring for her, a gentle little red-haired girl in overalls and work boots who sat on my lap while I read her Golden books and Bible stories. Eric's parents helped us buy a little house near Drake University. The house had three bedrooms, two of which were tucked under the eaves upstairs, rooms where I could wallpaper and wax the wood floors, perfect bedrooms for kids. It was the most natural thing in the world to begin planning our next child. It never occurred to me that I was only nineteen and Eric had just turned twenty. Or that Eric was a carpenter's assistant with no job security beyond the building season. Our calling was to have families, to raise our children in the Lord. I wanted to please God by being a mother. We began praying for a son.

When I missed my period, Eric and I were very happy; somehow my conception seemed to be a stamp of God's approval. God had opened my womb, just as the Scriptures said. I felt like Mary or Elizabeth. I wanted to sing the Magnificat. I wanted to find a Jewish rabbi who would bless me. I longed to offer two turtledoves on the altar of the temple. Everything was full of significance, weighty with promise. I was having a child for the Lord.

"Children are a blessing of the Lord. Blessed is the man who has a quiver of them," Phil said when we told him.

"Praise God," the sisters said. "All your children shall know of the Lord, and great will be the peace of your children."

Our parents were less happy with the news.

"Oh," my mother said weakly. "Another baby."

"You need to keep that thing in your pants," Eric's mom told him when he made the announcement. His father cleared his throat. Later that night, we offered up prayer again for our parents, pleading with God for their salvation, asking Him to open their eyes to the majesty of His plan.

And then I became very, very sick. My body, rail thin already, rejected the new presence in my womb and the flood of hormones in my blood. Morning sickness was a horrible misnomer; I vomited every hour of the day and sometimes woke up in the night to dash for the toilet. Eric would sit up and groan in sympathy when I pushed back the covers in a desperate rush. Afterward he would hold me and pray for me. His body against mine brought the nausea back again; I wanted to push him away, to snap at his sweaty commiseration, but I was unable to move away. He held me damply the rest of the night. When I woke, I rushed to the bathroom again.

The prescription antinausea drug that I had taken during my pregnancy with Allison was considered suspect in my circle of health-conscious sisters and brothers. Our bodies were the temple of the living God – we were charged by Scripture to care for them appropriately. We wouldn't even take an aspirin if we could help it. We ate whole wheat and lentils and tofu. We didn't drink caffeine or alcohol. Nobody would consider taking a drug to ease nausea, especially a woman who was growing a child of the Lord in her womb.

"You just can't do it, Carolyn," Rebekah said. "Who knows what they could eventually find out about that drug? It's not worth taking a chance with your baby." She bent down and kissed the top of her baby son's bald head. They both looked at me with expectant smiles. I wouldn't hurt a baby, would I?

"There are a lot of natural remedies for morning sickness," Rebekah added. "There's this herb, I forget what it's called, but I know a sister who has it. She swears it worked for her – I'll find out the name of it and get you some."

Then the whole room was abuzz with ideas and suggestions, promises of help. I sat in the middle of them all, my cup of peppermint tea untouched on my lap. The morning sunlight streamed through the windows around me. I was surrounded by light, my sisters' smiles, and God.

My next prenatal visit, I told my obstetrician that I wouldn't be taking the antinausea drug he offered. "God will take care of me," I told him, swinging my thin legs over the edge of the examining table. I had lost eight pounds in the first eight weeks of my pregnancy.

"God expects you to use your head, too, Carolyn," the doctor answered. "If you lose too much weight, it won't be good for the baby."

My hand flew to my belly. I held it there and smiled. "Don't worry, my baby will be fine, really, Dr. Allen. Just fine."

He cleared his throat and filled out my chart. "I'll see you next month. Keep taking the vitamins. Eat several small meals all during the day, OK?"

I nodded and dimpled and listened to him talk about my baby, the baby whose limbs were being knit even as we spoke. The God Who made that baby would keep him whole and see him safely through.

"Don't worry," I said again, and left his office. I was nineteen years old and I weighed ninety-five pounds. My stomach churned the saltines I had eaten for breakfast and I knew they wouldn't stay down, but I walked out to the car full of joy. A baby. God had given me a baby. A son.

Meanwhile, chaos had taken a firm grip in our household. Allison was a normal toddler and required a lot of care. I established myself on the living room sofa, bedsheets, pillows, and quilts covering the scratchy plaid Herculon. I hoped Allison would play quietly at my feet and nap beside me, but that wasn't what happened at all. I tried to entice her by reading to her or by putting a *Sesame Street* record on her little record player. None of these distractions lasted very long. She slid off the sofa and whirled away from my grasp. As she ran from the room, I called after her, but she didn't answer. When

I heard a commotion in the kitchen, I pulled myself up and slowly made my way there. Allison had emptied the cupboards as fast as she could get them yanked open. I leaned against the counter and looked at the mess: pots and pans, dishcloths, and boxes of cereal turned on their sides and spilling their contents. The nausea overwhelmed me again and I made my way to the kitchen sink, where I dry heaved for a while. Allison stood at my feet and gagged with me.

"Mommy, aagh, aagh," she imitated. She hunched over, holding her tummy, and made retching noises. "Mommy – you're funny."

I picked her up and took her back to the couch. Once there, I wiped away my tears, called Rebekah, and told her I needed help.

The sisters rallied and took over. They drew up baby-sitting schedules for Allison's care. A different sister cleaned my house every weekday. Meals were brought in each evening, including weekends. I was incredibly grateful for their intervention, but I struggled with the idea of being so dependent. I listened to Camille move around my house, vacuuming and dusting and polishing. When I heard her enter the tiny bathroom outside my bedroom, I cringed. Sure enough, she began to scrub the toilet. I heard the familiar swishing and felt my face burn with sudden humiliation.

"Camille!" I called. "Eric can do that."

"Almost done!" she sang back. The toilet flushed and then she came into my room, peeling off her rubber gloves. "Don't worry about it, sis. I've cleaned toilets before, you know."

"But not mine," I said weakly, too nauseated to lift my head from the pillow and look at her. "Camille, I guess I'm being proud or something. But I find it very hard to accept all this. I want to be the one helping, not the one helped."

She crossed the room and kissed my forehead. "It is humbling, I know, Carolyn. But this is good for you; it keeps you from being confident in your flesh. There is such a thing as being too self-sufficient, you know. That's not what Jesus wants for us."

"He is the vine; we are the branches," I whispered. My stomach seized upon itself, cramping into a fist-size ball.

"Exactly, darling," she said. "If you won't let me wash your toilet, Carolyn, I'll have to wash your feet, like it says in the Word. Do you want me to do that next?"

"No." I laughed weakly. "I can still do that."

"You're going to get better soon," Camille promised. "Your name is always circulating on the prayer chain – people all over Des Moines are praying for you. It's going to happen, sis. Believe it!"

Her cadence, so similar to Phil's, and her confidence buoyed me. I felt the presence of God, a warmth settling into my limbs like syrup.

Camille tucked the blankets firmly around me. "Thank you, Jesus," she prayed as she pressed her cheek against mine. "Thank you that you have already begun to heal my sweet sister. Amen and amen."

I listened to her sing, "Jesus, Jesus, Jesus, Sweetest name I know . . ." as she regathered her cleaning supplies and left the room. The nausea began to come back in earnest, and as wave after wave began sweeping over me, I concentrated on Camille's voice as she moved through the rooms of my house. I told myself it was an angel in all her radiance, blessing my little home, bringing order and light and hope as she sang praise to Jesus in the highest.

When Eric came home that night, everything was spotless. Rebekah sat on the floor, playing with Allison. Freshly baked bread and fresh string beans and a pasta casserole were laid out upon the stovetop. The table was set.

"Hey, little girl," I heard him say when he walked in. I could hear him talking to Rebekah, but I couldn't make out what they were saying. Her laughter, his laughter, and then the sound of the front door closing. He came back to the bedroom with Allison in his arms.

As usual, I was in bed with my Bible, my books, and some needlepoint. A pitcher of water and a stack of Ritz crackers on my bedside table. He kissed me on the forehead – the place I liked best. We never kissed more than a peck on the lips, a dry and quick peck to say hello or good-bye. He sat on the edge of the bed very carefully.

"The house looks really nice," he said. "How was your day, honey?"

"Better," I said. "Camille prayed for me, and I really felt the presence of the Lord."

"Oh, honey," he answered. "I'm so glad."

"Camille thinks God has already begun healing me," I said slowly, unsure if I should be saying it out loud. "Maybe I should try to eat some dinner tonight."

"Oh, boy, Allison, did you hear that? God is making Mommy's tummy better!" Eric tickled her stomach and slung her over his shoulder. "Let's go get her some dinner, okay?"

"Mommy better?" Allison asked, and turned to me, her flawless face so trusting, so ready to believe, that it broke my heart.

"Yes, baby," I said, and knew that Allison believed me. "Whoever will not receive the Kingdom of God like a little child will never enter it." I would believe. I would say it aloud: "I'm going to get better now."

Eric brought me a tray, and I ate what I could. When I threw up later, I ran the water loudly and flushed so Eric wouldn't hear. "I'm getting better," I told the woman in the mirror. I wiped the tears from my face, brushed my alkaline vomit from my teeth, and said it again. "I'm getting better. My healing has begun."

I made my way back to bed and listened to Eric putting

Allison to bed. He sounded unnaturally cheerful in a forced performance for Allison's sake. We're both performing for someone else, I thought. I nibbled the bread and prayed for the son in my womb. Please, God, make him strong. Make him a man who will not settle for less than everything.

Paulina was on the cleaning schedule the following week. I laughed when I saw her name. Paulina didn't clean her own house – she was going to clean mine? She was the most exotic woman I had ever met – a dark-eyed beauty who was a first-generation American in her family of Eastern Europeans. Paulina's father, a fiery and temperamental pastor, had sent his daughters to an evangelical college in Oregon. There Paulina met and married bland, white-bread Stu. They had been giving birth ever since. Paulina was now pregnant with their sixth child, and she was not even thirty. Her household was overflowing with babies, opera music, planters of herbs and sprouts, whole-wheat flour in bins on the floor, and books everywhere. The whole house smelled of yeast and suspicious earthy odors. Her dark European furniture, mostly castoffs from her family, was covered with carvings and inlays and spread with tapestries. It was like nothing I had ever seen in Iowa. Dust and newspapers covered every surface. Half-eaten food, rotting fruit, smears from little kids' fingers. When Paulina sent me to the refrigerator for wheat germ or something, I always braced myself. Her refrigerator had never held a can of soda or even a tub of margarine. Instead there were parcels of grains and cheeses, dark black pastes with splatters of oil glistening on the surface, brown dried fruit that looked like human ears, bottles of murky amber juices, and a silver pitcher of grayish goat milk.

I would pull out what she had asked for and carry it back to her wherever she was, usually nursing a baby and sometimes two, the toddler and the current infant. I wasn't always able to hide my total distaste for the odd foods and chaotic house, the lack of cleanliness and order. Sometimes I would have to pull back the eager child who embraced me at her door and lead him to the kitchen, where I would wash his sticky face and hands. I did that cheerfully enough; I didn't want to hurt Paulina's feelings, but I needn't have worried.

"Oh, Carolyn," she said, giggling. "You don't like messes, do you?" She waved at the house. "Poor Stu. He's not wild about it, either, but I think he's adjusting. But his mother – oh, his poor mother. She brings rubber gloves and Pine Sol in her suitcase when she visits. She cleans the whole time she's here, and I don't say anything. Bless her heart, I'm sure she never pictured Stu living in circus like this."

"I'm sure she loves you," I said. "She knows you love her son – what more could she want?"

"That's what I say." Paulina laughed, and her white teeth dazzled the room. We – her children, Allison, and I – all stopped for a minute. Paulina was as passionate about Stu as she was about her children, music and books, and the Lord. "And, Carolyn, I do. I love that man."

How could exotic Paulina fall for a man like Stu? What did she see in his square head and expressionless face? It was a mystery to me. I was so young, so inexperienced, so naive in the ways of love, that I eventually gave up trying to figure it out. Besides, the most important thing was that God wanted Paulina and Stu to be together. Every other consideration paled next to that.

The morning she arrived was a particularly bad one. I had been up in the night, vomiting more than once. My head hurt and I had begun to worry about the baby. I placed my hands around my softball-size womb and told my son how sorry I was that I was feeding him less than nothing, jarring him, disturbing him with my perpetual heaving. God, I prayed, please have mercy. I looked down at my legs; they were spindly, and my usually knobby knees stood out even more graphically. I had heard one of the sisters whisper to Eric last week that I was "skeletal." I was scared of what might happen to the baby if I was not able to eat soon.

"Carolyn!" Paulina said as she appeared in the doorway of my bedroom. "I'm here!" She was wearing a red cape, her shiny black hair streaming over her shoulders. Titus, her youngest son, was straddling her hip. All of Paulina's babies looked the same: enormous square heads and wide-spaced green eyes – not especially appealing babies. I blamed Stu's genes for this.

"Hello, sis," I said, hoping my disappointment wasn't too evident. I couldn't imagine how she could get anything done with nine-month-old Titus along. Despite the health regime at Paulina's house, her children always had colds. Even from across the room I could see that Titus's nose was running. I didn't want Allison to get sick.

"I had to bring Titus," Paulina said cheerfully. "He's a bear if he doesn't get to nurse every couple of hours. I knew Elaine was here baby-sitting and I thought Allison would like having another kid around."

"Sure." I nodded. "She likes babies. She's so excited about this one," I said, stroking my stomach. "She wants to call him Rocky."

Paulina laughed and I relaxed. So what if she had brought her messy baby? So what if she didn't get a lot accomplished in my house? And God could protect Allison from Titus's cold. Paulina could have been doing so many other things that day, but she had chosen to come here and clean my house. She was my sister and I loved her.

"What should I do first?" she asked as she gathered her hair into a topknot. "The kitchen?"

Paulina, like Camille, sang as she cleaned my house. "I'm my Beloved's and He is mine. His banner over me is love. . . ."

She had a strong, operatic voice, and she was not shy about using it. When I closed my eyes and listened, it was easy to imagine the whole house being filled with light and goodness as her vibrant songs became a current, sweeping out the misery, igniting great fountains of hope, causing joy to cascade along the walls. Her voice pulsed within me, and I began to praise God with her, to put the baby in His hands, and to genuinely trust Him with my health and the baby's health. I felt buoyed with confidence as I lay in my plain bedroom with its white bedspread and pale walls, the picture of Jesus in Gethsemane the only adornment. "Praise Jesus," I breathed. "All will be well."

But when I raised my hand to wipe away tears from my face, my arm passed in front of my eyes and I was shocked again. It was a prisoner-of-war arm, a bone with flesh stretched over it, oh, God, oh, God.

Trust me. I will never leave you or forsake you.

I will. I will trust God with all of my heart. Satan would destroy my confidence, but I would not be swayed from following the Lord. Praise Jesus. Praise the holy name of Jesus.

Again, I felt enveloped and sheltered, like a child who has crawled into bed with a parent. It was all good. There were no forces that could reach me here. I slept.

When I woke, I heard the front door closing. Then my bedroom door opened slowly. Paulina peeked in.

"Are you awake now?" she asked.

I nodded. "Yes."

"Elaine left to do errands, but, praise God, she took both of the kids with her," Paulina said. "Can you believe that? Wasn't that nice of her?"

"It was," I said, stretching. I felt better. I wasn't used to sleeping in the daytime, but I hadn't been sleeping well at night, either. And even my stomach felt better. I reached for my water and drank the rest of the glass.

"You were thirsty!" Paulina said as though she were praising a child. "But you need to eat now, Carolyn. What sounds good to you?"

For months now, nothing had sounded good, but suddenly I was hungry.

"A bologna sandwich on white bread with Miracle Whip and lettuce," I said quickly.

Paulina did not flinch at the mention of meat, especially nitrate-infested cold meat, or white bread or cholesterol. Instead she nodded. "I think that's exactly what you should have, then," she said. "Your body knows what nutrients it needs."

In an unparalleled act of Christian charity, Paulina left for the neighborhood grocery, bought the sandwich makings, and returned to fix me lunch. I ate it hungrily and thanked her several times.

"You're welcome," she said. "I should take some of this stuff home and make Stu a sandwich." She giggled. "I think he's afraid to admit that he lusts for white bread occasionally. I don't mind, though, as long as he still lusts for me."

"Is that all right, I mean, when you're married?" I asked, and leaned toward her. I blushed at the foolish question, but there, it was out.

"Well, yes," she said softly. "I don't mean that we lust for each other in a bad way, like we're consumed with sex or something." She laughed. "But let's face it, sex is a pretty good idea."

I just looked at her, longing to ask what it was like to have your husband be your lover, the one who made your heart pound, the one who kissed you and took your breath away. Imagine living with your lover – it was a fantasy, an unattainable fantasy. I closed my eyes and sighed.

"Sex with Stu," she began exactly as if she'd heard my thoughts, "is so amazing. He has an incredible penis."

I had never heard a sister say the word *penis*. I couldn't quite believe she had said it. I opened one eye and looked at her. She giggled. "Well, he does! I've been drawing it lately."

"Drawing?" I asked hoarsely.

"I have several pen-and-ink drawings of it – they're all over the bedroom right now. Oh, my goodness, Carolyn, I forgot to take them down the last time my mother-in-law visited. She saw them, all right, but she didn't say a word." She began laughing very hard. "You should have seen her face when she walked out of the bedroom!"

"Oh, I can imagine," I said, picturing how I would look if I had seen the drawings. I tried not to, but I kept seeing those pictures in my head. Stu's penis in all its glory taped all over Paulina's messy bedroom. And when the lights were out, they were lovers.

"Could you eat another sandwich?" Paulina asked. She was pulling lint from the front of her sweater; I noticed for the first time how full and round her breasts were. Stu probably loves her breasts, I thought, and saw his hands cupping them, his mouth on them.

"No," I said loudly, interrupting my perverted thoughts. "I mean, no, Paulina, I hope eating this one wasn't a mistake."

But it was. The nausea returned later that day. I threw up violently and wept. I had reached my breaking point. That night I told Eric that I needed a healing from God. We had to go to the Elders and ask for the laying on of hands and anointing with oil, the New Testament sacrament of healing of the sick. My husband held my hand and said, "Yes, we'll go, we'll ask them to do it as soon as possible."

The Elders' prayer was arranged for the following Sunday. I would be attending church for the first time in months. I combed my hair – was I imagining it, or was it thinning? – and dug out an old container of blush to smooth across my cheeks and forehead. I didn't need to wear maternity clothes, even though I was almost six months pregnant. I wore a white blouse and long ashy green skirt with an elastic waistband. I looked frail, anemic, my veins purple against my white skin. I couldn't look away from my haunted face. "You've suffered," I consoled my reflection. "But that's what makes you worthy to be called His own."

I held my Bible on my lap as Eric drove us carefully to church; we were renting an actual church in those days. We sat in pews instead of folding chairs, and we had a real stained-glass window. My husband glanced over at me at stoplights and squeezed my hand.

"I love you," he said.

"I love you," I answered, and I meant it. He *was* my best friend, the boyfriend of my troubled youth, and the father of my children. But none of these roles would ever make him my true mate and lover. God, in his unfathomable wisdom, had denied me this. "Come to me, ye who are weary and heavy laden." Yes. I would come, and I would accept this divinely appointed yoke.

But if there would be no miracle for my marriage, there would be a miracle for my body, I felt sure of it. God was going to heal me and raise me up. He would touch me and bring health and vitality once again. My baby would be born whole and perfect. God was going to do something extraordinary today.

The sisters made their way toward me as soon as Eric and I walked through the door. They folded me in their arms and stroked my hair. "You're here," they kept saying. "Oh, we've missed you." No one mentioned my ghastly appearance or commented on my sticklike arms poking out from the three-quarter-length sleeves. They patted my hands and squeezed them and told me that they would be praying for me all day.

149

They were not allowed to be a part of the Elders' meeting where the prayer for my healing would take place but promised to hold their own prayer meeting.

"God is able to do exceedingly beyond all we ask or think," Camille said as she put a sweater over my shoulders.

"His arm is not too short to save," Rebekah reminded me as she walked away to join her husband.

"Healing is in His wings," Paulina whispered into my ear.

"Yes," I kept saying. All morning, I agreed with the saints. God was a mighty God, amen and amen.

It was hard to concentrate on Phil's teaching that morning. I was filled with anticipation, the rush of adrenaline tempering even the omnipresent nausea. I was going to be ushered into the presence of God in thirty minutes, now fifteen, now ten. I moistened my lips, smoothed my hair, adjusted my stockings. I took a deep breath and felt my body trembling. The Almighty God, me, five minutes.

After the service, the Elders gathered inside the small room that held the baptistery. When I walked in, I was immediately overwhelmed by the smell of damp concrete and mildew. I suddenly felt queasy and panicked. What if I threw up right here, right under the hands of my brothers? I took a deep breath, swallowed hard, and set my jaw.

"Are you all right?" Tom asked. He stood up and walked toward me. I waved him off, afraid even to open my lips to talk. I closed my eyes and took several more breaths.

"Where do you want me?" I finally managed.

"Sit here, Carolyn," Tom said, leading me to a chair in the middle of the room. I smiled my thanks and sank into the worn upholstery. The Elders pushed back their own chairs and began to gather around my chair. They wore their regular casual clothing, jeans and oxford shirts, Adidas and Nikes on their feet – I realized I had half expected vestments, hooded robes. As they took their positions around me, I could smell their aftershave lotion, their mints, the fabric softener on their shirts, and I regretted that I had arranged the whole thing. Everything was too homely, too obviously Iowan, for me to believe I was in the Holy of Holies.

"Sister," Phil said after the Elders had taken their positions around me, "do you seek healing from the Lord?"

"Yes," I said. "I do." The sudden formality flustered me. I felt even more uncomfortable.

"We will anoint you with oil and offer prayer as we are instructed in the Word, which promises that the fervent prayer of the righteous will raise you up," Phil said confidently, his voice strong and authoritative.

I fought an impulse to answer, "Okey-dokey, then, let the healing begin." I didn't know where the hysteria was coming from, but I was clearly out of my element. I believed in the juxtaposition of earthly and heavenly matters. This sacrament was one such intersection, and instead of entering it boldly and full of faith, I was reacting like a foolish child.

It was crazy, wasn't it? A little crazy? I could take a pill and I wouldn't puke anymore. I had taken that same medication with Allison and she was healthy as could be. Why was I putting myself through this? Who were these people? Why was a fat guy approaching me with cooking oil? *Satan.* I recognized the Tempter's voice. *Get thee behind me.*

"Praise God." I said aloud, hoping to silence the Father of Lies.

The Elders, all five of them, looked at me tenderly. Tom held a small vial of golden oil. He tilted it and put a drop on his finger. Then he stretched out his hand toward me. When his finger touched my forehead, I felt a surge in my body.

Something ancient in me rose up. I felt caught up while some distant cognizance tried to record the unrecognizable force coursing through me. Good? Was this what pure goodness felt like? Love without restraint? I had never encountered it before, not once in my twenty years had I suspected there was an obliteration of self that felt frighteningly, exhilaratingly *right*.

My head swam. I couldn't hear anything but my name and God's Name, spoken by each of my beloved brothers as they interceded for me to the Lord. I was aware that the Elders were all on their knees surrounding me, and I knew their hands were on my shoulders and my arms, but I was in the presence of God in such an exalted fashion, I cared for nothing else. I was filled with fire, a masculine flame, incredible strength intentionally tempered with gentleness – it was as though God held back from consuming me with His love. I hovered on the brink and thought only this: Take me. My infirmity had brought me so close to God. My body had never been so weak, but now I could see that my spirit had never, never been so strong.

"Please, Father," I heard them say one by one. "Touch our sister. Raise her up. Have mercy. Heal her."

And sitting there in that worn maroon velvet chair, I was not so convinced of my need for physical healing after all. Knowing God and being in His presence was sufficient. I repented of my earlier doubts. God was Who He said He was. I was guilty of trusting in my weak and sinful flesh. I wept under the Elders' hands. I knew that I had received a healing I hadn't even been looking for.

And then God did more. Later that week, the nausea began to ebb. Each day I felt stronger and stronger; within two weeks the nausea and vomiting were gone completely. The last two months of my pregnancy I could eat, clean my house, take care of Allison. I was incredibly grateful for my physical healing, but even more I continued to savor the moment God had fallen upon me. I replayed the healing scene with the Elders over and over and wished I could live it again.

The church rejoiced in my healing. We all liked to tell the

story of what God had done. The sisters used it to encourage others who were suffering. Phil and Tom would mention it during their teaching. I felt so humbled and grateful that God had used me to bring glory to Himself. I was the vessel of clay the Master had chosen to use. When I thought of my petulance and my resentment and my irreverence even on the day of my healing, I was overwhelmed at His mercy to me.

Joshua Eric was born an absolutely beatific baby. He held my finger while I nursed him. He studied me with such passionate intensity, I was awash in grace, determined never to doubt God or His ability to heal for the rest of my life. "Oh, Jesus," I sang quietly. "Jesus, Jesus, Jesus. Sweetest name I know. Fills my every longing. Keeps me singing as I go."

SAINTS

Eric and I stood on the front porch of a nondescript clapboard house on Sixth Avenue. The neighborhood was definitely working class, the houses white and beige, streaked with car exhaust from the unending traffic that passed by. We pressed the doorbell, but I couldn't even hear if it worked over the sounds of semitrucks changing gears and speeding toward the freeway entrance a few blocks away.

"Hi!" A woman in a head scarf stood in the doorway, her smile so bright that in an odd bit of synesthesia, I thought I heard it, the earth cracking open, a lightning bolt, something odd and wonderful and significant. "Carolyn and Eric, right? Oh, you're so cute. Praise God you belong to Him. Come in. Come in."

Eric and I ducked into the doorway of a strange little jungle of rooms, all decorated with large, glossy posters of bear cubs and children, hot-air balloons, waterfalls, and a Scripture under each one. "Love bears all things." "Become as little children." "Keep your mind on things above." "Jesus is my best friend." We followed her into the kitchen, where she poured us glasses of iced tea and shoved a plate of grainy flat cookies toward us. They were dark brown and filled with little sink holes. No leavening, I guessed.

"Charles should be home any minute," Anna said as she scooped up one of her babies from the floor. "He's so anxious to meet you. We both love meeting new saints."

"Are you sure this a good time?" I asked. The Elders had arranged this meeting. They had thought it was a good idea for

154

Eric and me to become close with a couple older than us in the Lord. We had been believers for five years, but we still had so much to learn. Anna and Charles were ten years old in the Lord. They could show us how to keep on the narrow road.

"It's a perfect time," Anna assured us. She wore a peasant skirt and a short-sleeved blouse, and I could see her arms were motherly, fleshy but firm. "We thought we'd talk you into staying for dinner – sweet corn and veggie burgers, how does that sound?"

"Great," Eric and I said together, and then laughed. Anna laughed with us, her face so delighted, so serene, that her laughter rang in my head the rest of the night. She was a woman who could help me to become closer to God. That was all I wanted in the world.

After dinner, Charles pulled out his Bible. It was a large black leather King James, the gilt from the pages completely worn off. He began to give us passage after passage to help us pursue righteousness and resist sin. I watched his hands on the pages, the quick flip to a cross-reference, the way he could look at a page and instantly find the verse he was looking for. By the end of the night, I was far more familiar with his hands than I was with his face. Anna, on the other hand, glowed with the presence of God, a radiant bride of Christ, as she sat across the room, nursing a baby, putting in a word here or there, asking Charles a question as though he were the wisest man on earth. She was so humble. As I helped her with the dishes, I couldn't stop myself from praising her, from telling her how much I sensed the presence of Christ in her.

"He must increase, I must decrease," she said, scraping our chewed-up corn cobs into the trash can under the sink. She wadded up the greasy napkins and looked at me. "Carolyn, I'm nothing without Christ. I'm trash."

It was a moment I would never forget. I was overwhelmed

by her humility: a woman like Anna, someone whose very presence had created a home of love and harmony and goodwill. Her girlish face, her winsomeness, and her generosity would have brought her attention anywhere. We stood over the remains of our meal, the empty boxes, the bones and discards of many, many days. I nodded at her statement and then looked down into the depths of the garbage can. "Me too," I whispered happily.

Eric and I held hands on the way home. We were elated and somehow felt compelled to anchor ourselves to the earth. We were connected to the whole of the universe, and we were never going to be afloat again. God was ordering our days, our relationships, our future. It was all we could have ever hoped for in a world where our peers were dropping out, disappearing, killing themselves. We had salvation. We had everything.

A winter night some months later, I was stirring soup when the phone rang. Eric answered. Even though I could not hear what he was saying, there was something about the rhythm of his words that made me uneasy. Too many pauses. Too few words. No laughter at all.

I turned the soup down and walked into the living room. He had hung up the phone but did not turn around.

"What is it? Who was that?" I asked. He shook his head but still did not turn around. He waved toward the children, who were playing quietly across the room. Allison looked up and smiled. She was five but had already developed an empathetic smile. She had a servant's heart, always ready to do something for others. Joshua lay on his belly, pushing a Hot Wheels car back and forth while he hummed "My God Is So Big". I touched Eric's arm and he finally turned around. He reached up for his glasses and pulled them off to wipe his eyes. I was scared for the first time in a long time. We walked into the kitchen.

"It's Anna," he said. "She has leukemia, the worst kind possible. The doctors say she doesn't have much hope."

"The doctors don't know anything. Anna's a Christian. God will heal her," I answered confidently and without so much as a trace of sorrow. I felt almost relieved. Nothing was without a solution in our world. Nothing was impossible with God. God would not let Anna die. He would use her to glorify His name. How wonderful that would be.

"I thought you'd be upset," Eric said. "I thought it would be hard for you to believe that God was still in control." He began to brighten.

Praise You, Jesus, I prayed silently. You give us strength for all things.

"Should we pray?" Eric asked, and we did. We prayed in the kitchen as the steam from vegetables and broth misted us, warmed us, reminded us that our God was *Jehovah Jireh*. He gave us the fruit of the earth. He healed us. He could raise someone from the dead if necessary. We were not living in a random universe. Everything happened for a reason, and God had *promised* that "all things work together for good to those who love God." One had to be patient to see what God would do, what miracles lay just beyond our vision.

That spring, Anna lay dying in Iowa City. She had had a bone marrow transplant and developed encephalitis. She was bald, her mouth coated with painful ulcerations. She could not speak or eat; tubes ran in and out of her body. Rebekah and I had traveled two hours to stand at her bedside and hold her hand while her brain was being attacked. We did all the talking while Anna looked at the ceiling, her feeding tubes, the pictures of her babies on her bedside table.

"You should see your house," Rebekah said. "Spotless, Anna, spotless. The sisters are over there every day, cleaning, polishing, even painting. They've painted your laundry room. I hope that's OK."

We waited for a smile or nod, but Anna did nothing.

"The kids are fine," I said after a moment. "More than fine. You really don't have to worry, Anna. They're having a lot of fun staying with us – all the new toys, I guess. Not that they're not glad to see Charles when he comes to pick them up, but they're always smiling when he drops them off in the morning again." Anna didn't react.

"Did you have them all last week?" Rebekah asked me.

I answered, and then she asked another question, and somehow we gave up on the idea of talking to Anna. Instead we spoke and let Anna listen. We talked about things she would be interested in: our walks in Christ, our Bible study, our children, a recipe or two. We exchanged dinner ideas over the body of our failing sister.

Rebekah and I agreed that the Lord would heal Anna; it was just a matter of time. Only God knew when He would be glorified the most. We had to trust Him to answer our prayers. I prayed without ceasing. I could not stop asking God to heal my sister, my discipler, the woman I aspired to be.

Anna lived. Her brain was permanently damaged, but she was alive. She could go home and care for her children. She would speak in a monotone the rest of her life. Her face would never register emotion again, but she was alive. And the church celebrated. We had a prayer meeting that lasted all night long. One of the Elders reminded us that God's ways were not our ways. There was a good reason that God had allowed Anna to contract encephalitis. God would be glorified by Anna's infirmity because in our weakness, He was made strong. I watched Anna as she sat across the room with Charles. It was just like the parable Jesus told. Anna was the clay vessel in which the Master chose to place His candle. All the cracks, all the thin places and worn places, allowed the light to shine brighter than it ever could in a perfect vessel. Jesus would shine in Anna, radiate more than He ever had before. I trusted Him. Charles trusted Him. And, Anna, Anna had always trusted Him more than any of us. We prayed long into the night. We sang hymns with our eyes closed. Some of us fell to our knees. Only Anna did not weep for at least some time in the long night.

How Eric and I loved the saints in those early days. Being introduced to someone new was not a matter of sizing someone up, testing the likelihood or possibility of friendship; instead the friendship, the kinship, was assumed. The bond was already in place – all we had to do was acknowledge it, shake hands on it, open our arms for an embrace and yet another embrace. We were loved. *"God loves you and I love you and that's the way it should be. . . ."* We sang this at the beginning of our meetings and then again at the end.

Life in Des Moines in the 1980s was like a decade-long family reunion. We ate, we sang, we played, we loved. Our children were born into this fold. My babies were rocked by dozens of loving women and tossed in the air by laughing fathers. Year after year of growing closer to people we already loved and meeting new saints we loved instantly – it was the utopia others had failed to achieve. We were often thought of as a cult, both by mainstream, liberal churches and by unbelievers. We looked like hippies and we had a lot of kids and even sat cross-legged in our folding chairs sometimes – that seemed to be enough to be called a cult, but there was no sinister element, no mind control, there was just this: love.

Eric and I saw some people outside of the church – my family, for instance. My mom and stepfather were definitely a part of our lives. Mother was happy in her church; we talked about spiritual matters and passed Christian books back and forth. She was pleased that I was living for God. My sister married and moved to Iowa City. Her husband thought Eric and I were Jesus freaks and more than a little annoying, so we didn't see them very much. My brother married at a very young age and began raising little boys with a dark-haired girl named Cynda. My dad was on wife number three, but we liked her a lot. She was perky and energetic; she listened to me more than my dad did. They ran a bar in Allendale, and one Christmas we spent the evening there, all the Christmas lights on, the jukebox playing "Blue Christmas" as we ate Buffalo wings and sipped Shirley Temples. Eric's parents were buying motor homes and apartment buildings; we didn't see them much at all. We loved our families of origin and we would never turn our backs on them, but both Eric and I felt our real family was definitely the church.

And it was inevitable that we would have some relationships in the church that were closer than others. Some brothers and sisters were so singular that you couldn't help be drawn to them.

John was tall, angular, with the face of an aesthete. He was the single guy, bravely so, amid the families in our group. He loved God. He pursued God with a zeal that was apparent to all of us. He often fasted in order to pray. He painted houses for a living, but he wouldn't even pack a lunch – he spent his lunch hour petitioning the Lord for the rest of us. He prayed for our children, this man with paint-splattered clothing. His hands were wide and expressive and often held open in praise to God. He sat alone at our gatherings with his head bowed in prayer. His devotion thrilled me. I admired his heart for God and the comments he would offer after teaching. He understood the Scriptures – that was clear. When he asked Eric if he could spend time with us in our home, I was very happy. I pictured the three of us encouraging one another, reading our Bibles into the late hours, talking happily and earnestly of the Kingdom and our part in it.

Eric and I loved our small house on Park Avenue, a one-block dead-end street lined with shade trees and long sloping yards behind the modest homes. Allison and Joshua shared a yellow bedroom. Eric and I slept across the hall in a pale blue room with white curtains and a miniature closet under the eaves. There was even a bedroom in the basement for overnight visitors. I was eager to have visitors, especially Christian brothers and sisters; opening our home to someone like John made perfect sense.

The summer we spent with John showed me that I was missing something very vital. I had begun to depend solely on God for the intimacy I hadn't found with Eric. Eric and I were not intimate, not the way God wanted us to be. It was true that I could achieve a oneness with God that took away the loneliness I felt with Eric. When I was close to God, I hardly noticed my impoverished marriage. But when God felt far away, I was overwhelmed by the vacuum that rushed in.

Eric and I didn't have much to say to each other. Each day was pretty much like the next, an endless succession of days spent in the Lord. ("Are you in the Lord, honey?" "I am. And you, Eric?") How could I complain of kindness and civility? Of course we were kind to each other – we were brother and sister in Christ if nothing else – but there was more than that. We shared the same sense of humor. Eric did a perfect imitation of Donald Duck sneezing that had made me laugh since I was fifteen. He was my friend, someone who loved me when no one else did. The ancient Hebrews characterized God's love with a single word: lovingkindness. Eric loved me this way, and if I felt smothered by it, there was no way to protest, no calling out for mercy.

John was young and intense and *holy*. He despised compromise. He was like a prophet saying, "Love God. Serve Him at all costs. Sacrifice everything for Him." I liked that a lot. If I couldn't have erotic, I could have holy, and sometimes I couldn't tell the difference between the two. I felt alive around John, tuned in, and yes, turned on.

When John came into our lives, talking and admonishing and challenging, it was like a rushing wind that filled the house. He had a standing dinner invitation any night of the week. We ate dinner night after night on the patio of our little house on Parkwood. We grilled vegetable kabobs and sliced homegrown tomatoes and drank tall glasses of iced tea with sprigs of mint I picked from the yard. Thomas of Aquinas, Augustine, St. Francis – suddenly our table talk was full of the ancient fathers and their doctrine. I learned about Brother Lawrence, the ancient cook for a monastery who practiced the presence of God as he peeled vegetables. We talked about philosophy and the need for a First Cause. It was my first real experience with a meeting of the minds. I felt the spark, the fire kindled, the burning, between John and me. It flared over our heads, good God, I didn't know why Eric let it go on so.

In fact, Eric would often go to bed early and John would stay for hours afterward. The two of us would sit across from each other in our webbed lawn chairs, our Bibles on our laps. He would talk and I would ask questions, thrilled with his keen insights. One rainy night, we moved into the living room. I fell asleep on the sofa while he was talking. I awoke when John bent over me to kiss me gently on the forehead. It was such a brotherly thing to do – I thought about it for a long time afterward. It occurred to me that if I had to count football player Tony, John was only the third man in my whole life to kiss me. I looked at his lips the next time I saw him and realized again that his lips, his mouth, had touched my face. It was an inappropriate thought and one I forsook immediately, but it came back.

Eric seemed glad that I was entertained. In a way, I think, he felt the pressure was off. My intensity wore him out. My need to see what the Scriptures said and my insistence on knowing the whole counsel of God were pretty exhausting. Although he still revered the Word, he had begun to pursue music more than his studies. His idea of getting into the Word was to take the words of a psalm and set them to music. He sat in the porch swing and strummed a background to the theological discussions that I was having with John. Eric loved us both; he was content to listen and felt no compulsion to join in with his own deep thoughts or comments.

The discourse of true intimates raged on, and Eric strummed along.

Toward the end of summer, we invited John to join us on a trip to the park with the children. It was a pleasant August day, not overbearing in heat or humidity, and we took a picnic lunch with us. The three of us watched Allison and Joshua play in the wading pool.

"We don't belong in time," John said, almost at once. The park was nearly deserted – it was late afternoon and the shadows from the jungle gym and monkey bars stretched across the grass, creating long prisons of light and darkness. Joshua dove under the water, his four-year-old body as lithe as a dolphin's. I watched him and savored his movements – he was my son, my only son, and how I loved him.

Eric nodded. "Amen, brother."

I thought another minute before responding. "What does that mean – we don't belong in time?"

John paused. He leaned back and looked up into the sky, waiting, I supposed, for some fresh revelation from God.

"What I mean is this – we are not creatures for whom time is a natural environment. We don't know how to exist in time very well – that's proof that we are eternal by nature," he said, taking another swallow of his iced tea.

I felt uncharacteristically lazy about making my way around his logic, interacting with a new idea. I was just about ready to pull out the potato salad, and I was thinking of the new potatoes, the icy onions, the pungent mustard and cold mayonnaise in my grandmother's ceramic mixing bowl. I forced myself to answer.

"How could we not be used to time?"

Eric looked relieved that I had responded. "John," I could imagine him saying later, "is just too heavy most of the time."

"The children, for example. Look at them in the water. They're having a great time, but it's because it's a novelty. They're not used to being surrounded by water. They're surprised by it," John said. "If they were fish, they wouldn't be surprised. It would be natural to be surrounded by water if you were a fish, right?"

"Right," Eric said, and yawned.

"We're surrounded by time, but it doesn't feel right. We say things like 'Time flies,' or 'Doesn't it just seem like yesterday that so-and-so happened?' That's because this small confine of time on planet Earth isn't our natural element. We're meant to live in eternity," John explained.

"Oh," I said, looking at him in delight. Eric walked toward the children, who were squealing in the water, their lovely brown arms flashing in the sun. Our brother smiled at us and it all seemed quite clear that we would live forever, but never could we be more filled with love and peace than we were at this very moment.

Believers on planet Earth are foreigners in a strange land.

"People who say such things show that they are looking for a country of their own. . . . They are longing for a better country, a heavenly one. Therefore God is not ashamed to be called their God, for he has prepared a city for them" (Hebrews 11:14, 16).

As we became more and more bonded with the fold of the believers, we didn't want to be anywhere else. Those people understood us; we understood them. We had a coded language and shared goals. We were serving the Creator of the universe. As far as the world was concerned, we had become zealots. Some people in our families grew impatient with our dogma. My father and sister avoided anything but the most cursory of relationships with us. When we were visiting, they always tried to keep the conversation on the kids or sports teams. They nodded their thanks at our gifts of Bibles and religious literature, but they never read them. I would look for our gifts the next time we visited and find no evidence that even the front cover had been lifted; the pages were smooth, creaseless, absolutely unread. Mother was happy with me, though. She saw me as a younger version of herself, someone who would do the right things in her marriage and who would raise her kids to follow God. One of my mother's greatest regrets was that she did not know Jesus when we were small.

Eric and I wore crosses, carried large Bibles, and spoke in biblical cadences. Even our daily language was a series of truisms: God was in control, we said when the windshield cracked; God is sovereign, Eric reminded me if our plans were foiled for the weekend; Praise Jesus, I said when he came in the door at night. We were grateful, I think, for these things to say to each other. There was no longer anything else to say.

God had taken John from us, just as mysteriously as He had plunked him into our life the summer before. A pretty young nurse had begun attending Fountain of Joy. When John saw her thick eyelashes and sapphire eyes, he asked her if she would like to join him in prayer later that evening. His perfectly serious request was received in the same manner. Within weeks, they announced that God wanted them to marry that year. After a holy six-month courtship, sans kissing on the lips, they married. John nodded at me at church, shook my hand as he did Eric's, but all the lovely spiritual discourse was over between us. I missed it.

165

My only recourse was to pore over my own studies. By this time, we had accumulated quite a library. We owned Bible concordances and Bible dictionaries. We studied Berkoff's *Systematic Theology*. I bought a Greek interlinear New Testament – the original Greek alongside the English translation. Eric decided to memorize Scripture. He carried twenty Bible verses in his left back pocket at all times. He used the time he was stuck in traffic or waiting in line at the grocery store to memorize the verses. He knew many, many verses by heart now and quoted them readily when the situation warranted it. ("Thy Word have I hid in my heart that I might not sin against thee" was a favorite.)

At one point, we were attending five studies a week. I had my women's group. Eric had his discipleship group. We never missed the big Wednesday night Bible study. Then there was the core group's meeting, where we got together with the band members to keep each other accountable in the Lord. Finally, on Saturday morning we woke up early and met with a small group of stalwarts who wanted to study theology from the seminary textbooks Phil had supplied.

We dropped Allison and Joshua off at Eric's mother's. She loved the kids and was always pleased to have them, even if it meant Eric and I were off to another brainwashing session. No, she never said that, but she let us know that she had been surrounded by religious fanatics all of her life and wasn't thrilled that her son and his wife had become fanatics as well. We kissed the kids good-bye and rushed out the door. Phil didn't like us to be late. Eric drank coffee from his thermos as he drove. I was happy to have this place to go. This place to be. Someone was expecting us – that novelty never escaped me. I belonged at long last.

We met in the nursery of a large downtown church for this particular study. The room smelled of baby powder and disposable diapers, teething biscuits and sour milk that had

166

been drooled into the carpet for generations. The walls were hung with pastel posters of wide-eyed children shepherds and a gamine Jonah beside a cheerful whale who spouted a heart-filled jet of water. Fortunately, the room was also filled with rockers for all the volunteer workers. We each chose a rocker, unbuttoned our coats, and opened our textbooks.

"Let's pray," Phil said.

The room was filled with our soft sighs and our acknowledgments of God and His presence. When no one spoke aloud, we all prayed in silence. I sensed the cavernous building around us, the cold stone and corridors, the stained glass, the chalice on the altar, all of it lifeless until God entered. And there we were, unlikely little Christs, rocking in the heart of the church. "Praise you, Jesus," I whispered. I felt Him sweep through me, the tingle, the now familiar thrill of knowing He was here in our midst. I was caught up in this reverie when I heard Phil speaking and realized we were done praying.

"So, Carolyn," Phil was saying. "Tell us about dispensational theology."

"We can divide the history of God and man into seven dispensations and determine God's method of relating to man through each of those dispensations," I said quickly, shy and surprised that he had called on me. I was one of only two women present. This study was really supposed to be for the men, the only ones who could teach, according to God's Word. No one said women couldn't come, but no one especially invited them, either.

"What does that mean?" Phil asked. "That sounds like God changes. We know from the Scriptures that He is the same yesterday, today, and forever."

I was silent for a moment as I waited for someone else to chime in. I bit my lip and looked down. Phil laughed.

"Hey, little sis, you're right. Don't back down," he said, smiling at me. Two of his teeth overlapped; I noticed for the first time. He laughed again. "You'd get eaten up in seminary, you know that? Stand firm, all of you. 'Study to show yourselves approved, a workman of God, unashamed.' Or in your case, a workperson," he said, winking at me.

It was subtle enough. I had been put in my place, but lovingly. I knew God had made man to be my head – there was no way to argue with those teachings found in the Scriptures. I had heard teachings on a woman's submission dozens of times, and I believed that to be God's will for me, but I registered a voiceless protest coming from within me from time to time. I repressed that rebellion. I hushed it, I spoke on top of it, I mocked it, but I never quelled it entirely.

I smiled at Phil and made a helpless face so he would laugh again. I didn't speak again the rest of the morning. Phil didn't call on me, and I didn't have the nerve to answer any more questions, even if I did know all of the answers. They were my answers this time; I hadn't copied from anyone. I didn't need to.

The study was over at eleven, and Eric and I hurried out to get the kids. We took them to McDonald's for lunch. We looked like any other couple, except people probably thought we were too young to have two kids, but we were loving and careful parents. Eric made the kids laugh by counting french fries like the Count on *Sesame Street*. I wiped their faces and kept their shoes tied as they ran around the play area. I acted surprised every time Joshua appeared in the window of the jungle gym.

"Joshua! How did you get there?" I asked, my hands on my hips, my face filled with righteous surprise. And then he'd collapse with hilarity. A sturdy, solid little boy, he'd laugh until he began hiccupping, making Eric and me laugh, which set Joshua off again. Allison, half-buried by red, yellow, and blue plastic balls, echoed our laughter just because it was ours.

Nobody watching this could know my mind was filled with

God. Nobody could know how badly I wanted to get home to pray, to fall on my face in my prayer closet, to have time alone with Him. I kept prayer journals, great lengthy entries where I wrote out my prayers, where I dated the requests and the answers, where I asked God again and again to please give me true intimacy in my marriage. There was never a corresponding date of God's answer to this request.

Rebekah and Joseph Mahon loved each other – that was apparent. They were our age, married right out of high school just as we had been. He was, like many of the brothers, a carpenter. She was a housewife. They lived in a crumbling gray asphalt shingled house on the east side of Des Moines that smelled of cats and furniture polish. One of the couples in the church had given the Mahons their old kitchen table, white Formica with four bright orange vinyl chairs. Rebekah and Joe were thrilled because they loved nothing more than having the brothers and sisters over to break bread. Eric and I sat on those orange chairs a thousand times and discussed the things of the Lord over bowls of soup and glasses of herbal tea.

Joe was red haired and freckled, but his nature was anything but impetuous and fiery. He was a content man, a serious and studious one, and he loved Rebekah as though it were his vocation. Not far removed from his pursuit of God was his desire to be a godly husband.

"Rebekah, my love," he said when she walked in the room. "The greatest of God's gifts to me."

"Oh, Joseph," she said giggling. She stroked the back of his head, and he reached up to put his hand on top of hers, stilling it, holding it there beneath his fingers.

I stopped blowing on my soup and swallowed a large spoonful of minestrone. It scalded my tongue and throat. I grabbed my tea and drank quickly.

"Are you all right?" Eric asked.

Rebekah and Joe looked at me with equal concern.

"I'm fine," I said. "Great soup, Rebekah."

"As I was saying, this woman, her price is far above rubies," Joe continued. "Aren't we blessed, Eric, to have these women for our helpmeets?"

"We sure are," Eric said in his Donald Duck voice.

We really laughed then.

Why had God seen fit to give them this love and withhold it from me? Why did God think I could live without it? I couldn't. I absolutely couldn't do it even for a day, not unless He gave me the strength. I crumbled another cracker into my soup.

"I was thinking of something today," Joe said in his usual measured way. I knew he was introducing an analogy. He was pretty good at them. It would have something to do with a tool or maybe a dovetail joint and how that's like the Holy Spirit and us. We all looked at him and waited.

"Whenever I get ready to build a house, I start with a frame, right? I mean, you can't just start putting up walls and plumbin' and wirin' the thing, can you?"

"Sure can't," Eric obliged. "You'd be in trouble if you did that."

"We know this, don't we, brother? We gotta have a foundation. We gotta have something to pour the cement into, don't we? A frame, right?"

Joe didn't need us to do anything but nod at this point. The three of us took turns.

"So I build a frame for that cement and then, only then, can I get at what I want to do, build a house."

I nodded. Yep, that's what you want to do, build a house.

The payoff was coming. Joe shifted and looked at us closely, a dramatic pause.

"Well, that's what we do when we can't love somebody. We build ourselves a frame," Joe said as he held an imaginary hammer, pounding it firmly up and down the length of an imaginary two-by-four.

"We begin to behave as though we love that person. We sacrifice for them. We pray for them. We do everything the Scripture tells us to do for one another. And then, brother and sisters, *then*, God comes in and pours the cement. God provides the real thing, the kind of love that's solid and genuine. All you gotta do is lay down that frame."

For a moment, I wondered if Joe was talking to me alone. Could the church see that I wasn't loving my husband the way I should? Was Joe telling me to lay down the frame in my marriage? I looked at him warily, but he wasn't looking at me at all. It was Rebekah he was watching, Rebekah whose fingers he was playing with on the white Formica table.

I excused myself to go to the bathroom. As I washed my hands, I knew I had indeed laid down the frame of genuine love for my husband. I had never betrayed him in any way. I loved him truly, as well as I could. But I had been waiting a very long time for God to fill up the frame with the real thing. I was always disappointed, mad at myself, at Eric, even, fearfully, at God. I felt filthy with hypocrisy sitting in that little house late into the night as the four of us discussed the Kingdom. The internal dialogue I kept going in my head drowned out the other three voices around the table. Again and again, I forced myself back in their midst, gritted my teeth against the reality of my life.

Rebekah generously took it upon herself to come over once a week and teach me all I needed to know about being a Christian wife and mother.

One afternoon, I casually remarked that I hated finding pennies around the house, that I had taken to throwing them away when I found them in the cracks of sofa cushions or at the bottom of junk drawers.

"Oh, you can't do that," Rebekah said gently but firmly. She scared me a little with her firmness. She was my age, slender, with exceptionally thin arms and legs and pale blue eyes, but she seemed so much older.

I laughed and took another bite of my carob-and-honey brownie.

"I'm serious, Carolyn," she said. "It's against the law to throw away money, and as a Christian, you are charged to obey the laws of the land."

It was another example of worlds colliding. My flesh reeled back at the rebuke, but my new spirit accepted the wisdom my sister in the Lord had just given me. I grimaced in regret.

"Oh, I didn't know," I said. "Really, Rebekah, it never occurred to me that it was anything I shouldn't do."

Rebekah nodded solemnly and began flipping through the pages of her King James. "Shall we look at the virtuous woman passage again?"

Sometimes I felt as though I had so far to go, so much to know, so much to forsake, that I felt like crying, but then I would reread one of the Gospels and see Jesus, His selflessness and goodness and mercy for sinners. It still broke my heart to read about His life. It still made me want to be the bride of Christ at all costs. He was my true Husband, and only He could satisfy me, I knew that.

The sisters nursed each other's children. It was a kindness we performed for one another when we baby-sat. We didn't have to fool with bottles or formula. We often said this: Breast milk is breast milk, and we each have what our babies need. On the few occasions when I had to leave him, the sisters had breast-fed Joshua when he was an infant. I didn't think about it too deeply – everyone took it for granted that this was the thing to do. Joshua was now close to three years old and still nursing; it was no longer a matter of nutrition, he just liked it. I didn't feel like a nursing mother necessarily, so I was surprised when Paulina asked me to watch her newborn, Jeremiah, for the afternoon.

"Ohh, Paulina. I don't know. Allison's been a handful lately and Joshua's whiny with an earache. He wants to nurse a lot," I said, and gave her a pitiful look. "My mom has a fit. She says he's way too old."

"I know." She laughed. "Our mothers used to wean when the first tooth came in. Thank God our little ones give it up when they're ready. I really do need the help, though, sis. I'll hurry back; he'll probably nap the whole time I'm gone anyway because he had me up all night long."

She reached for Joshua and pulled him to her side, stroking his red hair while she waited. Joshua adored her. Paulina had always made time for him, squatting beside him and listening carefully whenever he had something to say to her. Paulina had been so good to me when I was sick with Joshua. How could I refuse her a small favor like this?

I agreed to watch her baby and didn't regret it until he awoke with an odd cry. It sounded like a disembodied yowl I had once heard in the undergrowth of my backyard, strange enough to scare me back inside. I lifted Joshua off my lap, soothed his protests, and walked slowly toward Jeremiah's bassinet.

"Hey, Jeremiah," I said, lifting him up. I patted his back, but he reared away, crying and flailing. I cooed to him. I tried to give him his pacifier, but he tongued it out, screaming louder and louder.

He felt different from my babies; his body was hard and angular, his luminous gray eyes feral and accusing. He didn't smell like my young. He was of Paulina, yeasty like her, foreign and grown in humus not my own. I knew instantly there was no way I could nurse a baby that was not mine. That was freaky. *He's God's child. You love God.* Of course I love

God, but I don't have to feed the whole world with my breasts.

"Don't cry, Jeremiah," I pleaded. "Please don't cry, settle down, honey. Shh . . ." I jumped up and walked with him around the room. I put on some music. I tried the baby swing. Nothing helped. He screamed until he was purple. His nose ran furiously while saliva and tears mixed, making his face slick with mucus. I tissued the mess from his face; when my fingers came close to his mouth, he jerked to attention and turned his face for a nipple, the only thing he wanted. In his disappointment, he cried harder than ever. I begged him to stop.

"Shh, Jesus is here, Jeremiah," I said. "Jesus, Jeremiah, Jesus."

His screams were deafening.

Feed my sheep.

I was just making that up. That wasn't God talking to me.

Whoever gives a cup of water in My name, gives it to Me.

"Jeremiah, what's this? Is this your tummy? Watch out, I'm going to kiss your tummy!" I tried to play with him, distract him, but I could hear the hysteria in my voice. Both Allison and Joshua were watching now. Allison stood with her hands over her ears.

"He's hungry, Mommy," Allison said. "He wants to nurse."

It was that simple as far as she was concerned. The sisters thought it was simple, too. God was telling me to feed him. But the truth was, I just didn't want to. Whatever was still pure Carolyn in me, the selfish core of me, it wasn't bending on this issue, no matter what. I sat in the rocking chair and pressed Jeremiah's head against my breast. Once again, he tensed, rooting for my nipple. I jerked back and pushed him away. He wailed in astonished hunger, his face pinched white and bloodless.

I rocked him until Paulina came back, and I tried to under-

174

stand my actions. I had long ago stopped thinking of myself as an individual with desires distinct from the others. I didn't know what to do with the rebellion inside of me, the strange surge of self-direction. All I knew was that I could not nurse my sister's baby. I could not allow his lips to take my nipple into his mouth. I could not give him my milk. My body was my own. I was not submitting to God for His use, not with my whole heart, not with my whole mind, and certainly not with my body. I wept along with Jeremiah, barely able to compose myself when Paulina returned. I held the baby out to her.

"He wants his momma," I said tearfully. She quietly took him from my arms, pulled open her blouse, and fed him.

LOVESONG

"Make a joyful noise unto the Lord," read a Scripture near and dear to us at Fountain of Joy. It was the age of the guitar man, only in our case, a holy guitar man. Our worship sessions never included an organ; instead an acoustic guitar accompanied "Amazing Grace" or "Take Time to Be Holy". The brother would play softly, plaintively, urging me to submit, to become one, to forget I was an individual. It worked. No matter how out of sorts I was when worship began, I always surrendered to the Spirit before it was over. Somewhere in the fourteenth stanza of "Lord, We Adore You", I felt an odd internal click that the combination was complete and that my will finally gave over to His. My pettiness and self-centeredness disappeared, and everything became easy. I sang with my brothers and sisters; I smiled at my children; I told Jesus that I *loved* Him so and I always would. The answering wash of peace made me cry. *Oh, Jesus.*

The brothers and sisters in Fountain of Joy loved Elijah's Chariot, the Christian band that assembled and disassembled biannually. Eric was like everyone else in the band, enthused and eager to make music for the Lord but distracted by his job and family. The band was a *ministry,* and it was a struggle to find time for ministry in the midst of our day-to-day lives. At the same time, there was a demand in the local Christian community for the kind of music Elijah's Chariot could provide. Contemporary Christian music was beginning to take off in the seventies and early eighties all over the country; professional Christian musicians were cutting records and holding huge concerts where fans paid secular music ticket prices to see Nancy Honeytree, Lovesong, or the Second Chapter of Acts play. I didn't like the idea of professional Christian performers and found the whole arena rather unsettling, especially when someone would identify himself as a Christian music fan. Only Jesus deserved fans, I wanted to protest.

Eric and I went to one of these concerts, shelling out twelve bucks each for the tickets and walking straight by the T-shirt and cassette sales table. The Second Chapter of Acts had scheduled an appearance in our little city, appearing at Hoyt-Sherman auditorium. We loved the music of the trio, two sisters and their blond brother, a delicate boy with heart-shaped lips. They were long-haired hippies like us, modestly dressed, no makeup or pizzazz of any kind, just lovely, simple voices, guitars, radiance, and gentleness. Eric and I sat in the balcony of the one-hundred-year-old auditorium in the narrow wooden theater seats and were soon caught up. My favorite song was the one Annie sang, Snow White's song – "One Day My Prince Will Come" – but the song was not about a fairy-tale prince at all, it was about a young girl's longing for her Savior's return. We were used to music in church basements and shabby apartment living rooms with the ever-present voice of at least one person who could not carry a tune. This trio's harmony, their musicianship, and the lighting made for a surreal experience. The Second Chapter of Acts' performance was close to perfection – indeed, it was perfection as far as I was concerned – but I was not prepared for Matthew's guitar solo. Right in the middle of a song, the girls stopped singing. Matthew walked downstage and began to play a solo on his electric guitar. A *long* solo. It went on and on and on. Wait a minute, I wanted to object. Why are you doing this? This isn't bringing my heart and mind to Jesus. It's focusing on you, Matthew. I'm only thinking of your hands on those strings, your anguished face as you fret like a sweaty rock star. I want to be thinking about Jesus.

I looked at Eric and raised my eyebrows. He nodded, acknowledging my confusion. He began shuffling his feet the way he did when he was nervous, and one hand went into his pocket to clutch his change. The guitar solo continued. By now some of the people in the audience had begun to cheer softly. Matthew fell on one knee, laid his head next to the guitar's body, and played even harder. Applause. Shouts. Excitement all around us.

What is this?

I was angry at Matthew, but I was also angry at the crowd when they burst into applause at the end of the solo. When Matthew bowed, I was filled with indignation. *How can you take credit for the talent God has given you? This audience should be praising God, not you.*

Suddenly the atmosphere reminded me of the secular concerts Eric and I had once attended. The adulation, the frenzy, the energy that was almost sexual, how was this concert any different?

Then Matthew held up his finger. He pointed toward the vaulted ceiling, held his face to it as though he were seeing the very face of God. He began to clap. The audience roared with approval and clapped with him. It was the loudest applause of the night. The musicians on stage clapped, those on all sides of us clapped, Eric and I sheepishly clapped.

When I was lying in bed that night, I realized how judgmental I had become, how ready to throw the first stone. There was a cold, fiery core to me that I referred to as righteous and uncompromising, but I wondered if that was true. Something about Matthew's performance had made me afraid.

Our world of Christian music was not tainted by money or fame. Elijah's Chariot's latest gig was for a student organization at the nursing college. Their venue was the anatomy lecture hall. Because the band was scheduled to play mid-afternoon in the middle of the week, I was able to find a sitter and go along. It felt strangely familiar, being the girl with the band. Eight years earlier I had watched Renegade and wondered how soon they'd play "Hot Water" or if Eric's solo on "I'm a Man" would go well, wearing a halter top, the red knit one that outlined my breasts perfectly, and cutoffs that barely covered my ass.

This time, I sat anonymous and silent in the back of the auditorium and watched the five people on stage, all modest and winsome; the two women wore white blouses and long blue skirts, the guys wore khakis, white shirts buttoned up to the top. The band smiled all the time, smiled at each other, smiled at the student nurses, smiled in the absence of anything to say. Phil was such a good talker – glib, charming. He introduced each song with a little story like the one about writing this song in boot camp in North Carolina, how the pine woods smelled and how the moon shining on the Quonset huts reminded him of the radiance of our Lord and Savior, the Alpha and Omega, amen. His voice trailed off while Eric played a hollow-sounding prelude on the electric piano. The sisters began to sway in their rustling blue skirts, and Phil and William joined in with guitar. The music was pure, sweet, simple, nothing like bone-crushing, loud, strobe light-flashing Renegade.

"We've got to turn our backs on this world and live for Jesus," Phil said, and his amplified voice broke my heart with its clarity. "Nothing else is worth it, sisters and brothers. All of the wealth on earth cannot buy a single ticket to heaven. 'What will it profit a man if he gains the world and loses his soul?'"

That Scripture always made me think of a West Des Moines suburbanite surrounded with bags of money, a shiny new

179

convertible, jewels on her fingers, Cole-Haan shoes on her feet, laughing, talking, drinking a glass of red wine, and all the while, an evil spirit hovered with a stopwatch, waiting to claim her yuppie soul at the appointed time. And then all of those accumulated riches would mildew and rot or be frittered away by others – what good did they do the stripped and terrorized socialite who was now in hell, being taunted by Satan, eternally separated from all that was good?

"My wife and I have given ourselves to His service. Our family will serve God," Phil said, reaching for Camille's hand. She took his hand and moved to his side. This was a number they did in every set, a duet where the man promised to look out for his helpmeet, and the helpmeet says I will be true to thee, that kind of song. I knew it was inappropriate, but I thought it was kind of sexy the way their voices melded so seamlessly and how they watched each other's lips so earnestly and with such interest. I tried to imagine Eric and me performing together like Phil and Camille. We would be awkward and wooden, smiling perfunctorily at each other and waiting for the moment when we could say, with great relief, "Praise God," and move to separate sides of the stage.

In the last set, Phil set down his guitar and sat on a stool in the center of the stage. The rest of the band members moved offstage. I looked around the audience. The girls were not much younger than me. They wore ponytails and blue jeans, cardigans buttoned over their shoulders. I looked for Bibles in their laps, a sure sign of a believer, but spotted only a few. They had probably never heard such frank discussion of spiritual things; they probably went to churches that were dead, stagnant, given over to liberal teaching. Get ready, I said silently to the pale-faced girls. You're going to hear the gospel today, oh, yeah.

"So, what can you say about Jesus?" he asked. "What do *you* say? He was a good man? Someone we should read about and try to emulate? Someone like Mohammed? A prophet, maybe?"

Oh, Phil, I thought. What eloquence God has given you. I prayed for Him to open hearts. I prayed for protection from Satan, who would snatch the good news right out of the girls' ears. *Oh, let them hear, God. Let them hear and believe.*

"Maybe we should look at what Jesus said about Himself," Phil continued. "He said that if you've seen Him, you've seen the Father God. Hmm . . . and here's a Scripture in John, chapter eight: 'Before Abraham was born, I am!' The Jews recognized what he was saying. He was saying that he was Jehovah, the God of Israel." He flipped through the Bible, not really reading, just glancing at the pages he knew so well. "And look here, later on in John, Jesus says, 'I am the way, the truth, and the life.' A bold statement, wouldn't you agree? I don't know, folks, if we can say Jesus is simply a good man. Can you imagine somebody walking around downtown Des Moines saying things like that? Some joker who says, 'Hey, come and listen to me. I am the way. I am the truth. I am the life,'" Phil imitated, puffing out his chest and slurring his words. "That guy's either nipping the bottle or he's crazy, delusional with some messianic complex. But you're not going to call him good, are you?"

Phil paused and looked intently at the nurses in the audience. "So what are you going to do with Jesus? He can't be good and crazy. He can't be good and a liar. Jesus is either who he said he was, God, or he's some scheming nut case."

It was very quiet in the auditorium. I stared at a large diagram of the digestion system, but I wasn't seeing it, I was praying for the Holy Spirit to sweep through the auditorium and turn it upside down for God.

"I know what I believe," he said, and reached for his guitar. He began playing softly.

"I believe," he sang.

"We believe," the rest of the band picked up the refrain from the audience and rejoined him on stage.

"We believe in the one true God eternal, the Lord Jesus Christ, our Lord," they sang.

"Sing with us," Phil said. The nurses were primed and ready. Maybe they didn't know the words, but that didn't stop them. Their voices rose up like a river of song, rushing around that auditorium, snaking under the stadium seating, crawling up the walls, pouring down over our heads, over every one of us. Phil let the praise run over him, watching it pool at his feet.

"Oh, Holy Spirit," he breathed into the microphone. "Rain on us."

Even though the singing drowned Eric's accompaniment, he kept playing. No one could hear him, but he didn't notice. You can knock it off, I wanted to say to him, they don't need you. It made me realize again that Eric and I had completely different approaches to life. I would have stopped playing the minute I suspected my efforts were wasted, but not Eric. He kept going.

I smiled at the nurses as they filed out, noted the tears on their faces and heard the tremulous faith in their voices. "Wow," they kept saying to each other. "Amazing. Unbelievable." God had moved! God had brought new souls into the Kingdom, and we had been a part of it. Phil and William laughed as they bundled cords. Camille hummed to herself as she polished her flute. Eric was giddy, answering questions in his Donald Duck voice. This was what life was all about – Elijah's Chariot had just been used by the Almighty God for work that really mattered.

"AAAhChooo!" Eric sneezed as Donald Duck. It cracked me up, as it always did, and I laughed with everyone else. I smiled at Eric and he smiled back. This was when our marriage felt right – when we joined with the saints in serving God. I wished we could live in a Christian crusade all the time.

We could set up camp in the revival tent, sleep in separate bunkhouses, and sit by each other to tally up the newly won souls each night.

"Good night, Brother Eric," I'd say with affection. "Get a good night's sleep, OK?"

"You too, Sister Carolyn," he'd answer. "Go in God." And then he'd walk away, content to be alone. I would watch his squared shoulders as he disappeared from my sight. I would pray for him each step, so great was my agape love for my brother Eric.

"Are you ready to go?" Eric asked. It was dark in the lecture hall. Everyone had left but us.

I hesitated, not wanting to let go of my daydream or the extraordinary afternoon.

"OK," I said. I stood up slowly and stretched. I remembered the way the Holy Spirit had filled me that afternoon, the lovely rush of warmth, euphoria on a Wednesday. Phil would call that a mountaintop experience. "It's good," he always said, "but it's not everything. You can't go from mountaintop to mountaintop in the journey. You'll be doing a lot of walking in the valley."

Eric held his hand out to me to pull me back into the valley. What else could I do but take it?

THIS DARK WORLD

Late one night, we had spontaneous sex, out of the blue and with no condom. A silent encounter, a quick and desperate coupling in our tiny bedroom. No kissing, only a series of efficient and experienced caresses and then it was over, only it wasn't over. I was going to have a baby. In the church, that meant celebration. In my heart, it meant dread. I did not want another baby. I loved Allison and Joshua more than anything, but I couldn't imagine going through another pregnancy. Plus, five-year-old Joshua was beginning school and I had been looking forward to some free time. I tried to believe what Eric believed: It was God's will that we had not used birth control that night. Indeed, many of the believers we knew practiced no birth control at all, trusting God to open and close the womb as the Scriptures say He does. I couldn't help but remember how ecstatic I had been when I'd learned I was pregnant with Joshua. I had been so sure that God was doing something amazing in our lives.

God *was* amazing. I hadn't changed my mind about that. I was grateful beyond all measure that God had chosen me to be His child. And I understood the concept of childlike faith: the kind of faith that Jesus called us to. From the beginning, I accepted the idea that I couldn't understand everything; my puny human brain was just not capable of God's omniscience. It was enough to know that God knew what He was doing. All of my questions had been answered. Well, most of them. After eight years of walking with the Lord, I was past the honeymoon and the glow was fading, just a bit. Little objections and tiny contradictions nagged at me, and I couldn't always repress my doubts.

The tapestry analogy was popular. Our lives being a complex woven tapestry, we must realize that we see only the underside of this tapestry. We see the knots and tangles, the thread that dangles. But someday God will take us to heaven and we will see the other side and we will understand what it was He was doing, how splendidly He was weaving our lives into something beautiful. Losing a job may look like an ugly knot from our side of the tapestry, but oh, wait to see what beautiful design is on the other side.

Even so, I couldn't help but question the underside sometimes. Why did my all-powerful God turn a blind eye to tragedy He could have prevented? That spring, a beautiful Christian woman was killed in a traffic accident on her way to church. She had been raising four holy, God-fearing children. Her husband was not a believer and would not raise the children to follow Jesus. What kind of sense did that make? What kind of providence was that?

Hush, I told myself. It will make sense someday.

It takes a toll on you, this battening down of the hatches, the deliberate decision not to mull over inconsistencies or mysteries. And heaven forbid your questions were ever voiced. A questioning spirit revealed you for who you were: a doubter, a Thomas, someone of little faith, someone who demanded answers here and now.

"Why do you suppose God let Pamela Wooten be killed by a drunk driver?" The question burst out of me. I knew Rebekah knew the answer. I knew she would help me understand.

She was silent for a moment.

"When your kids were babies," Rebekah began, "you took them to get immunizations, didn't you?"

We were in a paddleboat at an all-church picnic. The lake

was bright green with algae, the paddle wheel dripped with it, great fluorescent strings of green. We pedaled in unison, waving to our children on shore.

"Yes," I said slowly. Was she going to give me a lecture on not trusting God? Several families in the church didn't immunize their children, instead vowing that God would protect their kids from disease. I couldn't remember how Rebekah felt about the issue.

"Well, did they like those shots?" Rebekah pressed. Our cotton summer skirts had hitched up. I took a rare look at our legs. Mine were tan and in need of shaving, hers were white and thin, two small knots of muscle in her calves. Up and down, our legs pushed the still, thick water.

"Of course not," I answered. "They screamed."

"They had no way of knowing why you were letting them get hurt, did they?"

"No," I said, sighing at how inevitably didactic everything had become.

"They trusted you, and you let someone else hurt them," Rebekah said slowly, squeezing my arm to emphasize the word *hurt*. "But you had a reason for allowing that pain, didn't you? Your motivation was something your children had no way of understanding."

"Right," I said. "All they knew was they hurt. And that I stood by and let them be hurt."

"You were trying to prevent worse pain, maybe even death, when you allowed the doctor to put a needle in your child," Rebekah finished needlessly. I watched the willows and the way they bent with the wind, their helpless branches fluttering in submission.

"Don't question God," Rebekah said firmly. "Do not."

I knew the drill: We were occupying an orderly universe, and we had to believe there was a reason behind God's action or inaction. We had to proceed on faith, trusting His love. It was hard to admit, even to myself, but the orderly universe had lost some of its thrill for me. My zeal was flagging. Often I was not content with my little house, my husband, the brothers and sisters. Being pregnant compounded everything. I couldn't remember a life outside of this one of duty. In a silent act of rebellion, I accepted the antinausea prescription wordlessly from my obstetrician and had it filled on the way home from my first prenatal visit.

For a while, I felt a little guilty every time I swallowed one of those pills. It was self-imposed guilt, no doubt. Eric didn't care if I took the pills or not, but to me, it had become a question of faith. Did I not trust God to take care of me? Was I bringing shame to the Lord in the whole spiritual realm? I knew from the Bible that the whole cosmos was teeming with activity we could not see. God and His angels were waging war with Satan and his legion of demons. I worried that God was mocked in some way every time I did not obey Him. And the opposite was true as well. Every time I obeyed God, the angels would fall at His feet in adoration. ("Oh, God, you are truly great. Even Carolyn obeys you!") I imagined the cosmos swirling about me, all eyes on the little gladiator of faith.

"I will raise my throne above the stars of God . . . I will make myself like the Most High," Satan had vowed when he was still Lucifer, the highest of all angelic beings. There was a coup d'état in heaven when Lucifer tried to be equal with God. He was merely a created being, not God-like, but he was powerful and egotistical enough to believe he could take on God. Wrong. He was cast out, he and a group of braggarts who also grabbed the opportunity for promotion. Satan's pride and his evil intent had doomed him. After a brief period of ruling on earth, he would ultimately be condemned to the everlasting lake of fire that God prepared for all who do not worship Him.

Satan intended to make the most of his time on earth. He hated God, hated mankind, and especially despised believers because God loved them. Thus, Satan's twofold plan: 1) Prevent man from hearing and trusting the gospel; 2) In the event of failing here, try to make believers as useless as possible. Make them doubt, rebel, prone to secret sins. We believers were often aware of this "oppression". We would confide in one another that we were being oppressed, dogged by the Father of Lies.

Once in a while, even in those early years, the whole idea of living by faith struck me as an absolutely ridiculous idea.

Wait a minute, I would think, stopping in the middle of putting clothes into the washing machine. Wait just a doggone minute. You're living your life, the only life you're ever going to have, based on some guy who died in the Middle East thousands of years ago? What kind of bullshit fairy tale is that?

The clarity was terrifying. I could respond only by hissing, "Get thee behind me, Satan." I would finish stuffing the washer with a vengeance and then climb the stairs two at a time to get to my Bible, reading until that ridiculous question of the Tempter was flushed out of my brain.

The Elders in the church constantly reminded us that "our struggle is not against flesh and blood, but against the rulers and principalities of darkness." I didn't know how to picture a principality; it was a vague idea at best until Christian novelists began to write about demon activity with long, detailed sagas of creepy, gargoylelike demons who invisibly roamed city streets and flocked outside of questionable venues such as theaters, discos, and nightclubs. After that, I could imagine the reptilian monsters lounging at the doors of the Civic Center downtown. I watched people go in and out and wondered who carried a demon home unaware.

We purged our homes periodically because we had been

taught that even inanimate objects or books or music could be a conduit for demon activity in our homes. This world, after all, belonged to "the prince of the power of the air" – Lucifer, Satan, Beelzebub. Eric parted with long-stored rock albums, dozens and dozens of them. In the beginning, he gave them to Lisa, but then we became convinced that nobody should listen to music that so clearly glorified Satan, promoted lust and alcohol and drugs. We burned most of the remaining albums in a trash can in the backyard: Santana, Edgar Winters, the Allman Brothers, the Who. I tossed in a few questionable books to keep it going. I liked it when the battleground of faith was so clearly drawn, when the Enemy's weapons were tangible and I could burn them with fire or throw them away. It was so much easier than swallowing my pride or being patient or forgiving the undeserving.

Eric's parents had given us a Lalique crystal figurine for a wedding gift. It worried me daily. A beautiful woman embraced by Pan, a satyr: It was clearly myth, bestial, lowly, and base, but there it was on a shelf in the dining room hutch. I picked it up sometimes, turned it over in my hands, held it up to the light, looked closely at the face of the woman and the face of Pan. Pan's face was unmistakably demonic. One day I told Eric that we had to get rid of it.

"But how?" he asked. "Mom will notice if it's not out."

"It's a gift, isn't it? We're just choosing not to display it," I said, feeling more and more righteous. At moments like that, I longed for a lion's den, a fiery furnace, a pit in the ground where my faith would clearly triumph.

"Well, what do you want to do with it?" he asked. He knew me by now, knew when the martyr was making her way to the surface.

"We have to do something. I mean, the Bible says our struggle isn't against flesh and blood. This statue could bring demons into the house. It's not worth it, is it?"

"No," he said. "We'll get rid of it."

That night I took the expensive crystal and placed it in the trash can among diapers, banana peels, and eggshells. I looked down at it for a few minutes and wondered at my own audacity. Although my faith wavered from time to time, tonight it had not. There was nothing I wouldn't do for God, it seemed. I put the cover back on the trash can and turned out the porch light.

When the sisters got together, as we did every other day or so, we would pray. We prayed for our husbands first of all, and then we interceded for our children. We asked God to make our babies and toddlers righteous soldiers of the cross, stroking their little shoulders and faces as we prayed aloud. We asked God to protect them from Satan. Sometimes we would go through room by room of our homes, casting out any evil spirits in the name of Jesus. We stood in our children's bedrooms, letting our hands fall upon toys and dolls as we prayed, especially any toys that could attract demons. Somebody always knew somebody who had seen a Cabbage Patch doll dance across a sleeping child's bed. The Smurfs made the women in the church nervous after a report in a national Christian newsletter had dug up dirt on them. Their blue color was an indication that the Smurfs were the dead walking, soulless little zombies, hardly appropriate entertainment for our Christian children.

I was skeptical. It was one thing to get rid of mythological figures like the Pan, but cartoons? I remember thinking this time I would not go along. I saw the looks of alarm on the faces of the women around me. No more Saturday morning TV, said Mary, an attorney's wife. Satan is not going to get my child.

A spurt of laughter made its way out of my mouth, but I coughed quickly and managed to look as concerned as the sisters. I didn't want anyone to think that I didn't take spiritual warfare seriously. And later that night, I threw away a Smurf coloring book I found in Joshua's closet, just in case.

As far as I was concerned, there were enough clearly defined battlegrounds in spiritual warfare, I didn't need to make up any. Halloween was a pagan holiday. Who could argue with that? My own research revealed its druidic origins, infant sacrifice and the like. Why take part in a day that glorified Satan? I didn't let the children trick-or-treat on Beggars' Night. I wrote a note to their teachers every October and explained that I did not want my children coloring pictures of witches or ghosts. The teacher just gave them Thanksgiving pictures to color instead. Allison and Joshua came home from school with their colored pictures of cornucopias and Pilgrims weeks ahead of the other children. We left the house on Beggars' Night and ate pizza at a deserted Happy Joe's. If a clown or witch wandered in off the street, the children would not say a word. They kept eating their pizza, but they did not take their eyes from the masks and makeup. They knew better than to smile or point.

I knew that Satan was not likely to make any real inroads into our family with rock music, erotic art, or demonic toys. No, the way Satan could destroy us was by my own hand. I could open the door and invite him in. I could pull up an easy chair for him and say, "Let's talk."

"Sure, little sis," Satan would say, his scales glistening beautifully. A mistake to think Satan himself is hideous, no, he's the angel of light, all believers know this. He appears to be beautiful and rational and sympathetic.

"I love my husband," I would begin.

Satan would yawn. "Yes?"

"But I don't *love him* love him," I would say, though it would be hard, my throat closing up in an attempt to silence me.

"What you need is a nice little love affair," Satan would say, his eyes narrowing.

"Oh, no! No, I'd never do that!" And then I would know

191

that I had invited certain disaster. I would stand up, show Satan the door.

"Why did you ask me to come over, anyway?" Satan would throw over his shoulder, slithering across my hardwood floors. "I would have been glad to help you out."

"I just don't want to be married to Eric, that's all," I'd finally manage to whisper as we stood at the door.

"Divorce, dear. It's all the rage in the church these days, haven't you heard?" He would lean close to me and his eyes would be full of compassion. "It happens."

And then I would slam the door hard and lean against it, my heart pounding, the forbidden word echoing even though Satan was now on the other side.

Eric and I were affectionate with each other. We called each other honey and dear and sweetheart. We held hands in church. He was a devoted husband, but I did not know how much longer I could deny that I was not drawn to him in any intimate way. I heard the other sisters talk about their husbands and I watched their faces, yes, there it was: yearning, sweet and sanctified, for their mate. I had never experienced this, not beyond the first months of teenage infatuation. I didn't want him to kiss me – I didn't want him to reach for me in bed. I was not romantically in love with my husband, but I had to be content to be his wife, to be the mother of his children. I had no other options. Divorce was the deadliest of sins. I would destroy all of us. I would destroy my children's future happiness. I would be a tool in the hands of Satan. I knew this and I tried to deaden myself, tried to tell my breasts and thighs that they would never be fondled by hands they would welcome. Never. I could endure this trial. I could resist the Tempter, the Father of Lies. I would not entertain the devil.

When Lauren was born, the women in the church gave me a

baby shower. They had coordinated their efforts months before and presented me with a homemade quilt and matching bumper for her crib. Sheets, a car seat cover, even a mobile, all made of green gingham and appliquéd with a rainbow and white clouds. We drank coffee and ate little sandwiches with real watercress. Some of the women had jobs by then and were wearing plain blue or black suits and flats from work. Although some still held to the Scripture "You are called to be a peculiar people," some of us had stopped equating outdated, hippiesque clothing with holiness.

In fact, it often struck me that Fountain of Joy was pretty much a microcosm of the real world: Our number included the truly unlovely, the poor, the indigent, and the handicapped, but also professionals who had graduate degrees. Probably the most glamorous couple was Molly and Rick. Eric and I were awestruck when Molly showed up at one of the Bible studies. She was the girl in the film *I Wish We'd All Been Ready*. She had been working part-time for a Christian booking agent when she was cast as the lead in the film. Molly was lovely – she had long, sun-streaked hair, full lips, and a body that managed to call attention to itself even in the modest clothing she wore. She had a real job downtown and sometimes traveled to the West Coast. I was proud of her for being willing to be counted among the few who would lay their lives down for Christ. She was outgoing and confrontational – I knew she must be doing great things for the Kingdom as she went out into the world. When the Elders divided us into groups of ten or twelve and placed us in house churches that would meet midweek, I hoped we would be put into Molly and Rick's group. Instead, Eric and I were assigned to Tom and Dora's house church.

Tom and Dora could have easily found work in Hollywood by accepting roles as born-again Christians. They were exactly what you would imagine a Fundamentalist to be, both in looks and demeanor. Tom dressed neatly; he hitched his pants high around his middle and kept a neatly folded handkerchief in his front shirt pocket. His dark hair was boot camp short with bangs cut perfectly across his forehead. He carried his well-read study Bible everywhere. It went to the grocery store with him; he plopped it in the child seat next to the current toddler in the family. "You never know who God might put in your path," he often said. "I want to be ready with the Sword of the Lord."

And Dora was everything Proverbs 31 said the virtuous woman should be. She kept a garden, made clothes for her household, and raised her children to be light in this dark world. Extraordinarily tall and thin, she wore long house-dresses of pastel cotton, Donna Reed dresses from someone's attic, and brushed her red, curly hair back from her face, holding it in place with stretch headband. She wore absolutely no makeup, and her face was wide and simple, radiant with only Ponds cold cream. Dora always wanted to pray. She suggested prayer whenever we walked in her door.

"Hello, Carolyn! Hello, Allison and Joshua and baby Lauren! Let's pray, shall we?"

So the eight of us, her three children and my three children, knelt on the stained Berber carpet to ask the Lord's blessing upon our visit. My children had grown up in people's living rooms worshiping the Lord. They spent every Sunday morning in this particular living room, sitting cross-legged on the carpet, singing songs about David the shepherd boy slaying Goliath or obedient Samuel who was abandoned to priests. Praying on a weekday in the same room never fazed them at all. Afterward Dora gave each of the older children a piece of homemade fruit leather with instructions to play in the back-yard. I held six-month-old Lauren on my lap and gave her my keys to play with. It was time to fellowship. Dora quizzed me about my week, my quiet time with the Lord, and my Bible study. I answered her questions and waited for her to volunteer her own experience. Physically, Dora wasn't much older than me, but spiritually she was much older and wiser. It was a well-understood dynamic that I was not to hold her accountable for her walk, rather I was to submit to her leadership and authority.

After we had duly fellowshiped, we talked babies and recipes until it was almost time for our husbands to come home from work. We gathered the children and prayed for the second time that afternoon. Joshua put his sweaty arms around my neck, his damp head pressed on mine. I breathed in my boy and said, "Amen."

One of my first serious conflicts with a brother or sister occurred when Tom, who was helping Dora baby-sit my children one afternoon, paddled Lauren, who would not lie still for her diaper to be changed. Unaware of this incident, I took her home and later discovered the large purple handprint on her leg. I gasped and asked Allison what had happened that day at Tom and Dora's. She told me that she had seen Tom spank Lauren. She had protested, but Tom scolded her for interfering.

"Allison," Tom had said, "I am teaching her to obey. You mind your own business."

I wept as I put Lauren's snowsuit back on, and I rushed out the door to confront Tom.

I knew that I should wait for Eric to come home. I knew I should let him handle it. There was a prescribed chain of authority that I was completely disregarding by driving over to Tom and Dora's on my own, but I didn't care. This was my baby. When Tom answered the door, I lost all submission I had ever claimed.

"She's eleven months old!" I screamed. "She doesn't know why you hit her – she doesn't have the ability to connect pain with her actions!"

"Sister, calm down," Tom said. He held a peanut-butter sandwich in his hand, and peanut butter smudged his lower lip. "I'll get Dora."

"This doesn't have anything to do with Dora. Allison told me that she saw you hit Lauren."

"Carolyn, I didn't hit her. Come on. I disciplined her in the Lord. Come on, you know me. I love your children as much as I love my own. Calm down now. Sit down and take a deep breath," Tom said as he backed onto the sofa. He patted a place beside him and reached for the Bible. "Dora!" he yelled over his shoulder. "Come in here."

I stayed where I was. Lauren squirmed in my arms and threw back her head.

"Do you want to see what you did, Tom? Do you want to see the mark you left on her?"

Tom stood up and reached for Lauren. I pulled her back. Dora came in at that moment.

"Did you know that Tom spanked my baby today?" I demanded. They had never heard me speak in anything but a gentle, reverent tone. "There's a huge handprint on her leg," I said as I began crying again.

"Sis," Dora began, "babies bruise so easily. You know that Tom would never hurt her – he loves her."

"She's eleven months old!" I wailed. Lauren joined me in crying. Tom and Dora's children begin to make their unobtrusive way into the room, and I saw at once that it was useless, that I could not make them see that what Tom had done was wrong. I could see the monklike composure that had settled about Tom's mouth and eyes. His hands were even folded over his belly. Dora wouldn't look at me any longer, so I turned and left.

I drove home feeling as bruised as my daughter. I wanted the luxury of hate. I wanted someone punished, but I knew that I had no option in the matter but to forgive. I cried out to God for His help to forgive Tom and then, before I pulled back into my driveway, I said the words aloud: "I forgive him." If I still struggled with forgiving him, it meant that I was operating in the flesh, and I refused to allow that to happen. "I forgive him," I said more firmly. I said it even as I wept. And then unbidden, this question in my heart: If Tom were God's chosen shepherd, how could he be so cruel and how could he be so wrong? Whose fallibility did this reflect, man's or God's? I faltered for a moment, and everything seemed ridiculous, all of it, following God, trusting the brothers and sisters with my children's welfare, living a life out of the first century. My defenses were down, and I was being attacked. "Get thee behind me, Satan," I said aloud, and slammed the car door shut.

THE SISTERS

It was high time I found a disciple. It was my responsibility to pass on what I knew about the Lord and the Word. One of the elders suggested Jackie, but she was a physical education major with no kids and she lived in a house with wood heat. She'd come into my living room wearing a flannel shirt and smelling of hickory smoke while she tromped across my brand-new carpeting in her muddy hiking boots. I tried not to notice or care about the mud and to be holy and remember that people were more important than things. But once I started getting a few nice things, it was a lot harder to dismiss them as inconsequential and of little true worth. I still did the "It's gonna burn" mantra, but sometimes I caught myself lingering over an Ethan Allen catalog, dreaming of a house filled with subtle and expensive accoutrements.

Then Brianna moved in right across the street. She was just my age and she had kids close to my kids' ages. I'd given up on having someone like that in the neighborhood – all of the other neighbors were either gone in the daytime or retired and fussing about any kids who took a shortcut through their yard.

I was entranced by her loveliness. She had creamy skin with delicate freckles and tiny, perfectly manicured hands that reached for mine.

She was a nurse. She tried to run at least three miles a day. Her kids were monsters, but she loved them with all her heart, and weren't my three the most adorable things she ever saw.

But there was this: She was a Catholic.

To a Fundamentalist, a Catholic is the biggest challenge. It is far more difficult to convert a Catholic to true born-again Christianity than it is to convince a pagan to come to the light. A pagan knows he's lost, but a Catholic is convinced he's OK: He has the guarantee of the church that he's square with God as long as he obeys the rules, keeps the sacraments and all that. A little sprinkling when you're a baby, and bam, you're on the way to heaven, no personal conversion experience necessary. Brianna wasn't just a Catholic; she had grown up in parochial schools and even attended a Catholic college. Everyone in her family and her husband's family was a Catholic. I didn't think there was much chance she'd come around to the true faith, not when she discovered the rigors it would involve and the inevitable cost of her family's love and approval.

That didn't stop us from being friends, though. Instant friends. I loved her easy way with the children and her generosity with time and possessions. She was always bringing me treats from the bakery or outgrown clothes for my children or tomatoes from her garden. She acted like a Christian, but I knew she wasn't. She had never even read the Bible – how could she be a Christian? She didn't know anything about the Bible; she knew only about a bunch of saints I had never heard of. I told her to forget saints; they were made up by a corrupt Catholic Church in the Middle Ages to keep peasants in line.

"You can't pray to Mary, Brianna," I said as we lay in the sun and watched our kids in the wading pool. "She's just a woman, no more special than you or me."

"She is the mother of God," Brianna said, pulling herself up on one elbow. "That's pretty good, isn't it?"

"She isn't the mother of God. She was the mother of God's son, Jesus. There's a big difference."

We talked all summer. She rarely objected to any of my dogma – indeed, she was a little sponge. I was delighted that she was interested in spiritual things and even more pleased when she began reading the Bible I gave her. I told her that her Catholic Bible wasn't the real thing – that it had been adulterated by the Apocrypha and other illegitimate work. She took my word for it.

She began taking my word for everything. Daily, I praised God for opening her heart, for drawing her to Himself.

Before the first frost, she had made a decision. She wanted to be a New Testament believer like me – she had prayed to ask Jesus to be her personal Savior, and she was now born again. I had my disciple at last. For the next three years, Brianna and I sought God exclusively. Like girlfriends who dieted or exercised together, Brianna and I goaded each other on. We gave pep talks and hugs and reminded each other that following Christ was the only thing that counted. Eventually we became Christian mystics, exploring the hinder regions of orthodox Christianity. We wouldn't stop until we had experienced everything, even the Baptism of the Holy Spirit and the gift of tongues.

We began ordering our days and lives and children together. I would go over to her house as soon as Eric and John left for work. Eric was pleased with our friendship – John less so. He told Bri that I was a fanatic and she should try to meet some of the other neighbors, too. He invited people over from work, but Brianna just witnessed to them and served them soft drinks and popcorn, telling John she was no longer comfortable having alcohol in the house.

Brianna and I pledged to pray for John daily, pleading with God to open his eyes. As soon as we settled the children in front of *Sesame Street*, we would kneel on the kitchen floor and pour out our hearts to God. We praised Him for being majestic and all-powerful and forgiving and loving. We interceded for the lost, beginning with John and working our way through our list of unsaved relatives. We asked forgiveness for our failures, our laziness, our evil hearts that turned constantly toward evil. And then we prayed for our children and asked for God's hand to cover them. If the children wandered in, we pulled them next to us and urged them to talk to Jesus with us, but they would usually twist away, rummaging for cereal or doughnuts and then leaving the same kid-sticky, cluttered kitchen that Brianna and I fully believed to be the throne room of God.

Sometimes after prayer, Brianna and I took advantage of the children's preoccupation and went to her bedroom. It was still early in the morning and the bed would be unmade, and we would crawl back inside and pull the covers to our chins and talk some more. I felt so close to Brianna. She was beautiful and holy, and she loved me. We laughed at how goofy it was to be in bed together morning after morning, but I needed it. Brianna, my disciple, was also my soul mate, and her presence in my life eased my loneliness in a way that Eric never had.

"Bri," I began one morning as we lay side by side, her elegant Laura Ashley comforter pulled to our chins.

"Hmm?" she murmured. We could hear the TV in the other room, our children laughing. An inch of snow had fallen since we had begun praying in her kitchen. The bedroom brightened with the snow outside. The furnace droned steadily. God loved us.

"Sometimes I wonder, Bri. What's it like to make love with John?"

She laughed. "What a weird question, sis."

"I mean, what's it like to make love to someone you're in love with?"

"Well, you know. You're married."

"It's not the same with me and Eric. We're not . . . well, you know, we're not romantic or anything."

"What are you saying?"

"It's just that you *love* John – I mean physically. You're attracted to him," I said, and closed my eyes. I didn't want to see her face in case it would be condemning or judgmental.

"And you're not attracted to Eric," she finished.

Tears seeped from my clenched eyes. "No."

I waited, but she didn't say anything.

"Just once, Bri. Just once to want him to reach for me, to want his hands to touch me, his kisses . . ."

She remained silent but reached for my hand under the cover and held it tightly. After a while we got up and we never talked about our husbands and sexual desire again. There was no remedy for my situation but a miracle, and the miracle seemed too much to ask for from a God Who had His hands full with a failing world.

Brianna pushed open my front door without knocking and called my name. I was folding clothes on the kitchen counter and yelled for her to come in there. Zucchini bread baked in the oven. My favorite radio Bible teacher, Dr. Dobson, expounded upon the need for righteous teenagers to take a stand in their high schools. I was humming and happy and content. Brianna walked into the kitchen and looked troubled.

"We have to talk, Carolyn," she said.

"Go ahead, sis. What?" I walked across the kitchen to start water boiling for our tea.

"I don't want any tea. Carolyn, I have to rebuke you," she said.

My heart began to beat faster. "Why?" I asked, stopping where I was in the middle of the kitchen.

"Because you're dressing too provocatively, that's why," she said in a rush.

You have to understand that the sisters were not exactly into high fashion. We wore long skirts and loose trousers and blouses. The holier sisters wore bandannas or grandmother scarves on their heads, a symbolic act to show submission to one's husband.

"What do you mean, Brianna?" I felt myself getting defensive, shot a quick prayer for forgiveness to God, tried to humble myself, empty myself of pride. "I have no idea what you're talking about."

"That blue dress. That dress you've been wearing to church lately."

What the hell? my flesh sputtered. I swallowed that protest and spoke slowly. "What's wrong with that dress, Bri? It's long enough; it doesn't have a low neckline."

"It has all those flowers on it! They're really attention-getting. And it fits very closely. I just don't think the brothers should have to deal with you wearing that dress. Remember what Nate Thomas said during sharing time a few weeks ago?"

After Phil had finished teaching, he'd opened up the floor to anyone who wanted to share what was on his mind. Nate had announced that he had a special message from God for the sisters. I had felt the thrill of a prophetic message for a minute before I realized the message concerned the same old theme of woman, the temptress, the weaker vessel, woman, the daughter of Eve.

"Sisters, you know I love you," Nate began. "I have labored in prayer for each one in this room. God has used you in mighty ways in my life. Mighty ways. Your servanthood inspires me, your tenderness and sensitivity amaze me, your love for Jesus moves me."

The brothers smiled and patted their wives in approval. I anticipated Eric's touch and bent over quickly to fool with the ankle strap on my sandal.

"It's because I love you that I rebuke you. 'He whom I love, I chasten.' Sisters, you're not dressing modestly enough. It's not fair to your brothers who love you. Scripture clearly instructs you to not look to your outward adornment, but rather your inner beauty.

Do you want to make your brother stumble? Do you want to lead your brother into sin?" Nate looked crestfallen and weary. "Do you, Paulina?"

"No, Nate. Of course not," she answered, shaken.

"How about you, Sarah?" He turned to his wife.

"No," she murmured, clutching her Bible with white, bloodless hands.

Nate named us one by one. Each sister shook her head, chastened, saddened to be reminded that she had such power.

"And Carolyn. Surely you wouldn't tempt a brother?" Nate smiled at me.

"Never," I answered. I had let my mouth fall open and raised my chin to him. "Never, Nate."

None of the sisters wanted to talk about it afterward; we all just exchanged guilty looks – half-ashamed, half-bewildered. I went home that night with mixed feelings. It was embarrassing, for one thing. I was trying to follow Christ. I was taking care of my family, training my children the best I could, trying to be charitable and generous and do everything that was expected of me, yet I was assumed guilty of being a Jezebel. Always, the church seemed to hold women suspect. Now this. Brianna, my *disciple,* standing in my kitchen telling me that I was wearing something I shouldn't have been. I tried to be calm.

"Attention-getting? Are you serious about this? Bri, some brothers would have a hard time if a sister wore a gunny sack!" I was exasperated, on the verge of real anger, something I thought I no longer experienced.

"Think about it this way, Carolyn. You wearing that dress makes me stumble, and Scripture says you shouldn't do anything to make a brother or sister stumble," she said firmly, not backing down a bit. "I love you, sis. It freaks me out to see my spiritual mother wearing something that turns heads."

There was no way I could argue with her on this point. I was responsible for her nurture in the Lord, and if wearing that dress was a sinful thing to her, then it was up to me to get rid of the dress. I couldn't become a stumbling block for Brianna, no matter how foolish I thought her conviction. I took the blue dress to Goodwill the next morning. I didn't know if I was rebelling against God or submitting to Him, but I wore a long paisley skirt and long-sleeved white blouse to church every Sunday for months afterward.

Dora thought the house church sisters should pray together every other day. My house was chosen as the central location, and the time was set at six in the morning. We began praying together at the beginning of December and continued through the long, cold Iowa winter.

The sisters left their sleeping babies and slow-moving husbands and pulled on coats and scarves and boots over their nightgowns. They started their reluctant cars and drove through the dark and quiet neighborhoods on roads packed hard with tire-treaded snow to make their way to the dead-end street where I lived. We met in the family room beside the standing furnace, and the room was filled with the fragrance of wet wool and coffee and the milky smell of our pajamas. We prayed ourselves awake and then hugged each other, wishing each other a good day. The neighbors pulled back the curtains to watch the stream of women, bulky in their winterwear, faces creased and puffy from sleep, a thermos of coffee in their hands, leave my house in a single file. The sisters squinted in the sunrise and cheerfully climbed into their cars to make their way back home.

Then a couple of hours later I would be at Bri's and we would be praying again. Our lives were saturated with the Bible and prayer, we spoke in antiquated language and lapsed into prayer in the middle of a conversation.

"Billy had another tantrum today," Brianna said. "I didn't

know what to do with him. He was so angry; I think he scared himself because he had absolutely no control. I finally carried him to his room for an all-afternoon time-out."

"It's the spirit of rebellion," I said. "The sin of Lucifer."

"Oh, Father-God, I just beseech you to protect my son. I cast out that spirit in the name of Jesus and . . ." Her head bowed. Mine followed. If our children walked through the room, they knew to wait until we were done. Sometimes I would hear them as they hushed each other and tiptoed through the living room with the curtains drawn, the television muted, their mothers desperate in prayer.

That was normal. Jesus was our truest love. He was the lover I had always longed for, the One Whose whole world was consumed with *me*. If people in the mall passed me without glancing my way, Jesus was tracing my steps, counting them, keeping track of me every minute of every day. If others grew distracted and disinterested in what I had to say, not Jesus. He would prompt me, "Keep going. This is interesting. And have I told you how beautiful you are lately?" How could I not revel in an all-consuming love like that? I felt desirable, fully lovable.

And out of gratitude, I was willing to go all the way with Jesus.

Baptized in the Spirit, that's what they called it. Overcome with the Spirit. The second baptism. Associated with Pentecostalism in the early part of the century, the orthodox church did not give this experience its sanction. It was a Holy Roller phenomenon, an exuberant and excessive display of people swooning and speaking in tongues. And besides that, it was highly unnecessary; one did not need a second baptism to partake of Christ's salvation. Further, the gifts the early church experienced, tongues of flame and ecstatic utterances – those existed only as long as it took to get the Bible put together. People needed something like that before they had the Word of God.

None of that dry doctrine mattered to me. There were too many other people who claimed that the baptism was the ultimate step in following Jesus. When a believer surrendered this completely, the Holy Spirit just moved in and filled up all the crevices, swept out secret sin, kept the place clean for God. I read testimonies and accounts of people with lackluster Christian lives who had become spiritual giants after the baptism. Oh, I wanted it all right. So did Brianna. And she wasn't content just reading about it. She asked questions and found Aglow, an organization of women who had experienced the baptism of the Holy Ghost. She told me the next meeting was the following week and that she thought we should go. I looked at the brochures. Doves swooping down across the page, flames interspersed among black-and-white photos of hair-sprayed women dancing with their hands in the air. I told her I wanted to think about it just a little longer.

Brianna was baptized in the Spirit on a Tuesday in a convention room at the Holiday Inn.

"How could you do it without me?" I asked. "I wanted to do it together."

"The Holy Spirit was moving, Carolyn," she said. "What was I supposed to do – tell God it wasn't such a great time?"

"I guess not," I said. "It just feels weird. You've done it and I haven't." I didn't know how to explain the odd jealousy I felt. I was on the outside of something Brianna and Jesus shared together. I hated that.

"Well, you're going to," she said, hugging me, "because it is absolutely fantastic. Jesus is more than we ever knew, Carolyn. It's like a drug high, I swear, only you never come down."

"And well, how about, well – tongues?"

"Ahh. Amazing. It's like singing, only the angels are praising God for you, and you just kind of float through the middle of it." While she told me, I could see that she was living it all over again, a dreamy smile on her lips, her eyes fluttering closed.

"Can you do it for me?" I asked, not knowing if that was allowed or not.

"Of course. Oh, no problem. I want to do it all the time," she said, and looked at me. "You'll love this."

We put a lot of stock in the Spirit bearing witness. It was our way of validating someone's word or experience as being truly of God. When Brianna prayed for me in an unknown tongue, the Spirit bore witness. I thought it was the most beautiful thing I had ever heard. I knew without a doubt that God was the author of those words, and I also knew that I would not rest until I had experienced it as well.

I asked God for the gift. I told Him I was ready. And then I waited.

For two days my chest burned as though I'd swallowed fire; I was filled with a strange expectancy. I went about my daily chores, took the kids to school, made a beef stew, but there it was, this otherworldly feeling, a tingly urgency in the center of my rib cage. I told Brianna it was just a matter of time.

And I was right. I put the kids down for a nap and grabbed my Bible. I hurried to the family room and opened my Bible to read aloud a psalm when suddenly, instead of reading Scripture, I began to speak in a new language. The words were halting and strange. I sounded like a Bedouin, singsongy, a chant, something I was not inventing. I could stop speaking if I wanted to, but when I made a sound in the back of my throat, there would be the prayer language again.

"*Koonah alli stonakah*," I sang. I felt as though I would

burst with joy, and I ran to the bathroom mirror to see my face. It was as radiant as a bride's.

The next day and the next and the next, I awoke with anticipation. I slipped out of bed and ran to the bathroom to pee and wash my face. I brushed my teeth and ran a comb through my long hair, and then I rushed downstairs to find Jesus. When I began to pray, to call upon him, I felt dizzy with desire. My breathing quickened, my heart pounded, and a surge of physical desire swept through me. I closed my eyes in pleasure and murmured "Jesus" until the prayer language began to flow, a trickle and then a torrent.

By the end of that summer, there were seven women in our circle who had been baptized in the Spirit, and all of us had the gift of tongues. To my surprise, Paulina came forward and admitted that she had a closet prayer language she had been using for years. She had been afraid to admit it to any of us until now. Dear, unique Paulina taught us so much about tongues and their interpretation. Other women came forward as well. Madeline Parker, a gorgeous woman with wavy hair and a model's elegant body, all arms and legs and cheekbones, had recently moved to Des Moines while her husband completed his internship at a local hospital. She was delighted to discover there were other tongues speakers in the church. We sat in her student housing apartment, holding hands, praying one by one and sometimes in unison. Once in a while one of the sisters would offer an interpretation of what someone else had prayed. Several women perched on the camelback sofa. Others knelt on the cobalt blue area rug Madeline had bought in Greece on her honeymoon. Incense burned in tiny glass saucers placed on the cherrywood coffee table.

"We adore You, King of Kings. Behold your maidservants, let it be done as you wish," a sister offered as an interpretation of what had been prayed in an unknown tongue. We nodded and cried and prayed harder.

Most of our husbands didn't know, or if they did know about the exact nature of our prayer sessions, they were not convinced it was something we should be pursuing. I had told Eric about my baptism in the Spirit, with disastrous results.

At first he was silent, gathering his forces, and then he began.

"But we don't believe in tongues," he said quietly. "That's a gift for first-century Christians, not for us." By now, we knew all the ancient creeds, the sacraments, all things orthodox.

"Eric, it's real. I've been going to Aglow meetings. All the sisters there have the gift – it's just a prayer language, that's all," I said. I was so in love with God. I had begun to think of Him as my true husband. I was Christ's eager bride, something I had never been for Eric.

"It can be counterfeited, you know," Eric said. "You know – Satan. The angel of light. You shouldn't mess around with it, Carolyn."

"This doesn't have anything to do with Satan, Eric," I said sharply. "I feel closer to God since I started doing it."

"We should probably talk to the Elders about it," Eric said, twisting his finger into his ear. Faster and faster he turned it, not looking at me at all.

"Do you want to hear me?"

Eric stopped digging at his ear. "What did you say?"

"I said, 'Do you want to hear me?'"

"Speak in tongues?"

"Yes."

"No, I don't," he said. "Carolyn, it's weird. It would give me the creeps to hear you jabbering away."

"C'mon. Just listen." It was suddenly important that he hear me. "I can do it right now, if you want."

A car passed by; its headlights swept the room and flickered across our faces.

"Let's pray, okay?" I asked as I crossed the room and sat

210

beside him on the sofa. I reached for his hand. He looked at me, his face flushed bright red. He took my hand.

I began praying in English: Father God, I love You. I wanted Eric to know about me and God. I was now a mystic, a saint of old. I began haltingly to speak in tongues. *Ahgleeahtoe. Famiaglotta. Komee Komee Seena.* I lifted my hands toward heaven. I wept, but still the words came, rushing out of me, pushing past my trembling lips. I forgot to measure Eric's response. I forgot the children were asleep upstairs. I knew only that I was in the presence of God.

Eric dropped my hand.

"Stop it," he said. "Stop, Carolyn. I don't like it." He stood up and walked across the room. "It doesn't sound right."

The words dried up. I felt them lodge in my gut, felt the exotic, lovely words writhe in my acid and fade away. Eric seemed frightened of me. He scratched the back of his head, shifted from one foot to the other, looked as though he wanted to run.

"It is right," I said. But I could no longer convince myself. Everything was suddenly foolish. Our house smelled of hot dogs. We could hear the laugh track from a neighbor's TV. Finally, Eric shrugged.

"It won't last," he said quietly. "You'll see the light."

I had been dazzled by the light for the past few months. What did he know?

For a while, I disregarded Eric and his reaction, but then one morning I woke up and felt a surge of fear. What if Eric was right? What if the prayer language was all wrong? What if we had all been the gullible, easily deceived women the Bible claimed we were? We were the naive ones after all, who had believed Satan in the Garden of Eden. I prayed and asked God to please show me if this gift of tongues was from Him. I had to know once and for all if I had manufactured this experience because I wanted it so badly or, worse, if Satan had been giving me a counterfeit experience to distract me from my service of God. I prayed all week, several times a day, and asked for confirmation of this gift. Thursday night it snowed heavily. The streets were clogged with feet of heavy snow – tree branches broke, cars stalled, and businesses closed.

Eric and I took the children to Waveland Country Club, where sledding was allowed on the hilly golf course. We pulled Allison and Joshua behind us on their red vinyl saucers. I looked at their faces, their mittened hands, the hats on their heads, and I wanted to keep them like this forever. Oh, to pull them behind me on the icy snow, to know they will look up and meet my eyes with nothing but delight, nothing but acceptance and love. I was lost in these thoughts when we finally finished dragging the kids and sleds to the top of the highest hill. The course was packed with hundreds, maybe thousands, of children and their parents. It didn't look like anyone was working that day. The grown-ups were all red faced and had ice in their eyebrows. They were wearing mufflers that were unpacked once a year, double-breasted dress coats that were not the kind to play in. Our goofy, fat-fingered gloves and earmuffs became ice encrusted, just like our kids'.

Eric and I tried to find a likely place to take a run down the hill. I rode with Allison; he rode with Joshua. I squinted against the sun, trying to see how people were landing at the bottom.

"Carolyn!" a woman shouted over the heads of several stocking-hatted adults.

I turned to see a woman I knew only casually. She was the secretary of the children's Christian day school. She didn't know Eric and didn't greet him. He turned away and retied Joshua's hood. I left Allison on her sled to say hello to the woman I knew only as Jo.

She grabbed my shoulders and pulled me close to her face.

"I have to tell you something," she said. She seemed amused about something. Maybe she was pregnant and had to tell even me, a near stranger.

"What?" I said, turning to check on Allison. The legs of a dozen strangers surrounded her, but I could see the top of her pink hat; alert and precious, she was waiting for me to come back.

"Carolyn, I've been baptized in the Spirit. I have a prayer language, and it is changing my life. I'm so in love with the Lord!" She had tears in her eyes, the angular, no-nonsense secretary who had written me a dozen reminders of overdue tuition, tardies, field trip forms that had not been signed.

It was one of the moments that are singular, a sound bite for the deathbed, the day you know you will not forget, the day you will remember is Friday, the month you will remember is January, the date you will remember is the eighteenth.

My own eyes filled with tears.

"When I saw you," she continued, "the Lord said to go tell you, to tell you that this gift is real, this amazing gift of tongues is real."

I stammered that I had been praying for just such a confirmation; I told her that lately I had been confused about the whole thing, but no more, I vowed, no more.

We stood on the top of a hill and were pressed on all sides by children and their parents, and it was winter in Iowa, a day no one was working. No one but God.

Oh, how I loved Him. I loved my children. I loved my husband as my brother in the Lord. I didn't have the distraction of earthly passion. All of my consuming fire could be for the Lord Jesus. I comforted myself with this as I neared thirty. I saw myself in middle age and old age as an odd sort of virgin, a nun, a keeper of the flame for my Savior and Him alone.

Fountain of Joy held a weekend retreat in the snowy

countryside of southern Iowa. The sisters had made a huge pot of potato soup with whole-wheat dumplings and we'd just eaten it with hunks of bread and a green salad. Nate walked by me and stopped.

"C'mon," he said.

"Me?" I didn't know whom he was talking to. We were all lazing before the fire with our Bibles open before us. Camille was trying to get a game of charades started, but no one could rouse the energy.

"Take a walk with me," Nate said. He was wearing his parka, a muffler already tied around his neck.

Why would Nate ask me to take a walk? I tried to avoid him. First, he made me nervous – he was a chiropractor and everyone called him Doc – that was intimidating enough, but add to that his Ralph Lauren model looks, all blond and windblown and aloof. He was someone who would have completely disregarded me in the real world. I knew that and interpreted his dutiful smiles to me as simple PR in his unofficial campaign to become an Elder. Second, he was the brother who had issues with the way women in the church dressed. That third-degree session still rankled: "Surely you wouldn't tempt a brother?" I looked down at my clothes. Was that what this was about? He didn't like the jeans I had begun wearing?

"What about Sarah? Does she want to go with us?"

"Eight months pregnant? What do you think?"

I glanced around the room; nobody stirred or looked interested one way or another if I was taking a walk with Nate. Eric looked puzzled for a second, and then he smiled. "Dress warm," he said. Nate's wife, Sarah, smiled and waved a pair of knitting needles at us from the other side of the room.

Nate and I walked through the snow, making footprints where there had been none. The sun was bright; Nate wore sunglasses, but I didn't have any. Each time I looked up at him,

I saw myself looking back, a small woman in a green coat, my eyes slitted and careful. I didn't say much, just listened as he talked about his desire to become an Elder, his vision for the church, and the role he thought the sisters could play.

Uh-oh, I thought. Here it comes. He's going to say something about my jeans.

"You are so teachable, Carolyn," he said as though he were bestowing the highest praise. "Whenever I have a chance to address the body, I always see your face before me. You're hungry. Receptive." He turned away from me then and looked up into the gray white sky. "I'm drawn to you."

I opened my mouth to say thank you, to give him a reverent and submissive gaze, the quickest of smiles, just a flash of gratitude, not too much or I would reveal pride and that would be disaster. But then Nate turned toward me and pulled me close. He held me longer than the standard three-second brother-sister hug. He was still holding me and he didn't appear to be loosening his grip. What was happening?

A near stranger holding me in the blinding sun and snow. I felt plopped into *Dr. Zhivago,* my mother's favorite movie when I was a girl. Why did he just keep holding me? He should let go, I thought. Or I should let go. Instead, Nate pulled me even closer, and if my head was muddled, my wanton body was not. I wanted to melt into him, even the thought of his lips on mine, on my breasts – I shook myself. I was Eve all over, tempting, being a tool of the devil.

I pulled away "I'm cold, Nate. I want to go back."

We walked back silently. Snow had filled one of my boots. I wiggled my toes, trying to keep the blood flowing. I could not believe any of this had happened. Had I imagined it? Was I making it up? I could still feel Nate's arms around me, the insistence of his embrace. I felt a brief elation, a dark joy. I'd forgotten that I had that power to draw someone to me. Long ago I had repented of that ability and had laid it at the foot of the cross. Only Christ deserved adulation. Only Christ. My lips formed those words, but my heart lagged behind. Nate had wanted me, I thought. Me, of all the women in the church. We kept walking side by side. I had a mad impulse to grab his hand. *Oh, Lord. Oh, Lord, help us now.*

Nothing has changed, I thought as we opened the door to the lodge and rejoined the others. The Bibles were still on everyone's laps. The fire was burning. Someone strummed a praise chorus, one or two sang along with their eyes closed and their faces serene. Nate and I stood there for a moment, stomping the snow off our boots, taking off our gloves. I unbuttoned my coat and felt Nate lift it from my shoulders. When I turned to look at him, I saw at once that everything had changed. His eyes no longer held any interest or warmth for me; it was gone, vanished, as though it had never been. He hung up our coats and strode across the room, his voice strong and loud. "Where is that beautiful girl I married? Where's my woman?"

I watched him reach for Sarah. How right, I thought. How perfect. Praise God. The draft from the doorway chilled me in spite of the warm room. I couldn't seem to move. Something had happened out there, some battle had been fought, some principality had tried to bring us down. And somehow I was the one who lost – that much was clear.

BETRAYAL

After my cousin Delia married, she moved to Chicago with her husband, a man we didn't know much about. Something happened in Chicago that no one in the family would discuss. My aunts and mother all said, "Poor Delia," and shook their heads. "No one should have to suffer the way she has."

I didn't want to press for information. I just told Aunt Jill to give Delia my love. I added her to my prayer list, and that's all I heard for a while.

One morning Delia put on a halter top and a pair of tight blue jeans. She packed two suitcases and began driving west. She didn't know where she was going, but when she saw a Des Moines exit, she took it and drove straight to our house.

"It's me," she said when I opened the door. "It's Delia."

"Dee! Oh, Dee-Dee. I'm so glad you're here," I said, and reached for her hands. "How did you know where we lived?"

"Christmas card," she said, and pulled out the card I had sent last year, a photo of the children with "WISE MEN STILL SEEK HIM" emblazoned below. "Your kids are beautiful."

"Thanks. Oh, Dee, come inside and you can meet them," I said, reaching for her hand. She pulled back and took a few steps backward on the porch.

"Carolyn, I have totally fucked up my life. You have no idea."

"I've heard you've been having a rough time, Delia."

"I don't have a husband. I don't have any money. No job. I don't know what I'm going to do," she said, and began to sob. Her face crumpled and she backed into the porch swing.

I sat beside her and put my arms around her. "I know what you're going to do. You're going to help me husk some corn for dinner. Then you're going to pick out the sheets you want on your bed."

She slumped against me, a dead weight on my chest. I stroked her bare back and told her she was going to be all right.

I was glad that Delia had come to me for help. We were close when we were girls, spending at least one week of each summer together at our grandmother's house in the country. We had played in the corncrib, picked cherries in the front yard, pears in the back, and climbed all over Grandma's steeply pitched and gabled roof. When we became teenagers, we exchanged bikinis in the middle of the Iowa River, giggling as we kicked and paddled, trying to keep our heads above water as we unfastened our bra tops. She lived in Kansas with Aunt Jill and Uncle Frank, eventually attending college in Lawrence while I was in Des Moines falling in love with Jesus Christ. I had sent her Christmas cards all those years but had seen her only once or twice. After her mysterious marriage, she just dropped out of sight. I hoped I could help Delia. I knew God could.

Eric and I told Delia the bedroom in our basement was hers for as long as she liked. "It's God's house," we said. "Everyone is welcome here."

She looked up from the floor, where she was playing Matchbox cars with Joshua.

"That's good," she said. "I don't have any other place to go."

Dee knew Eric and I were religious, but I don't think she had any idea how religious our household was until she had been with us for a few days. No cursing allowed. No wine or beer in the refrigerator. Our radio was set on the local Christian station, and she found out soon enough that I closely monitored the television for anyone's viewing. There was always a guileless soul ringing the doorbell with a big smile and a tofu concoction to share. If she'd had any other place to go, I think she would have been there fast. As it was, I just prayed for the right opportunity to share the gospel with her, step by step.

Eric agreed. "Some people have to fall to the very bottom before they will turn to God," he said. "We'll know when the time is right to talk to her."

After three months, she found a job as hostess in a supper club and was gone most nights. The rest of the time, she stayed in the basement. I'd see her on the way to the shower or find her in the kitchen making a snack, but that was about it. She was quiet and depressed, not anything like the giggling Delia of my youth. I felt so sorry for her. How she needed the Lord.

A week later on a Saturday afternoon, the three of us sat at the dining room table. Delia had to leave for work soon, but she had come up from the basement early to visit with us. I said, "How nice, Dee!" and poured her a glass of iced tea. Eric and I looked at each other over Delia's head. I nodded, and then Eric began.

Eric told her how much God loved her, how He had made a way for Delia to be saved. Jesus died for Delia; if Delia would have been the only person on earth, Jesus still would have picked up the cross and marched toward Golgotha.

"You have no idea how much He loves you, Dee," Eric finished.

Delia shook her head. Her face was tight and angry. She lit a cigarette and stared out the window at the swing set, where Allison and Joshua were playing.

"I love little kids," Delia said softly. "That's about all the love I believe in these days." She snubbed out the cigarette and stood up. I'd forgotten how tall she was and how provocatively she dressed. She didn't belong here; that seemed clear.

"Wait, Dee," Eric said. "Let me read you a few Scriptures. Please?" He was barefoot in his blue jeans. He looked to me for backup.

But before I could say anything, Delia interrupted.

"No," she said. "I don't want to hear it, Eric. I don't want to be rude, but I'm just not interested, OK? I have to go to work."

Eric looked stricken. His hand went up to the cross around his neck, and I knew that we were thinking the same thing: We're suffering for the Kingdom. Delia was an enemy of the cross; we had to come to terms with that.

"If you didn't want to hear it, you came to the wrong house," I said. "You know we're Christians. You know that we want our lives to count for Christ."

Delia sighed. "Yes, I know you're Christians. How could I not know you're Christians? You tell me every friggin' minute you're Christians." She stood in front of the door and didn't move. "I'm sorry, I just wish things could be normal between us. I wish we could go have a beer together."

"A beer?" I asked. I pictured Eric and me sitting with Delia in a bar. Delia leaning back blowing smoke circles, tipping a long-neck, Eric and I playing footsie under the table. A plate of barbecued chicken wings, a cocktail waitress with an attitude, but she's busy, so we let it go. I'm sipping some icy drink with an umbrella and telling the story of the time Eric and I almost got caught having sex in Tina's bed. We all laugh until we're lying in the booth sideways trying to get our breath.

Normal.

"We don't drink beer," I said.

"I know," she said. "Listen, I have to go to work. Later."

After she left, I looked at Eric and shook my head. "She's so hard-hearted, Eric. She's like Lisa – they're two of a kind. If TULIP is true, maybe they couldn't even believe if they wanted to."

"C'mon, honey, let's not get into that," Eric said. He knew I was about to start in on hyper-Calvinism, something that I had begun to take real issue with. I devoted an entire notebook to my own Bible study of TULIP, an acronym for the five tenets of the doctrine.

"If TULIP is true, I don't even feel like I know God," I said. I was suddenly furious and didn't know what to do, so I threw down the dishtowel I was holding.

Eric bent to pick it up. "You agree with some of it, Carolyn. Total depravity, perseverance of the saints."

"But I don't believe that Jesus died only for certain people and that others are doomed, even before they're born, they're doomed to go to hell," I said. "What kind of love is that? Why would God not give everyone a chance to get to heaven?"

"He's the potter, honey. We're the clay. He gets to decide what He'll make us into. If He wants to make us a slop jar, that's His call, right?"

"Slop jar?" I asked. "Spare me the hokey analogy. Jeez."

We looked at each other then. Not only had I spoken harshly, "Jeez" was as close to swearing as I'd come since Allison was a baby. Uncomfortably close to "Jesus", the word filled the kitchen and made us both cringe.

"Sorry," I said, beginning to cry. "I just love my family, that's all. I don't want to lose them."

"I know, I know," Eric said. He pulled me into his arms. "But we can trust God, Carolyn. Everything's going to work out in His timing."

God's timetable. It always came down to that.

Two weeks later, Eric found a fishing tackle box in the basement shoved under a workbench he didn't use. A padlock held it shut. It wasn't his box; he had never seen it before. He fiddled with the lock for a few minutes and finally broke it. The first tray held Ziploc bags of hypodermic needles. He pulled the next tray and the box unfolded to reveal dozens of plastic bags, each filled with a grayish powder lined up neatly in every crevice and every compartment.

Eric carried it upstairs and set it on the table.

"Where are the kids?"

"The big ones are outside. Lauren's taking a nap. Why?"

"Look what I found." He opened the box again.

It was true that Eric and I had been living a sheltered life since we were teenagers. We had never used drugs, and we didn't know anyone who did, but we both knew what we were looking at. There was too much; it was too organized. This was someone's business.

"Call her," Eric said.

When I called my cousin at work, she didn't try to bluff or lie.

"I'll take care of it tonight after work," she said. "I'm sorry, please, I'm sorry. It's not mine. I was just holding, oh, please." She hung up crying.

Eric and I sat at our dining room table with the box in front of us. My heart was pounding so hard that I worried it would stop. I put my fingers on my wrist to track my pulse. I told myself to take deep breaths, slowly in, slowly out. Eric couldn't believe Delia would bring drugs into our house, not that quantity, at any rate. What about our kids? What if they had found it?

"We were trying to help her," I said. "She totally betrayed our trust. How could she do that?"

"She's moving out, Carolyn," Eric said. "I want her to get her things and move out today."

I stared at him. I had never seen him so shaken. Even though I was angry and vengeful as well, Delia was still my cousin. What would Aunt Jill say if I just kicked her out?

"She doesn't have any place to go," I said. "She's trying to save some money for her own place. She just got a new job.

Besides, if we made her leave, Aunt Jill would know something happened."

"That's her problem, isn't it?" Eric asked, and I saw how close to tears he was. I reached across the table and squeezed his arm. He was trembling.

"Oh, God, help us," I prayed. "Please help us get through this."

"Yes, Father," Eric said, trying to keep his voice steady. "We need you."

We bent over the maple table, still sticky from that morning's innocent breakfast, and wept. I listened to the kids playing in the driveway. I kept thinking of how danger had been in my house; the devil himself parceled in tiny packages and all of this beneath the rooms in which we slept. I stood up and walked to the window.

They were cracking walnuts on the asphalt drive. Allison held a brick over her head and dropped it onto the pavement. Joshua was on his haunches, looking closely at one of the jagged shells. Allison said, "Get back, Joshua. More nuts comin' right up." How clearly I heard her little voice through the wavy glass of the ill-fitted window. My babies.

"Eric," I whispered, "what are we going to do?"

"Tell her to get her stuff and get the heck out," he said. He kept his eyes closed, pressing his temples with his fingers.

"That doesn't solve anything."

"What are you talking about? It's all we can do."

"Somebody's going to end up taking those drugs," I said, still not turning around from the window. Joshua was wearing his swimming goggles and pedaling his Big Wheel down the driveway. I couldn't see Allison, but I could hear her singing. "Somebody's kids will take them."

"We can't do anything about that."

"Oh, is that right?"

"What are you saying?"

"You know what I'm saying."

"You want to get rid of the drugs?"

"I don't want anyone's baby to be destroyed by them. Do you?" I walked back to him, knelt before him. "Eric, what if God wants us to do the hard thing here? What if we're just looking for an easy way out and this is all part of His plan to see what is in our heart, to see how willing we are to do the right thing?"

"What about your cousin? She's going to answer to someone about losing this dope. Do you have any idea of what you're suggesting?" Eric held my shoulders and looked at me. His face was flushed, his fingers dug into my flesh.

"Joshua!" Allison yelled from the side yard. "I found more nuts!"

"Yes," I said. "Of course I know. I just can't let my earthly family get in the way of obeying God. You know I can't do that. I think God's telling us to get rid of the drugs now. I don't know," I said. "What do you think? You're supposed to be the leader here. What does God want us to do?"

"I don't know, Carolyn," Eric said. "I just want it out of here."

"What does God want?" I sank into the chair and laid my head on the table. I lifted it again. "Oh, Eric, what does God want?"

"Let's go to the Elders," Eric said. "Phil's out of town, but Larry's around. I'll call him, OK?" He stood behind me and kneaded my shoulders. "Larry will know what to do."

After Eric got off the phone with Larry, I called Brianna to ask her to keep the kids for an hour while Eric and I went over to Larry's.

"We have a crisis, Bri," I said. "Please pray for us to have wisdom. The worst thing has happened."

"What? You've got to tell me," she said. "What happened?"

"I can't talk about it, really," I said, and broke down. "It's too dangerous."

"Oh, Carolyn," she said. "Be careful, OK? I love you. Be careful. I'll pray. God will give you wisdom, I know He will."

Fifteen minutes later we were in Larry's basement study. Eric and I sat in the two leather chairs that faced Larry's enormous desk. Larry, a cherubic sort, beamed at us. "Coffee?" he asked.

We shook our heads.

"Larry," Eric began, "we need your counsel."

"Hit me." Larry smiled. "Go right ahead." He leaned back in his executive chair, his hands folded across his chest and his eyes sparkling as if we were beginning a new game of Clue.

Eric told him everything that had happened since finding the box in our basement. I added some details here and there. I was gratified to see the sparkle fade from Larry's eyes, the dip the expensive chair took forward, and finally Larry's white hands twisting the telephone cord on his desk.

"And you're asking me what to do?" he asked when Eric finished. He shook his head and laughed. "I thought you needed my advice about tithing or sending your kids to Christian school or something like that," he said. "Not drug running."

I tried to laugh, too, or at least smile appreciatively at his attempt to lighten things up, but I could not. I was getting ready to betray someone in my family. My girlhood friend, my cousin Delia. We had taken baths together. We had dared each other to sleep in the west room, Grandma's haunted bedroom. Oh, what would Grandma think? And Aunt Jill would never forgive me for sending her daughter to prison. Even Mother would think I had gone too far.

Do you think I came to bring peace on earth? No, I tell you, but division. From now on there will be five in one family divided against each other, three against two and two against three. Jesus said that – He said this would happen in a family, but the reality was so cruel, I felt faint. I took my pulse again as I watched Larry's lips reading Scriptures, saw his head bow in prayer, saw Eric turn toward me.

"Is that OK, honey?" Eric asked.

"What?"

"Larry's going to call a narcotics agent at the police station and ask for advice – it will all be anonymous. He won't give any names, right, Larry?"

"No, Carolyn. I'll just tell him the situation, tell him you want to do the right thing, and see what he says," Larry answered. He seemed to be revived, calmer now.

"OK," I said. "Don't tell them where we live, either."

"No," Larry said. "Nothing like that."

While Eric and Larry made the call, I left. I walked out to the car and was surprised to see it was still afternoon. Sitting in Larry's paneled basement with the lamps softly lit, our hushed voices and long pauses, I assumed it had become twilight. I couldn't stop crying. There was no good solution to this problem, no way to please God and Delia, I knew that for sure. I slumped down in the front seat of our rusty Subaru and tried to pray. At first, I couldn't get past the word *please*. Please. Please. And then clarity cut through my malaise and doubt. Judgment Day, of course, that's what it came down to.

As much as I believed the sun would come up in the morning, I knew the very day I died would find me standing before the Lord to give an account of all my actions for every minute of my life. He would ask me specifically about this night; He would want a reckoning. What on earth would I say if we gave the drugs back to Delia?

"Well, Lord God, it just seemed like the easiest thing to do. . . ."

There was no way I could do that. I could face neither His

wrath nor His disappointment. We had to do the right thing tonight. We had no choice but to obey.

I sat up when I heard the front door close. It was Eric squinting in the sun and walking toward me. He shook his head as he walked across the lawn.

"Well?" I asked as soon as he got inside the car. "What did they say?"

"Two options, Carolyn. Get her to flush it or else give them our address, and they'll come over, arrest her."

"They said to flush it?"

"The guy said that if it was his cousin, that's what he would do. 'Don't tell me her name, don't tell me your name,' he kept saying. 'Just talk her into getting rid of it.'"

"Do you think she'll do that?"

"I don't know, Carolyn," Eric said. "I don't know what to think about any of this. I wish she had never put us in this position."

"Well, maybe it was God Who let it happen," I said, "to see what we'd do."

Eric glanced at me and then looked back at the highway. "Everything's so black and white with you. It's truth or a lie. It's God or Satan."

"Well, yes," I said. "That's exactly the way it is. There are absolutes – you know that, don't you?"

He didn't answer me and just kept driving until we were back at our house. He got out of the car and went into the house without me. I twisted the rearview mirror over and looked at my face. It was tear streaked and pale, but I saw what I was looking for: a face like flint, a determination to obey God no matter what the cost.

I gave the kids an early supper of grilled cheese sandwiches and pear halves. After their bath, we all snuggled together in

Allison's bed while Eric read a bedtime story. I loved this more than anything else in my life – the children fed and bathed and in my arms smelling of Baby Magic lotion and Ivory soap. Nothing bad was ever going to happen to any of us because we would never stop listening to *The Clown-Arounds* and *The Magic Turnip* and laughing at the same places. Even Lauren, not quite two, laughed when we did, a charming delayed reaction that made us laugh harder. After Eric closed the book, I handed him another.

"One more, Daddy," I said. "Don't we want another story?"

"Yes! One more, Daddy!" Joshua and Allison looked at each other with surprise; they couldn't believe their good luck.

But when that story was over, we kissed them good night, prayed, turned on the night-lights, and went to wait for Delia.

I still dream of that night. I see Delia standing in the living room as we tell her the way it will be. She collapses like one of the children's toys, just folds in upon herself, neatly, quickly, without sound, ready to be packed away. Eric and I are on opposite sides of the room and we take turns talking at her. She lifts her head to protest, but she gives up, deflating again. In my dream Delia gets smaller and smaller until finally I pick her up and place her carefully between the pages of our family Bible, the white one with the unfinished chart of our family tree. "You'll be safe here," I promise. I close the Bible and then I say to Eric, "Delia is saved, at last, at last."

That is the metaphor my mind has arranged. The actual event was one of missteps and stammering, a bad TV movie where none of us knew our lines, and the lines we remembered, we overacted. I was righteous and tearful. Eric, alternately angry and embarrassed at the whole scene. Delia could not believe that we wouldn't give her back the box and was dumbfounded at our insistence that she destroy the contents. "It doesn't belong to me!" she kept saying. "I'm just holding it for someone, don't you get that?" She was angry and then apologetic. She was brave and then pleading. We were implacable, though. "It's God we answer to," I said a number of times. After a couple of hours, Delia picked up the box and walked toward the bathroom. Eric followed her.

I sat in the rocking chair, the one Mother and Hal had given us for Christmas that year. I knew that she would be horrified if she knew what was happening at that moment, but I couldn't let myself think of my mother or my aunt, not my grandmother, either. I held my breath as I listened to the toilet flush again and again.

"I'll have to leave town, go back to Chicago, maybe," Delia said when she came back into the living room. The hypodermic needles rattled in the empty box. She lit a cigarette and circled the room, looking at family portraits. She picked up a Depression glass pitcher our grandma had given me and fingered the crack on the lip. "Broken," she said.

"Do you want it?" I asked. "You should have it. I have other things of Grandma's. Take it."

"Jesus, Carolyn," she said. "I don't know what I'd do with it right now."

"Eric," I said, "put that in Delia's car, will you? Here, wait, let me wrap it up."

I grabbed some paper towels from the kitchen and wrapped the pitcher.

"There," I said when I finished. "Now you can take it."

Eric shook his head slowly. "This is crazy," he said. "Do you even want the pitcher, Delia?"

She shrugged.

"Of course she wants it. It's our grandma's," I said.

"What does that have to do with anything?" Eric asked. "This is crazy," he said again. He stood there for another minute, holding the wrapped pitcher, searching both our faces. He was like one of the daguerreotypes on the wall, his skin drawn back fiercely on his bones, his lips cracked to reveal only darkness, his eyes flat and hopeless. Finally he took the pitcher and left.

Delia and I stood alone in the middle of the living room. She pushed her hair back from her forehead. "My hair's a mess," she said. "Do you have a rubber band?"

I reached around and pulled the one from my own hair and felt my braid jerk apart.

"You didn't have to do that," she said, taking the rubber band out of my hand.

"Oh, Delia," I said. I reached for her and wept, overcome by the kind of sorrow I had forgotten about, one that could not be redeemed for good. "Oh, my God. I am so sorry." I breathed in her cigarettes and Chanel and held her.

And then she turned to go. Eric and I stood at the front door and waited until we heard the familiar squeal of her car's loose belts. Oh, she needs someone to look at that car, I thought. I began to cry again, harder than ever.

"God will take care of her," Eric said. He took a deep breath. "God will take care of all of us."

I nodded and wiped my face. I felt dazed. I didn't know if he was right or not. All I knew was my cousin was leaving town with a tackle box of needles and our grandmother's Depression glass pitcher. I wanted to hear God's still, firm voice telling me, "Well done, thou good and faithful servant," but all I could hear was the toilet running.

WILDERNESS

The next Sunday, Larry told the church that Eric and I and our family were in serious trouble and, through no fault of our own, our very lives were potentially in danger. Some of the brothers and sisters gasped. Others kept silent, bowing their heads, immediately beginning prayer, I supposed. Larry urged the body to keep praying for us in the coming weeks. He read I Peter 2:20–21 aloud: " 'If you suffer for doing good and you endure it, this is commendable before God. To this you were called because Christ suffered for you, leaving you an example that you should follow in his steps.'

" 'This is commendable before God,' " he repeated. "Our brother and sister Eric and Carolyn are commendable before God. I can testify to their faithfulness to God in the most extraordinary circumstances. Praise God."

"Praise God," Tom said from the back. Eric and I sat with our heads down, reluctant celebrities. I couldn't feel pride or satisfaction in sending my cousin out of town with a price on her head, no doubt. We were going to be eating potluck in fifteen minutes, where gracious, smiling sisters would ladle green bean casserole in warm dollops on our paper plates beside pieces of oven-baked chicken. The children would sip Kool-Aid and play Old Maid at a card table in the corner. Afterward we would take the children home and read our Bibles while they napped.

It had been the right thing to do, I knew that. Those drugs were off the street, swilling through the sewer system of Des

Moines. And that was what God had wanted me to do, wasn't it? I hadn't let my love for my family interfere with my love for God.

Oh, please, God. That was what You wanted, wasn't it?

Eric and I avoided talking about that night. Only the kids brought up Delia's name; they asked where she was and when she was coming over again. Allison made cards for her with glitter and paint, crooked hearts and rainbows, "I Miss You, Cousin Delia". I promised to mail the cards as soon as Delia called to tell me where she was staying. So far she hadn't called.

While the rest of the church sang the doxology, Eric and I studied the covers of our Bibles in our laps. I admired my name, the gold-plate sparkle of *Carolyn*. I didn't know what Eric was thinking; maybe he, like me, had decided to let it go, let all the hard stuff go. I wanted to coast for a while, just think about the material world. I was exhausted.

For me, that meant concentrating on the children and their activities. For Eric, it meant his career. After the Pleasure Island project had been completed, Richard had pulled yet another string and arranged a job for Eric in his friend's manufacturing plant in West Des Moines.

This time, however, Eric had thrived in the workplace.

As a child, he had loved science, especially physical science. For years he had kept a discarded library book, *The World of Atoms*, on the back of the toilet. We believed God had blessed Eric's love of science and his quick mind to make him a valuable employee at J.W. Manufacturing, makers of thermos jugs and coolers. Eric had become the go-to guy, the trouble-shooter for the whole manufacturing process. He designed the plant layout, knew the vendors on a first-name basis, kept the guys on mahogany row at their desks where they belonged while he steadily increased production and profit in the plant. When J.W. relocated to Arkansas, Eric was offered the number two spot in the whole company if he joined them. It was a good job with a salary we never imagined possible for a high school graduate. But there was no way we could make a decision like this on our own. We went to the Elders to ask their advice.

They were of one mind.

"You'll never find a fellowship there like we have here," Larry said.

"Pursuing the world, the lust of the flesh, destroys many an earnest believer," Don added, softening his words with a little shrug and smile.

"We love you guys," Phil said. "How could the church get along without you?"

That, of course, was the powerful argument. We were loved. We were shepherded and cared for. Why would we go anywhere else?

But the job paid twice as much as what Eric was earning. We had three children. Eric might never have an opportunity like this again. And maybe God wanted us to go there; maybe we were supposed to be missionaries to northwest Arkansas. That seemed like a possibility. We knew there was a veneer of religion in the South, but they didn't know about real, radical, sell-yourself-out-to-the-Lord Christianity. We brought up these issues to the Elders.

"The fact is that you need the kind of fellowship you have here at Fountain of Joy," Phil argued. "You need us to help you keep following Christ." He spoke directly and with fire. His eyes bored into mine, and I looked away, as I always did with Phil. He seemed so holy to me, so close to Jesus Himself, that I was afraid he could read my mind. I fiddled with the latch on my purse.

"What if we could, Phil?" Eric asked. "What if we found a fellowship like Fountain of Joy in Arkansas? Would we have your blessing then?"

Phil was silent. The other two Elders began to nod thought-fully.

"We could make you a list," Larry said. "A list of questions that the church you found would have to answer the right way. If they did, then I think" – he looked at the others – "I think we could give you our blessing."

Phil remained silent, a most un-Christian smirk on his face. What's the joke, Phil? I thought. We'll be back, is that it?

"I'll write the list," Phil volunteered. "And the Elders will look it over and then we'll get it to you."

"We really appreciate it, Phil," Eric said. "We sure don't want to go anywhere God doesn't want us to go."

"I know," Phil said. "And I don't blame you for that. Running away from God's plan for your life means sure disaster."

We left the Elders with that word ringing in our ears. *Disaster.*

A couple of weeks later we were on the road to northwest Arkansas with our list of questions from the Elders. During the four-hundred-mile trip, Eric and I talked about a life in the South, a new life away from our families, the church, everything we had ever known in Iowa.

"Neither of us has ever lived anywhere else," Eric said. "Iowa's all right, but there have to be more interesting places to live."

We had traveled a bit with the children over the years, twice visiting relatives in Florida and Washington State. I was drawn to the ocean like nothing else in the physical world. I was instantly seduced the first time I saw the aqua waters of the Gulf coast. I loved walking the sugar sand beaches with the bigger kids running beside me, tiny Lauren in her yellow bonnet squealing as her little toes sank into the wet sand. But oh, the coasts in the Northwest. I often thought about the day we had spent at Canon Beach climbing the rocks, jumping at the ocean spray, layering sand dollars between napkins in our cooler. The Pacific had kept me enthralled way past the kids' patience. I wanted to be lost there, half willing to sacrifice myself to that furious blue.

"By the ocean, maybe someday?" I asked.

"Let's start with Arkansas," Eric said, popping open a can of soda. "Hand me a pretzel, would you? Everybody's been telling me lately how beautiful Arkansas is. They have clear, running rivers; the Buffalo River is a national park. The Ozarks are supposed to be spectacular, too, the oldest mountains in America. Dogwoods and redbuds in the spring. Cost of living is low. Crime practically nonexistent," he rattled off.

"I hope God wants us to go there," I said, trying to remind both of us it wasn't a done deal, not yet. I looked at his satchel and thought about the sealed envelope with the list of questions. So much depended on those answers.

We drove through Kansas City and headed south on Highway 71. For hours and hours we drove through unremarkable countryside, no corn to comment upon, no fields of soybeans, just hardscrabble fields cropped clean by horses, goats, and occasional herds of cattle.

I tried to read, but it made me carsick. I nibbled saltines and thought about our kids. I hoped they were behaving for Mother and Hal. We had told Allison that Hal wasn't a Christian, and Allison had made it her mission to save her grandpa. She made him crosses out of Popsicle sticks and enclosed them in her famous glitter cards. "Jesus Loves Grandpa Hal".

It was strange to be without the kids. We were a family, not a couple. I kept turning my head around to the backseat, sure I had heard someone call out. I was so used to tying shoelaces, fixing snacks, and teaching life lessons, I was at a loss on my own.

"Do you think the kids are all right?"

"Well, yeah," Eric answered. "Of course they are. Hand me another pretzel, would you?"

I sighed and closed my eyes. I listened to Eric chew over the car's droning. I tried to picture us in Arkansas, the children growing up surrounded by beauty. Maybe we were going to a new Garden of Eden. Innocence and purity – how I longed for a place like that. Maybe Delia could come and live with us. I wanted to ask Eric what he thought about that idea, but I was suddenly too tired to stay awake.

After we checked into the Highway Host motel, we pulled out the phone book and scanned the churches listed in the Yellow Pages. "Fellowship" was a good indicator. If we found a church name with the word *fellowship* in it, that was a good sign. We looked for the word *Elder* listed as clergy. We found only one listing that mentioned an Elder. Elder John Peters was the shepherd of a Primitive Baptist Church. Their advertisement included a line in italics: *Where we still practice foot-washing!*

"Ugh," I said. "Do you think that's a metaphor? Or do you think they really wash each other's feet?"

"Sounds like they really wash each other's feet," Eric said, drumming the open telephone book with his pen. He scribbled down a number on the hotel stationery.

I pictured a roomful of tottering sisters and brothers with towels tucked around their waists, balancing basins of water and bars of soap as they made their way around a room of barefoot believers. "Sister, I'd like to wash yore pretty little feet right now," a toothless old man was saying to me. "And then it's your turn to scrub my pore old clodhoppers."

I shook my head. No way would that be happening. I wiggled my toes in my shoes and cringed at the thought of a stranger's hands on my feet.

"Would you let anyone wash your feet?" I asked Eric.

"What? No. Look, Carolyn, I have five, maybe six places I can call," Eric said.

"Are you going to call now?"

"Might as well," he said. "Well, let's pray first."

We prayed and asked God to give Eric wisdom to know if he was speaking to a true shepherd representing a true fellowship. I sat on the other bed and turned on the TV, then muted it so I could listen to Eric's side of the phone calls.

"We're interested in a New Testament church," Eric would begin.

"We are a part of an Elder-ruled fellowship. We stress community groups and discipleship. Accountability . . ." He was measured and cautious.

"Accountability. Someone who knows what's going on in our spiritual lives."

"Calvinists, yes, sir, I'd say so."

Eric answered more questions than he asked. Sometimes he asked only a couple and listened to a long answer, after which he would have nothing to say. He got off the phone quickly once and said, "Those people aren't even real believers. Guy had no idea what I was talking about."

Finally, only one possibility of a genuine New Testament church remained. The pastor had been open and friendly, and more curious than anything, he asked us to come and see him the next morning. We pulled into a Sonic and bought chili dogs, onion rings, two Styrofoam glasses of icy limeade. Back in the motel room, we called the kids at Mother's to tell them good night, but they were off with Hal, miniature golfing. We showered and laid out our clothes for the morning. Eric pulled out the envelope with the list of questions and put it inside his Bible.

"It's a spiritual wasteland down here," Eric said as we got into bed. I folded the comforter well back from our faces and gingerly arranged the pillows. I wondered what kind of wild sex had taken place in this very bed. I had read about the semen deposits on motel bedspreads revealed in laboratory tests.

"We don't know that yet," I said. I took off my watch and lay down. I planned to stay perfectly still all night.

"The Elders were right," Eric said, wrapping his arms around the pillow. He groped for the bedspread. "We've got it made in Des Moines."

"Good night, Eric," I said from my side of the bed.

"Good night, Carolyn," he said, his voice muffled from the depths of the comforter.

We pulled in front of Mount Calvary Chapel, a prefabricated lemon-colored metal building that reminded me of the hog confinement units Eric used to make. A large white cross in the lawn distinguished it from nearby commercial buildings.

"Ooh," I said. "Not so nice." I unwrapped a piece of gum and put it in my mouth.

"Can I have some?" Eric asked. We were both nervous. This was it; if the pastor of Mount Calvary didn't convince us that he was a shepherd after God's own heart, well, then we'd have to give up on the idea of moving. We sat there for a while, chewing our gum, until Eric twisted around and got his Bible off the backseat.

"Let's go, honey," he said. "God will reveal His will to us this morning, one way or the other."

A few minutes later, we were shaking hands with Pastor Griffin.

"Call me Jerry," he said.

"Jerry, we're the Anderses. Eric and Carolyn."

"Well, how about this? Have a sit-down. Tell me again what the Lord's doing in your life and how you ended up in Arkansas," Jerry said. Except for the southern accent, he could have been Pastor Jim. He was a huge man with a shock of black hair and a gap between his teeth. He wore an impeccably white shirt with gray flannel trousers, and every time he moved I could smell Brut.

Full circle, I thought. God has brought me back to Pastor Jim.

When Eric finished describing our quest for the right church, Jerry burst out laughing.

"Isn't the Lord good?"

We smiled and nodded

"Look at you two down here investigating the Lord's will for your life. I think that's amazing," Jerry said.

"Would you mind answering some of these questions from our Elders?" Eric asked as he unfolded the list.

"No, sir. I don't know how good I'll do, but I'll do my best."

After the first couple of questions, Jerry sobered up. He pursed his lips, blew out, and leaned toward us.

"Y'all aren't going to get the right answers from me, I'm afraid," he said. "I don't know of any church in this area that could give you that kind of accountability."

And that was the gist of the Elders' questions. How well would Carolyn and Eric be shepherded? Who would know if Carolyn and Eric were fading away from following God? Who would be aware that Carolyn and Eric were compromising in their walk? Who would pull Carolyn and Eric up short and say, "Straighten up. Obey God. Repent"?

"I'm not saying that I wouldn't be tickled silly to have y'all here, but I got to be honest. We just don't operate like that here. We love Jesus, sure we do, but well, I guess it's a different culture here. . . ."

He went on and on, but nothing he said was of any interest to me. Jerry and his church weren't going to be our ticket out of Des Moines. We were going back to pick up where we had left off with our predictable little lives. We would go to house church at Tom and Dora's and break bread with saltines and Welch's grape juice at eleven o'clock each Sunday morning, and Phil would say, "Are you in the Lord?" and we would alternately nod or hang our heads and the kids would grow up and then it would be Eric and me alone with our Bibles and our notepads scribbling notes about the Abrahamic covenant on dreary Sunday nights for year after year until we died. No big house with dogwoods in the yard and new neighbors who might invite us over for a mint julep before they found out we were religious. No new car or furniture and plenty of money to pay our bills, no new Brianna.

I still had my Brianna back in Des Moines, of course, but she had weaned herself of my tutelage to a great extent. Bri had charmed many others the way she had me with her sincerity and openness. It had been a gradual process, her growing away from me, one that was both gratifying and disappointing. It was good for my little disciple to be launched, to be God's handmaiden in others' lives. But I missed the way she needed me, the way her world had briefly revolved around my words, my actions. I wanted another Brianna in Arkansas, and for a while I had believed that possible, even likely.

We left the pastor's office and made our way back to the Highway Host.

"God doesn't want us to move down here," Eric said. His shoulders hunched as he sat on the foot of the bed.

I took a deep breath. The stale air rushed into my lungs: cigarettes, room deodorizer, the stagnant air breathed by people who were between things.

"I know," I said. I pulled the comforter completely off the other bed and curled up on the sheets. I cried because we had no choice in the matter. If God said no, then that meant no. Disaster, the Elders had said, would follow us if we disobeyed God. It was better to stay in Des Moines than to make a daring escape to Arkansas outside of His will. We'd get sideswiped by a semi on the way down. One of the kids would get bone cancer. Our beautiful new house would be burned to the ground. It was no use doing what your flesh wanted to; we both knew that.

As usual, Eric and I could not share disappointment any better than we could triumph. He turned on the TV and ate a bag of Cheetos, washing it down with a vending machine pop. Every once in a while, usually during a commercial break, Eric would issue some sort of statement or directive toward me.

"We have to have faith."

"God is sovereign."

"His will, not ours."

"All things work together for good for those who love God."

"Don't question Him."

"Please stop crying."

J.W. Manufacturing moved south without us. The best job Eric could find was in construction again. He was hired to build redwood gazebos in people's backyards. Really nice gazebos, he always said, the kind that will last forever. For three years he built gazebos, packing his peanut-butter sandwich in the same beat-up cooler he had used when we were kids. Most of the time, he acted pretty cheerful about the whole thing; he didn't question God or His will out loud, but I noticed a slight disappointment, a resignation, that I hadn't seen before. The physical labor alone was something he had to get used to all over again. One humid day in late July, he came home from work suffering from heat exhaustion. He opened the front door and said, "I'm sick, Carolyn. The heat got to me."

He was paler than I had ever seen him. When I reached for him, his arms and hands were clammy and cold. "I'm gotta sit down," he groaned. "My head is killing me."

I brought him cold compresses and ice water. I unbuttoned his shirt and pulled it open. "Allison," I called, "bring me that little fan from the kitchen."

Eric couldn't even talk, he was so weak.

"Shall I call a doctor?" I asked.

He shook his head. "Just need to rest. Thank you, honey."

"Oh, Eric," I said. "Please be OK." He was too frail to do construction; he should have been back at J.W.'s with an office and a secretary. My throat wadded up, and all I wanted to do was throw myself on his chest and cry. Instead, I left him there on the couch with the fan revolving toward him and away again.

He slept the rest of the afternoon and evening until I woke him up to go to bed. He sat up on the couch and tried to focus.

"Are you feeling better?"

"I think so. I've got to be. We have to finish this job tomorrow."

"Are you sure you should go?"

"Have to," he said, and smiled sadly at me. "You understand that, don't you?"

I nodded back, not trusting myself to speak.

So we just kept going. I tried to make his smaller paychecks stretch for everything we needed. I shopped garage sales and economized on groceries and tried not to fantasize about the kind of life we could have had in Arkansas. God had denied us entrance into the Promised Land, I thought often and without irony. How I had wanted to move on, to spy out the land, to claim milk and honey as my birthright.

But after the three years of wilderness, God brought us out. The president of J.W. Manufacturing called Eric again and offered him a salary and benefit package that made Eric say yes before we even prayed about it, let alone asking the Elders for their counsel. The whole thing was exactly the way God would work, we agreed. He just wanted us to trust Him, to wait for His timing, and then in one grand, elaborate gesture, our Father, our own *Jehovah Jireh,* said, "Come on down here to Arkansas. Put your feet up. Stay a spell."

Brianna gave us a going-away party. Sometime during the evening we made our way into the master bedroom, where we sat on the edge of her bed and held hands. She had a hard time saying anything. She started and then choked up, finally squeezing my hand as the tears ran down her face.

I brushed the tears from her smooth face with my fingertips. She was so lovely. I would never have another relationship with anyone like her ever again. No one would make me as happy as she had. I felt the presence of the Lord. I felt His hand on my shoulder and knew He was holding us tight.

"He's here," I said, blinking back my own tears.

"Thank you, Jesus," Brianna said, and we embraced, the sounds of a party outside the door, the streetlight outside of the window casting shadows on the walls of her bedroom, the mauves and colonial blue, the delicate stenciling, all lost, all swallowed up by the night.

TRAVAIL

We finished loading the moving truck the night before Thanksgiving 1983. Eric towed our Subaru behind the Ryder truck while I drove the ailing Pontiac as we made our way south in a fierce ice storm. The ground was thick with ice, rivers of sleet running through the prairie grass, crystal coating the naked branches of trees, and the whole world seemed an improbable and inhospitable place to live. At a rest stop, I tried to comfort restless Lauren, her cheek warm and moist against mine, while the older children drew pictures on the frosted window. Houses with chimneys, stick figures, apple trees – these surrounded us, and their homeliness broke my heart. I was giving it all up: the whole idea of home, of belonging, of being part of a landscape. I reminded God, You are my home, my only home.

We arrived at our new house in Arkansas around dinnertime. A J.W. Manufacturing pickup truck was parked in the driveway. When we pulled into the driveway, two men dressed in steel-gray coveralls got out of the truck and motioned me to park on the side street while they helped Eric back up the moving van, halting and waving him down the long driveway.

Our new house was cavernous, bigger and grander than I could have dreamed of in the Highway Host motel three years before. Eric and I had gone from a trailer to a bungalow and now from the bungalow to a four-bedroom, two-story house. Downstairs, three enormous bedrooms, a bath, and a family room with sliding glass doors to a deck. Upstairs, a living room that swallowed our few pieces of furniture and left yards and yards of white carpeting untracked. A cathedral ceiling of tongue-and-groove cedar in every room – another huge deck outside of the living room overlooked the woods and stream in the backyard. Every room had at least one picture window, outsize and bare of curtains.

The kids were delighted. They ran up and down the *Brady Bunch* house stairs and yelled to hear their voices echo. Lauren twisted to get out of my arms, but I kept holding her while Eric and two guys from J.W. struggled to get the piano up the stairs to the living room.

"Some house, Eric!" Darrell (according to the red script on his coveralls) said as they rested on the landing.

"Jesus H. Christ," huffed the scrawny one who had pulled his coveralls open to the waist and wore only a thin white T-shirt in the sleety twilight. "It's the biggest house I've ever been inside."

Eric coughed. We both hated the Lord's name being used in vain, but here was something new for the Anders. Someone was admiring our material possessions, maybe envying what we had. Neither of us was prepared for that. Nobody had ever looked at our car or our house and whistled in appreciation.

"We got a real good price on it," Eric said. "I don't know how well this old barn is built. Probably doesn't have a shred of insulation. And look at those windows, single pane. Well, I'll be paying for that all winter, I bet. Heat will go right through those windows."

"It's a beauty," Darrell said, just as if he hadn't heard.

"Well," Eric tried again, "it's the Lord's house, belongs to Him. He's just letting us live here."

"So the Lord's the one Who has to worry about the heating bills," White T-shirt picked right up. "Ain't your concern."

I stood in the foyer and listened to the conversation. Was White T-shirt a believer? In Iowa, people didn't say "the Lord" lightly. He couldn't be, though; just a minute ago he had taken the Lord's name in vain. It was my first taste of the South and its religious sensibilities. Although I didn't know it at the time, I would discover that in the South, everyone and his daddy believed in the Lord.

But that didn't mean they gave a lick about getting to know Jesus or being His disciple. Being a Christian meant you weren't a Jew. Being a Christian meant going to church on Sunday and doing what you wanted to the rest of the week. For Eric and me, it meant finding true kindred spirits was going to be one of the biggest challenges we had ever faced.

While Eric immersed himself back into the world of J.W. Manufacturing, I began to take measure of my new surroundings. I lived somewhere else at long last. This could be the new life I had always wanted. Even though icy skeletons of dogwoods dotted the yard outside my dozen picture windows, I felt a surge of new life at the opportunities to serve God in a brand-new place.

That optimism lasted for a few weeks, long enough for me to get the pictures on the walls and sew some curtains. I wrote long letters to everyone in Des Moines, encouraging them to trust the Lord, and then I sat back and tried to do the same: trust the Lord in the silence of my large house.

I missed Brianna. When the kids were in school and Lauren napped, the house was unearthly quiet. I sipped my cup of tea and stared out the window. Who lived in those houses? I willed their doors to open; I prayed for a sweet-faced Brianna to come out with a red scarf knotted around her neck, holding a plate of raisin oatmeal cookies as she strode up my driveway.

I ached for her.

So, more often than not, I called her when the afternoon seemed interminable and we prayed together over the phone. Bri told me what was going on in Des Moines; I demanded every detail, wouldn't let her leave anything out. Then I'd tell her about my house some more, the kids' new school, Lauren's progress at toilet training. For a while, I would feel comforted and loved, sure of my place in the world, but then it would be time to hang up. We always prayed together, and it was bittersweet. I now found it hard to pray on my own, longing for Brianna's echoing, "Yes, Lord."

Pastor Jerry's church had seemed like the logical place to start looking for a fellowship. We soon found out Pastor Jerry was no longer the minister; he had moved on a year or two back. So we didn't know a soul in the lemon yellow metal building, where we were welcomed like visiting dignitaries. Everyone wanted to shake our hand, marvel at how far we'd come – "Iowaay?" – and welcome us into their midst. There was something for everyone, it seemed: a men's discipleship group for Eric; the Ladies' Missionary Society for me; Awana, a children's Bible club, for the kids. The congregation was warm and sincere, smiling to beat the band, but it all left me strangely cold. These weren't my kind of people. These women who attended the Ladies' Missionary Society wore JCPenney and Montgomery Ward. They got their hair done at Hazel's Pin and Curl. I knew it was wrong of me to dismiss them because of clothing or hair. I knew that and tried to look past it, but I couldn't.

On the way home, I asked Eric what he thought.

"The teaching was solid," he said. "It would take some getting used to a hymnbook again."

"Do you think we'd fit in there?"

"Well, sure. They're believers, we're believers. That's all we need to fit in."

I sighed.

"You didn't like it?"

"Not really. It sort of reminded me of Allendale Baptist, nothing like Fountain of Joy. I'm just used to people who are more . . . hip, I guess. Like-minded. I don't know, it's just–"

"Blest be the tie that binds our hearts in Christian love," Eric sang, and turned to smile at me.

I nodded and looked out the window at the blueberry fields we were passing. Allison read the sign aloud: "Don't Be Blue. Eat Our Berries."

"Yeah, Mommy," Eric said. "Don't be blue."

"I'm not," I said, chewing on my fingernail. "God will lead us to the right church. I know He will."

But looking for a church, as the Elders had predicted, turned out to be an exhausting and discouraging task. We kept looking for the right fit. Sometimes we'd end up in a church that reminded me of the little white church by the trailer park – empty, trivial God talk, nothing real, nothing substantial to help me in my walk with God. The deacons shook my hand right off my shoulder with dreadful sincerity. The pastor's lackluster sermon nonetheless sparked a sporadic "Amen!" now and then; it was a loud and ungainly cry, not like the gentle chorus of "Yes, Lord" and "Praise God" we were used to. No guitars anymore, now there was organ music, great swells of chords filling the sanctuary as people filed in and out. No more folk songs or revised rock ballads. Now it was "Rock of Ages", "Great Is Thy Faithfulness", and "How Great Thou Art". I listened to a matron next to me warble "In the Garden", and I wondered if she had any idea of what it really meant to be intimate with the Lord Jesus Christ. She wore a charm bracelet and carried a Good News Bible – a paraphrased edition no serious believer would read. Ha, I thought.

After a few months of church shopping, I was feeling even more superior and tormented. Eric was discouraged but willing to settle for a Bible-believing church, no matter how Southern Baptist it felt. I suggested that we might like to have a house church of our own. Maybe we could get some neighbors to come, or maybe some of Eric's employees from J.W. would like to try it out. Lately, I had been thinking of

Tom and Dora's house church with great nostalgia, remembering those Sunday mornings when we sat in a circle while Tom or one of the brothers shared the Word. Afterward we had communion together, passing bits of saltines and a chalice of grape juice.

So we gave it a try: house church in our own living room. I wasn't brave enough to ask the neighbors I hadn't even met, and Eric didn't think it was appropriate to ask his employees to worship with us, so it was just our family. Eric lit the fireplace, I laid the crackers and juice on the coffee table, and we all gathered around. Eric got out his guitar and played one of the kids' favorite songs: "Ha, ha, ha, hallelujah. Ho, ho, ho, hosanna. Hee, hee, hee, He's my Savior. The joy of the Lord is mine. . . ." I loved watching the children sing. Allison was so serious about her praise to the Lord. She composed herself, put her hands in her lap, and sang each word distinctly and carefully, her face a study of piety. Joshua just grinned and sang for all he was worth, never really letting on that he understood a single word. Lauren nodded her head a little and joined in on the "Ha ha ha."

After we sang, Eric opened his Bible. He read a passage and then talked about it. Eric's explication of Scripture always sounded like regurgitated wisdom from Phil or Larry, nothing new, nothing bold or enlightening. Yet I nodded thoughtfully and directed the children's questions or comments to their dad. We were doing it for the children, after all. But I always hoped that Eric would teach me something I didn't know. In the early days after our conversion, the established patriarchy of Christianity had given Eric an advantage over me. I expected him to understand spiritual issues more clearly than I did, so it was no great surprise when he did. Gradually, however, I had outpaced him in my zeal and desire for the Scriptures. We'd started out together with our exhaustive studies, cross-referencing, and comparing texts, but Eric had faded somewhere along the way. His observations about the Lord and the Word were pedestrian, middle-school stuff. What I wanted was Phil's teaching. What I needed was Brianna.

I didn't see how Eric could fill their shoes. He wasn't the one who challenged me or excited me or stimulated me to be my best. Other people had taken those roles in my life. Living in Arkansas made me face the veneer of my relationship with Eric. Our husband/wife dynamic was thin to the point of nonexistence. What had once been a regrettable fact of life now became a question of survival. I was afraid of what might happen to me in Arkansas if my marriage did not begin to deepen. I began to pray in earnest, devoting whole prayer journals to asking that God do something to change things between Eric and me: "Please, God, have mercy. Make me love my husband the way I want to, the way You want me to. I'll do anything You say. I want my marriage to glorify You."

I looked for opportunities to build a frame for the love God Himself would pour out. If Eric was sitting on the couch, I would get up and sit on the couch beside him, ask him how things were going at work, and volunteer to pray for anything that was troubling him. I began planning weekly menus around the foods he loved best, pork chops and wild rice, lasagna, seafood salad. I let him play his guitar for hours and didn't nag him to stop or help me or do something more productive like read his Bible, maybe. I felt primed, ready to move at God's slightest nudging, but I didn't sense His prompting at all. For days and weeks, I circled Eric and watched him out of the corner of my eye. Now? I'd ask God. Now should I say something, do anything? . . . Now?

Eric looked up from his guitar but didn't smile at me. He was concentrating on the counterpoint to the melody, an impulse I knew and understood.

After a while I grew discouraged. Nothing changed between

Eric and me. I felt as though I would starve, and I didn't know where to turn for my daily bread. It would not be people this time; no slick-backed, shiny-lapeled deacon was going to teach me anything. I had to teach myself. How had other believers persevered in loneliness, torment, and drought? I began to read about the ancient saints. Oh, Bri, I thought, you would find this ironic.

I began with Brother Lawrence, the cook in a seventeenth-century monastery. "On numerous occasions I have been near to dying," he wrote, "but I have never been so happy. I have asked for the strength to suffer with courage, humility, and love. It is sweet to suffer with God, great though the sufferings may be. Take them with love. It is a Paradise to suffer and be with him."

" 'It is sweet to suffer with God,' " I mulled over. My suffering was hardly marked with courage and humility. I had been superior and impatient and hateful. I had let God down again. Anyone can serve God when things are going well, but a true believer obeys in God's silence and his seeming absence.

I found an edition of *Foxe's Book of Martyrs*, a sixteenth-century compilation of accounts of martyrdom. I was drawn to the accounts of cheerful death, the willingness of the early believers to die for the sake of Christ. Again and again, the saints defied those who would have had them recant, and how nobly the doomed did so, with what courage and pithiness of speech.

"And Elizabeth Folkes . . . on the stake . . . plucked off her petticoat, and taking the said petticoat in her hand, she threw it away from her, saying, 'Farewell, all the world! farewell Faith! farewell Hope!' and so taking the stake in her arms, 'Welcome Love!'

When all the six were also nailed likewise at their stakes, and the fire about them, they clapped their hands for joy in the fire, that the standers-by, which were, by estimation, thousands, cried 'the Lord strengthen them; the Lord comfort them; the Lord pour His mercies upon them,' with such like words and was wonderful to hear."

Oh, Lord, I was no Elizabeth Folkes. I was complaining and wretched, upset because I was *lonely,* because I was lacking *companionship.* Ohh, I sighed in disgust. I was spoiled and wretched. What was the matter with me? Would I ever be the kind of saint I wanted to be? I had been walking with the Lord so long, and here I was a dozen years later not that much further down the road. What would Elizabeth Folkes do if she were married to Eric Anders? Well, she would clap her hands in joy in the fire, that's what she would do. She would keep her eyes on Jesus and Jesus alone. There would be no pain, no destruction, because Jesus would keep her safe and make her his own dear bride.

As the winter thawed and the dogwoods began to bud and then finally blossom, I sat on the deck and savored my bone loneliness, counted it all joy, determined to forgo all human happiness if only I could know the presence of God the way I once had. I wanted to give my life in a blaze of glory; I wanted to say I cared nothing for this world or anything it could offer me.

But I felt something slipping.

The bedroom in our new house was large, with wide-planked, honey-colored pine on the floor. The ceiling was a deep red cedar and the walls were cream – a tiny border of vines and flowers stenciled around the room. My grandma's cedar chest at the foot of our maple bed. One of her quilts, the tulip one, folded on top of the chest. A thick comforter covered the bed; tapestry pillows and silk accent pillows with tassels were piled on the bed. Candles everywhere. Fresh flowers on the dresser, framed pictures of the children. This was the place of my deepest travail.

When Eric and I were alone in our bedroom, there were facts that had to be faced. I could not be my children's mother in our bedroom. I was not one of the sisters in Bible study. I was neither my mother's daughter nor Lisa's sister. I was not Carolyn Gilbert, the underdeveloped girl who undressed in a toilet stall. I was Eric's wife, and that was all. We shared a bed, an intimacy that neither of us had ever known with anyone else. A marriage bed, the Bible said, was the only acceptable venue for intercourse, an honorable and sacred place.

"The wife's body does not belong to her alone, but also to her husband," Paul wrote in the Book of Corinthians. "For the husband and wife will become one flesh."

It is one thing to be a life partner, to be committed for the long haul, to raise children and pay bills and go to family reunions or take out a mortgage, but it is another to be penetrated by someone you do not welcome. Whom could I petition to spare me this humility? Who would take pity on me? Not Eric. He loved me; he wanted this intimacy with me; he considered making love a rare, God-sanctioned pleasure in our lean world. Would the church intercede for me, make a way for me to live chastely within the bond of marriage? Of course not. It was God's divine plan, our edict to be fruitful and multiply. Jesus? Could I go to the Lover of my Soul and beg pardon from my husband's embrace? No, even Jesus would not spare me. He looked discreetly away when Eric's hands pushed up my nightgown. Even Jesus found another place to look.

THE TIES THAT BIND

No fellowship, no real friends. I knew we had to do something soon to find some people like us. I circled an advertisement for the next scheduled meeting of a pro-life group. Surely believers would be lining up for the cause of the unborn. Eric and I hired a baby-sitter for the kids and drove through the dark Arkansas countryside to find the meeting site: the community room of a local electric company.

I looked around. Freddy Kilowatt posters on the walls, bright fluorescent lights, a room full of folding chairs, but not very many people. A woman stood at the podium shuffling papers and whipping her long white hair over her shoulders from time to time. She looked up and smiled when Eric and I sat down. Her teeth were crooked and her eyes were shrewd. Not exactly friendly, but honest, I thought. She looked like a preacher, a truth sayer, as Phil used to call himself.

And Sue, this activist at the podium, turned out to be exactly that. A speaker of truth, an unapologetic zealot. She had a way of walking with her pelvis tipped forward, leading her into a room before she would stop, regally survey the other people, and then, only then, sit down. Ever since her conversion to Christianity ten years earlier, she had ferreted out compromise in any aspect and called it to the attention of others.

She would be my first friend in Arkansas. We were a mismatched pair from the beginning. I was halfhearted, willing to coast spiritually, but Sue was grim faced and determined to bully the world to its knees for Christ. Even domestic issues were occasions for her preaching, her not-so-subtle display of superiority.

One fall day we sat in my family room and discussed the training and discipline of children.

"Consider this, Carolyn. We need to motivate our children to obey the Lord," Sue began. "It has to be a matter of intrinsic motivation and not extrinsic."

I slid down in my chair. Sue was quite proud of her intellect and used it to make me feel small, stupid, and vapid.

"Sue," I teased, "don't use words over my head."

"Oh . . ." She flushed. "I'm sorry. I try so hard not to do that."

"Sue," I said, "I was just kidding."

"Intrinsic," she said kindly, "means inherent, the very nature of something–"

"Sue, I know what the words mean."

We looked at each other across the room. She began picking at a thread in her blouse, and I excused myself to refresh our lemonade.

Sue's husband, Bill, was a deeply tanned and rugged medical doctor. For years, Sue said, Bill had tried to believe in both God the Creator and the science of evolution. He had finally let evolution go by the wayside, but it had taken its toll. His shoulders were permanently stooped. He had lost his hair. His eyes were heavy lidded and downcast. If Sue had an answer to everything, Bill had a question, a thoughtful and unusual question that made me think harder than I had in years. When we got together as couples, I waited to see what Bill had for us to think about. The freewheeling discussions that sometimes resulted from Bill's questions reminded me of the early days of our conversion, before everything had become a recited catechism, a Roman numeral on an outline that was pulled out and referred to again and again.

I liked Bill a lot more than I liked Sue, but it was not possible to have a relationship with him. A close friendship with a brother was wrong, improper, ripe for disaster. Phil had warned us of this many times: "If you want to be a friend to a sister, brother, then you better be a friend to her husband. That's the best thing you can do for that sister: love her husband and stay away from her."

Even though Bill and I had a number of quiet conversations over the years, we remained in the strange netherworld between being real friends and being brother and sister. Neither seemed right. We smiled at each other sometimes, a quick, sad smile, and then we would turn away and talk to our mates, our children, reach for a Bible to keep us moored.

Sue wasn't happy with the local pro-life group. She felt the need for a Christian pro-life group, one with a sharp focus on the Word of God. Eric and I became charter members of the newly formed Believers for Life. We held monthly meetings where we planned picketing activities, educational outreach opportunities, and fund-raising efforts.

We ordered plastic fetuses, an accurate model of a three-month-old, the size of an index finger, a pink poly-vinyl thumb-sucking infant curled upon itself. I always carried a few in my purse. One look at this "baby" and a woman or girl who was considering abortion would know the abortionist had lied to her about carrying a clump of fertilized cells in her uterus and nothing more. My children liked to play with these little models, sneaking into the box in my closet and ferreting the pink bodies out of the packing peanuts. Sue frowned on that and told me that careless handling of the plastic fetuses was not that far removed from people thinking it was permissible to murder a real fetus. I agreed and promised to watch it, but not long afterward I found two fetuses in Lauren's Barbie doll case and one more lodged inside Joshua's remote-control car.

My least favorite assignment from Believers for Life was

picketing. A single doctor performed abortions in the area, and every Tuesday, at least one of us picketed his Fayetteville clinic. His office was located on a busy street with lots of traffic. We made our own hand-lettered signs: "Jesus Loves the Little Children – Dr. W KILLS Them", that sort of thing. So rain or shine, we marched up and down the street, enduring the honks and obscene gestures as well as the few thumbs-up from passerby. I liked to carry an ambiguously worded sign: "Equal Rights for All Women". Preborn women had the right to live as much as any other woman, that's all I wanted to say.

"Get your ass home!" some guy screamed from a pickup.

"Don't you have anything better to do?" a woman yelled not long afterward.

"Glory to God!" half an hour later.

"Fuck you!" often.

I marched and prayed, counted sidewalk cracks, and looked for dandelions. The fumes from the passing cars made me light-headed. I checked the time often to see if my two-hour stint was about up. I hoped I wouldn't see Dr. W because I had no idea what I would do if I met him face-to-face. My pocketful of fetuses wouldn't faze him. He knew what they looked like.

Eventually, I picketed less and did more public speaking for our cause. I discovered how much I liked to speak to an audience. Standing at the podium, surveying the audience, I felt alive and powerful. As a woman, I didn't have very many opportunities to preach, certainly not to a male and female audience, but now I had a platform, a legitimate topic, and I warmed to it.

"This baby," I would say, brandishing the fetus. "This baby has fingernails, did you know that? Ten little fingernails, perfect and pink. "*The Silent Scream,* the film you're going to see tonight, will show you what takes place inside a mother's womb when the abortionist inserts his scalpel.

The baby tries to get away. It leans. It lurches. You'll see how this little baby does *everything* in its power to escape death." I leaned forward and spoke those last words slowly and softly. The Wal-Mart executives and their pretty wives shook their heads miserably as they listened and then afterward wrote checks for a hundred dollars, sometimes more. I felt good about that and glad that I was saving the lives of babies. It was at least something. My own children were growing up. I had no real friends. I had grown weary of building a frame, toeing a line, and waiting for God. I was tired of being disappointed in prayer. More and more I caught myself looking in the mirror at a woman in her early thirties who was dying of boredom and couldn't tell a soul.

I resolved to start praying more, just regular, old-fashioned praying. I had no desire to use my prayer language; I couldn't even remember the last time I had used it, and it struck me as just a little spooky. Maybe someday I'd feel like doing it again, but not now. I also knew I had been neglecting my Bible reading in favor of my library books. I was visiting the library once a week and checking out books, completely secular books that had nothing to do with God or His Kingdom, but they were classics, I argued with myself. Dickens, Austen, Wharton. Books I would have read in college if I had gone. But they weren't the Word of God. They didn't contain light and salvation or the power to give new life. Oh, it was like that. Back and forth, arguing, discounting, rationalizing.

In the middle of this malaise, Eric came home from work and told me that he had met someone who was part of a New Testament church exactly like Fountain of Joy.

"Are they Elder ruled?" I asked, looking up from *Pride and Prejudice*.

"Yes! And they have house church, too," he said, smiling. He grabbed me and hugged me. "They've invited us to come next Sunday. They're meeting in a Seventh Day Adventist church – it's empty on Sundays, so it's perfect for them."

"What's the church called?"

"Mount Olive Fellowship," he said, shaking his head. "After all this time, honey. We're going to have a church again."

"I hope so," I said. "I hope this is what we've been waiting for."

We had been a part of Mt. Olive Fellowship for a few years when our worship pastor experimented with the lighting. An Arkansas boy with thick black hair he kept long in the back, he was loving and gentle and had become a true friend to me. He pulled up a stool, leaned over his guitar, and began to croon a love song. I felt something like the old electricity for Christ surging inside me. I sang along, my neck bent, my palms open, fingers curled upward and tingling. "You are fairer than ten thousand, the bright morning star." We repeated this over and over in the darkened church until we were all mesmerized, chanting, lost in corporate praise. And then I saw the couple in front of us. The husband was stroking his wife's back, and his hands were beautiful. Each finger fascinated me, the way they tapered so elegantly, the gloss of his nails, the firmness of the flesh on the back of his hand. Before I could stop myself, I imagined those hands on my breasts, those fingers between my legs. I sang to him until the lights were turned up. I sank back into the pew, ashamed and silent, resigned to humiliating fantasies like this one popping into my mind, no matter how old or established or respectable I became.

I was now an Elder's wife. Eric had been named an Elder a year ago. Eric and I both stood out at Mt. Olive, our zealotry, our apparent unabashed love for Jesus, our commitment to truth – these were qualities that distinguished us in the wealthy and rapidly growing group of believers at Mt. Olive.

They were well educated and genteel, men and women who respected tradition, whether it was the Razorbacks or Jesus. If it had stood the test of time, then that was good enough for them. But unlike some of the other churches we had visited in the South, we found true believers here, a pastor-Elder of great intellect and vision; Jeremy, the worship pastor; and a retired couple whose lives radiated love and worship of the living Christ. There were others as well who truly wanted to have a genuine and vital relationship with Jesus. If they were not spiritual giants, they were at least spiritual enough to recognize us as giants. Comparatively speaking, anyway, Eric was not just another suit on Sunday morning. He was a gentle, guitar-toting, memorized-Scripture-spouting kind of guy. If that wasn't good enough to become an Elder at Fountain of Joy, it was more than enough to be tapped at Mt. Olive for the weighty position of Elder.

Jeremy, the worship pastor, was the most creative Christian I had ever met. He was innovative, dedicated to the cutting edge, and eager to try drama on Sunday mornings. He asked me if it sounded like something I would like to do. I didn't know anything about drama; I had read a couple of plays in high school and that was about it, but I became Mt. Olive's drama ministry director. At first, I wrote pulpit dramas and recruited actors to perform the five- and ten-minute skits before the Elders began their teaching. When I had trouble finding amateurs who were willing to stand in front of the rapidly growing congregation, I decided I could probably act, and it turned out that I was right. Acting was fun, not so different from the way I had been living my life for years. I was Mary Magdalene one morning. I held my head scarf closed at my throat and wept as I told the congregation about this man named Jesus, this incredible man who didn't see me the way other men did. I did campy stuff, too. A librarian with half-frame glasses and an enormous behind who snorted Lily

Tomlin-like and cracked everyone up. I was the fat Christian aerobics instructor gobbling Cracker Jack in a bulging red sweatsuit. Nothing was below my dignity on a Sunday morning.

Jeremy loved everything I did. He praised my instinct and my talent and made me a part of the worship team, a group of Elders, musicians, and performers who met each week to plan the following Sunday's services (by now, two services; eventually there would be three). Since the pulpit dramas had become so popular with the congregation, there was always a lot of discussion and careful planning about that portion of the service. We sat at an oval conference table with clipboards and highlighters, taking notes and watching as Jeremy diagrammed the worship segment on the whiteboard. We would read the proposed drama script together, and to my delight, everyone would burst out laughing at every line.

"Can you imagine being married to a woman like Carolyn?" one of the Elders asked when we finished.

Everyone chuckled and shook their heads. What did they imagine? I wondered. That Eric and I sat around exchanging quips and antics? Nothing could be further from the truth, but I was gratified that they thought I was uniquely talented. Everyone seemed to think so at Mt. Olive. During the week, I received notes and cards from people thanking me for the skit and telling me how the humor had made them see their own foibles or how the serious drama had shaken them up and made them get right with God. I kept every note in a shoebox and read them often. My life counted for something, I told myself.

Brett was one of my actors in the Born-Again Players. He wore black jeans; that's what I first noticed about him. Next, his honeyed voice, sexy southern, not hick southern. He called his kids "darlin'", and it about stopped my heart to hear it. But then there were those green eyes that never left mine whenever we had a conversation. And despite his consistent effort to keep things spiritual between us, he felt it, too.

The sanctuary at Mt. Olive was lined with banners of flames spewing Christ. A bare wooden cross behind the pulpit. Lilies left over from a funeral that day filled the air with an aggressive sweetness, like a fresh car deodorizer. It was a Saturday night and we were in the middle of a dress rehearsal. Brett and I sat toward the back, waiting for our cue. We sat side by side on the church pew, his black-jeaned thigh tantalizingly close to mine. Only our shoulders touched. I knew and Brett knew that it was the absolute closest we would ever come to making love. He pressed against me slightly; I yielded and then pushed back.

"Project!" shouted the director to the actors on stage. "Louder, people!"

Brett's shoulder and the top of his arm. Mine against his. The tacit agreement to have innocent sex like this just a little longer. I did not turn my face toward him, but I could see his profile out of the corner of my eye. He looked as if he were in pain.

"We are performing this play as a service to God. It is a missionary project, people!" the director shouted again. "Carolyn, Brett, your scene is coming up."

Brett stood up quickly. I slid past him and didn't meet his eyes.

The three-act play depicted the events surrounding the rapture. There were eight of us in the cast, and all our characters had come to the truth of the gospel too late to be raptured. I played a hysterical woman, a neurotic who could not get over her bad luck of landing in the middle of the great tribulation. Brett played the leader of our group. This was the scene where he had the unpleasant duty of informing the rest of us that one of our double agents had been captured by the Antichrist.

My line was like most of my lines. I was supposed to cover my face in horror and say, "Oh, no!"

But there we were, Brett and I looking at each other under the spotlights. He was getting ready to tell me the bad news about Herman, the double agent.

I don't know what happened to me. Was it the lights in my eyes? Brett and the way he looked at me? The stupid name Herman?

"Herman's been captured. If he doesn't take the Mark of the Beast, he'll be killed tomorrow," Brett said.

"Oh, shit!" I said loudly. "I mean, Oh, no!"

Silence. The director cleared her throat. A little laughter. "What did she say?" whispered around me.

We finished the scene, and afterward Brett gripped my shoulders backstage. I could feel him laughing in the dark.

"Girl," was all he said.

Girl.

Those were the years of compromise, I'm sure believers would say. On one hand, I was earnestly and sincerely trying to please God with the work I was doing in the church. I maintained my integrity with orthodox belief, even though I had begun reading of divergent beliefs and studying books other than the Bible. I still attended Bible studies, still instructed my children daily in the ways of the Lord. I said everything I always had. But there was a persistent rebellion ever growing in me. Much of my interior dialogue was sarcastic, biting, and a little profane. I did not like hypocrisy in myself or others, but I could not deny it when I saw it.

Believers were intolerant of anything but our version of the truth. How many times I saw believers tighten their faces and close their minds to any variance of the norm. Not only did we hate abortion, we hated homosexuality, we hated Hollywood, we hated the politics of the Left. We hated. We hated. And then we had the nerve to claim that God was love and in Him was no darkness at all.

I grew tired of my forced friendships such as the one with Sue and obligatory potlucks and fellowships, home Bible studies. Many an evening I sat across the table from a banal couple and realized that I had just spent two or three hours of irreplaceable time making insipid and saccharine conversation.

Yet I had loved God for so long. I looked back at my life and saw His hand and knew He had brought me out of the darkness into the light. How dared I say I preferred darkness! The Bible said that such a retreat from the light was like a dog returning to his vomit. What kind of fool would I be to turn my back on the Kingdom? I panicked that I could even contemplate such things and resolved to spend more time in prayer. One day I decided that what I needed was a mystical jump start; I decided I would try to retrieve my prayer language.

I read a section from the Song of Solomon, a sexy scene where the bride is all hot for her bridegroom. I read and understood it as symbolism, an allegory for the love between Christ and the church. Then I bowed my head. I longed to feel myself overcome. John Donne: "Never will I be chaste unless Thou ravish me." But God was finished with the ravishing. There were no torrents of words in me, nothing in me to give at all. Nothing happened. It sounded as though I were clearing my throat, that's all.

I couldn't do anything with myself; inwardly I had become some out-of-control adolescent, one I barely recognized. I told myself to straighten up. When that wasn't successful, I cast around for other people's lives that needed to be straightened. My Fundamentalist nature demanded that someone somewhere repent. It might as well be my children. I was merciless with Allison.

I had always monitored her reading. She wanted to read everything she could get her hands on, and sometimes she read the wrong thing. I had found *Catcher in the Rye* in her book bag the week before. I told her it wasn't something a Christian young lady should be reading. I handed her the most recent issue of *Campus Crusade for Christ* teenage magazine instead. She took the magazine from my hand and leafed through it. As usual, I had edited the text of any material I found too mature for a fourteen-year-old. Smiling teenage girls with pageboys held Bibles as they chatted with wholesome-looking boys, but across the page there was a column snipped away. ("Dear Aunt Polly, My boyfriend wants to French kiss. Can Christians French kiss?")

I was determined that Allison be everything God wanted her to be. "Swear," I said to her one day. "Swear on the Bible that you will be a virgin until you get married."

She was fourteen by then and nearly fully developed. The skinny red-haired girl had become a beauty, full breasted like her aunt Lisa, and I was getting nervous.

"Mom," she protested. "This is a little embarrassing."

"I know," I said. "But it would make me feel better."

"OK," she said, putting her slender hand on my red study Bible. "I swear I'll be a virgin until I get married."

"Thanks, honey," I said. I walked out of her bedroom and slowly climbed the stairs to my own room, where I closed the door and threw myself down upon the bed. A deep sadness swept through me, and I broke down. I wasn't proud of what I had just done; it was wrong. That whole scene was way beyond being an involved mother; it had been intrusive, and I didn't think it had anything to do with the Lord. Why did Allison's growing up fill me with such panic? Once I started crying, I couldn't stop myself. I keened in my bedroom all afternoon. The kids did not knock on my door; no one bothered me for Popsicles or rides into town. I lay on my bed for hours and stared at the ceiling fan, following it around and around. I never had an epiphany, instead, a slow and reluctant truth that made me so ashamed and weary, I could not even turn to God.

I was afraid Allison would have a life like mine. Anonymous, long-suffering, of little consequence to anyone but a small circle of family and friends. A silent life followed by an acquiescent, obedient death.

"Oh, Allison," I breathed. "Not you, too. I can take anything else, but you must not have this life."

When Eric came home from work, he knocked softly on the bedroom door. I awoke to his concerned face leaning over me.

"Are you all right?"

"Yeah," I said. "A headache. I had a really bad headache all afternoon."

"I'll take care of the kids, OK? Just rest."

I never did get out of bed that night. I listened to my family in the other room. Eric pulled out his guitar and Allison sang with him. The dog barked to get out and the washing machine chugged. Someone screamed once, and I waited to see why, but nothing else was said and I fell asleep.

AGE OF REASON

Spiritual warfare raged inside of me for the next several years. A battle for my soul, I knew that, but most of the time I denied it was so. Eric's responsibilities at work increased – he began designing new layouts and hiring new workers for the projects he instigated. I wrote skits, found wacky props, made people laugh and cry on Sunday mornings. I decorated my house, searching for antiques and furniture bargains. I wallpapered. I did everything except pursue my relationship with God, but no one around me seemed to notice. I read my Bible for five minutes a day and called it good enough.

When Lauren began school, I took a job working as a teacher's aide in an elementary school. I surprised the professionals I worked for. I had never held a job, never even thought about having a career. Yet I was writing curricula and developing educational materials to help boost reading skills. I even began wearing all those funky clothes the other teachers wore: denim jumpers with appliquéd schoolhouses, corny necklaces made of blocks that spelled "TEACHER", Keds tennis shoes with white anklets. It was the most pedantic reinvention one can imagine, but it was revolutionary to me. It made me ask myself why I was pulling out staples from bulletin boards and passing out cartons of milk at snack time. Why wasn't I the one teaching?

I should have gone to school. I should have gone *back* to school. At thirty-four, it still wasn't too late. Eric and I talked it over – he was supportive and loving. "You can do it, Carolyn," he said. "I have no doubts." With his blessing, I enrolled in a community college for the following fall. I dove into it all at once, registering for a full load of credits. I resigned from my teacher's aide position and waited for September to come.

My new plan worked wonders for my spirits. I was going to do something at long last, take a concrete step toward becoming someone else. In the meantime, I let my spiritual dilemma slide. I would figure it all out someday. No one was being hurt by my inward struggle. The kids didn't know. Eric hadn't said anything. I could act like a happy carefree Christian; hell, I could do that in my sleep.

Late one evening Eric and I sat in the porch swing. We lived on a cul-de-sac and there was seldom traffic, so our street had become a haven for children who careened past on their skateboards and Rollerblades. That night the sound of their gliding reminded me of my flagging faith, both my desire and my fear of believing. I didn't want to coast anymore.

"I don't know what to do," I said, thinking out loud. I faltered, trying to think how to get out of this without Eric overreacting. "There's so much to think about."

"What do you mean?"

"I guess I'm trying to figure stuff out. See how God fits into everything."

"How God fits in? What's that supposed to mean?"

"I lost track of who I was, I think." I sighed. Too late now, we were into it.

"You're a Christian, Carolyn," Eric said as he leaned to push us forward. The swing creaked. "You can't just stop believing."

"Of course I believe," I murmured. "I want to believe." Fireflies calling out: *Here I am. See me.* I made a swipe at one near my face and caught it.

"It doesn't sound like it to me."

"Well, I do."

"Our whole life we've pursued God," Eric said. "Our

children . . . everything we've ever taught them. What would they think if you stopped following Christ?"

I could feel the bug moving in my clenched hand. It circled my palm, tried to find a way out. It signaled and I saw light leaking from the cracks between my fingers, but I kept my hand closed.

"I will take care of my kids, Eric. You know that. They're everything to me."

Eric sputtered, "You're crazy if you think you can live your life the way you want to, the way it feels good," he added, "and you won't affect our kids."

"I'll take care of my kids," I repeated. "Don't worry about that."

He let his feet fall heavily to the plank floor of the porch. "Oh, I'm worried, Carolyn. I'm plenty worried." He stood up and walked back into the house.

I opened my hand to let the firefly free, but it was already gone. It had escaped and I hadn't even noticed.

"So this is the college gal, huh?"

"It sure is, Jeff. She's bringing home straight As." Eric smiled, awkwardly pulling me to his side.

"Why, how about that? You studying with the kids at the kitchen table?" Jeff asked, smiling at me as though I were the cleverest little thing.

"Only after I do the dishes," I said, smiling, and excused myself from the church foyer, where the saints were gathered in little fellowshiping units. Jeff was a banker downtown, and he often told me how proud he was of me for having the gumption to go to college. He would clip the dean's list from the local paper and slip me a copy with a wink and a handshake. "Praise God, Carolyn."

Only our friends Dean and Violet, a retired couple, voiced slight hesitation over my higher education. I respected both

269

their marriage and their walk with God, so I listened to them no matter what they had to say. Dean treasured Violet and often told us so. I liked watching her watch him; her perpetually smiling eyes deepened a shade or two and just lingered on him.

We were sitting on their lakeside deck one hot evening when Violet whispered something to Dean and they disappeared inside the house. When they came back out, they were wearing orange clown wigs and oversize glasses. Dean carried a ukulele. The stereo blasted "Okie from Muskogee" from inside the living room. Violet and Dean lip-synched the whole song from beginning to end as Dean pantomimed playing the ukulele. Voilet fluttered her eyelashes at Dean, and he got on one knee before her to finish the number. They ended with a big kiss. Eric and the kids were laughing over their bowls of ice cream, but I could barely swallow.

Violet eased my loneliness. Sometimes I felt foolish when I realized my closest friend was over seventy years old, but mostly I just felt grateful. I wrote a poem in which I called her my harbinger, and I liked to believe it was so – my first true sister in the South, but perhaps she would be the first of many.

In the meantime, they took us under their wing, inviting us out to their condo for barbecues and long, lazy rides across the lake on their pontoon boat. When Dean and Violet's out-of-state kids visited, Eric and I were included in their noisy, laughter-filled reunions. I helped fix snacks in the kitchen with Violet's daughters-in-law and felt completely at home.

Dean was frequently ill. Each time he was hospitalized, I worried as though he were my own father. It seemed we were always getting the call that Dean had just been admitted into the hospital. When I got the news about his latest emergency, I prayed and fretted all day. As soon as Eric got home from work, we ate a quick supper and went to visit Dean in the intensive care wing of the hospital.

After hugs and Dean's assurances that he was fine, fine,

nothing major, just a bad reaction to a new medication, I relaxed and sat at the foot of his bed. Violet held my hand or rubbed my shoulders. Dean usually took the opportunity to tell a joke, but not this night.

"You're graduating next spring, Carolyn?"

"Lord willing," I said. "I think I'll be finished then."

"How are you going to feel about Carolyn having a degree when you don't, Eric?" Dean asked.

"I'm really happy for her," Eric said, and smiled at me.

"Are you sure you're going to be OK with that, Eric?" he asked kindly. "I've seen it put a real strain on a marriage."

"Don't worry about that, Dean," Eric assured him. "We've got this all planned out. After she graduates, she'll get a job, and put *me* through school."

Everyone laughed. I smiled, too, agreeing with them that it would be a fine, fitting thing for me to do and the only appropriate response to Eric's sacrifice. But then I froze because I knew it wasn't going to happen that way.

I wasn't going to stay in my marriage.

The man in bed was smiling past his pain, despite the tubes in his nose, catheters, an IV. The man who stood beside him and clutched his shoulder, the man I was married to, he was going to be hurt as well, crushed, and it was going to be because of me. I nearly swooned in grief as the realization hit. I reached for Eric's hand and told Dean and Violet that I was sorry we couldn't stay any longer, but we had to go.

Outside in the parking lot, I told myself that I could not do it. I could not leave Eric. It would mean leaving God. I couldn't be afloat in a random universe. I didn't have the courage to live one day if I gave up on the idea of God.

"Why did you want to leave like that?" Eric asked. "Aren't you feeling well?"

"I feel awful," I said. "I can't ever remember feeling this bad."

I was not a model born-again Christian in college. I bypassed many opportunities to speak up in class, defend the evangelical faith, or challenge error. One time I raised my hand in psychology class to say I believed in absolutes. When I put my hand back down, it struck me that I didn't know if that was true or not. Did I still believe in absolutes? Sometimes I wrote about my faith in composition papers, backing up my position with Scripture. My professors would return my papers with no response to my God-based rhetoric, but I hoped my words had made them think.

I was the one, however, who was being forced to think. A panorama of knowledge, this liberal arts education, spread on both sides of me. I loved it all. Unlike my fellow freshmen, I looked forward to class. Western civilization wasn't a morass of detail and dates; it was a story I had never heard, an incredibly interesting story of how we'd come to be.

I read everything in my literature survey courses, not just the assigned Wordsworth, Keats, Emerson, and Hawthorne, but also Lamb and Coleridge, Thoreau and Melville. I never missed a class. I was there early with my notebook open, reviewing my notes from the last lecture.

I kept trying to convince my husband and the church that college wasn't diminishing my faith. I stood up in the share service at church one Sunday and told all the believers about Constantine – did they know about Constantine and his miraculous conversion to the faith in the fourth century? He had seen a vision, a cross, with these words underneath: *In hoc signo vinces* – "By this sign shalt thou conquer." I was thrilled with the story and wanted everyone to share my enthusiasm.

"Don't forget that true wisdom is from above, Carolyn," Tess drawled in the hallway afterward. "The beginning of wisdom is the fear of the Lord," she added. I looked at her: a woman in her late thirties, satin skinned, with wavy chestnut hair, the quintessential southern belle with perfectly mannered children who ma'amed and sirred anyone over eighteen.

I nodded silently. There was no right way to answer such an admonition.

Give me a fucking break, I thought while playing along with a look of thoughtful reflection on my face. I was surprised at how naturally a forbidden word like "fucking" had become a part of my unspoken vocabulary. The contemporary poets seemed to use the word as naturally as any other. And I had come to believe it a fine word, a useful one. I liked the fricatives on my tongue when I whispered it in the car.

"Have a good week," she said, and I answered the same. After seventeen years in the church, I had grown weary of the look of holiness. It slid easily onto our faces and was just as easily stowed when not needed. Widen our eyes, bend our heads toward the person addressed, let our mouths fall open just a little, we could all do it.

That morning I was quiet as we drove home from church. I didn't have to stand up in the share service and reach for a microphone. I didn't have to try to edify the body with what I was learning, but I had made the effort. And then Tess had to call me up short and remind me that what I learned in school was basically worthless.

The stretch of Highway 62 seemed endless that day. I had no home on either end of the road. There was no place to be. Not the church, where I faked it. Not my house, where I did more of the same. There was no place the car could take me that would truly be home. Your home is where God is, I reminded myself as I clutched my Bible, resolving to be better, to do better. Then I'd count the telephone poles, the fast-food restaurants, the times Eric cleared his throat. I didn't want to think too deeply or repent too thoroughly.

DELUGE

In May of 1994 I graduated Phi Beta Kappa with a degree in English. I was thirty-eight years old. My family took lots of pictures that day. I am on the deck posing with my mother and Hal. My mother is smiling broadly, even though she has told me many times my first priority was my home, not my studies. I am holding my diploma. On either side of me stand my kids and Eric. I look elated, relieved, vindicated. My hair is very long and streaked gold. I wear a form-fitting black dress with gold buttons and black high heels. It is clear something is happening to me.

I had submitted a portfolio of my poetry and applied to the M.F.A. Creative Writing Program at the University of Arkansas. When I received the letter of acceptance that spring, I thanked God for letting me get into graduate school, and then I did my best to forget Him.

Nobody in the M.F.A. program knew that I was almost forty. The other students assumed I was ten years younger, and I was glad. I dreaded conversations with direct questions of how old my children were. I didn't want anyone to know. I wanted to be just another graduate student, but of course I wasn't.

My new colleagues found my history of Fundamentalist Christianity exotic. They asked me lots of questions, most of which I tried to answer without a great deal of detail or comment, just said that I was leaving it behind for good. I knew they would call my past life freakish. Religion simply had never been an issue in their lives. Some had attended liberal churches as children, several were Jewish, but no one admitted to having ever seriously considered the idea of God. I didn't understand that. You couldn't just disregard the whole concept of a Creator of the cosmos without reflection, could you? My colleagues and professors, for the most part, said yes, you could. Religion was a tool of the oppressor, the patriarchy, the Man. The masses were tamed and controlled by the idea of happiness in another realm; it had always been this way.

"But now you're free from all that," they always ended up saying. They expected me to be elated, the prisoner who had lost her manacles. I nodded my agreement, but I was always fingering my wrists, trying to decide if the absence of restraint felt good or terrifying. Most of the time it felt both.

"Luke thinks Carolyn's a babe," Sue, a translation student, announced from the front seat of the car. It was midafternoon and we had decided to find an early happy hour somewhere before the poetry reading that evening.

"*All right*, Carolyn," Don said. "Go for it, have an affair with Luke. He's hot."

Don had a compulsion to go out-of-bounds, to say things no one else would dare to say. He was true to himself in a way I had never been. I admired that. On the surface, we had nothing in common. He was thirty; I was ten years older. He was a Jew from New York. I was a former tongues speaker from Iowa. He had been a big-city music editor. I hadn't listened to any popular music in two decades. In spite of our differences, we had become close friends.

"I'm still married," I said automatically.

"So?" almost everyone in the car answered.

"So, I can't," I said.

"Why the fuck not?" asked Don. "Don't you think it would be nice?"

"Oh, Luke," Sue said. "What a stud. Hmm . . . imagine him giving you a pearl necklace, Carolyn."

Everyone laughed. I had no idea what the joke meant.

"She doesn't know what that is," Leonard said as he adjusted the rearview mirror to see my face. "Tell her, Sue."

"It's like this, Carolyn. You're having sex with a guy and he puts his prick between your breasts, comes, and then what do you know . . . a pearl necklace right around your slender little neck."

"That's lovely," I said, looking out the window. My colleagues had taken me on as a project of sorts, an aging and innocent initiate who needed to be introduced to the secular world. If I was shocked, and I was often, I wasn't going to let on.

Underpinning the writing program was an unspoken allegiance to the writers' legacy of being crazy and irresponsible. That meant a lot of drinking, some drugs. Ironic conversations, sanitized, of course, to be politically correct. Innuendo, constant references to past sex, future sex, kinky sex. Some of the behavior was just plain silly – people getting together and having a drink in their underwear, taking pictures, and giggling over them later. Some of it was dangerous, secret affairs and liaisons, infidelity.

"My God," Julie said loudly beside me. "Look – it's those picketers again."

We were driving past the abortionist's office. Three picketers marched, holding their signs: large photographs of severed limbs and heads, a weeping Jesus, a plaintive "Mommy, Don't Kill Me".

"Jesus," Sue said.

"This is so upsetting," Julie said. "I can't let myself think about it, I just can't. Those women – what are they thinking? They want someone else to decide what happens to their bodies?"

"Coat hangers," Sue said. "That's what we need. We could

276

throw them at these assholes. Do we have any in the office?" She looked at me.

I shook my head quickly and looked at my hands. They were shaking. What was I doing in this car? Why wasn't I protecting the babies anymore?

"Forget it," I said. "They're nuts. Anyway, I thought we were going to go get a drink somewhere."

"You're a wild thing, aren't you, Carolyn?" Leonard asked approvingly.

"Not so much," I said. "I just need a drink, that's all."

"Me too," said Don. "I want an ice-cold fetus straight up with a twist."

That night after the reading, I went to a party given in the poet's honor. I knew I couldn't stay long, but I liked seeing my professors in their own homes. I stood in front of their bookcases and found the books they had written tucked among the others. I was pulling one out when one of my favorite professors joined me. He had once studied for a master's in divinity but was now a respected novelist who disparaged religion whenever he had the opportunity.

"You'll grow out of this, Carolyn" he said, putting his arm around my shoulders. "Religion is small, superstitious thinking, and you live in a scientific world. That's kindergarten stuff."

I nodded, bit my lip, and smiled, grateful for his assurance. At the same time, I was thinking of Scriptures that would counter him. The short time I had been in the world, I had discovered that a pagan could be as close-minded as a believer, smug and intolerant, mocking something he had no way of understanding. My professor held his glass of wine, smiling at me indulgently, *tsk-tsk*ing my folly when he didn't know a thing about it.

On Sundays I would attend church, perform in my dramas, and accept accolades from the church members who told me how much my ministry blessed them. If he was in earshot, Eric nodded proudly.

I had become a hypocrite, the worst thing you could be. The kind of person whom Jesus spews from His mouth.

If I was going to leave Eric, I would first have to leave God. That terrified me, but I could not go on living my life of semicelibacy, the furtive and silent fumbling in the dark with no kisses in or out of bed.

I'd heard it preached hundreds of times: It was all a matter of dying to self. Lay down your life. Pick up the cross. Empty yourself. Become broken. Humble yourself in the sight of the Lord. Crucify your flesh. I just had to put aside my own desires in favor of God's. His Kingdom was what was important, not my fulfillment or pleasure. Besides, one day I would be fulfilled. One day I would reign with Him and be perfect. Why couldn't I just hang on?

In the end, only I knew. I hated the guilt I felt when Eric handed me my robe, asked me if I was warm enough, did I want anything from the store. I wanted more. His strange servility tore at my flesh, the memento mori an insistent thrumming in my organs. Every year I felt diminished; every day I felt less alive.

When Sue told me that Luke thought I was attractive, I began to think about that a lot. He was just a kid in his late twenties, but he was an extraordinary writer. It would be fun to mess around with someone like Luke, to pretend I was just another graduate student. I thought he might understand me a little. He was from Utah and he knew about a Fundamentalist faith; all his friends were Mormons, which allowed him to observe firsthand the tyranny of a church that will concede no salvation outside its creed.

"Let me get this straight, there's seven years' tribulation before or after the rapture?" Luke asked me one day while we were drinking coffee.

"Well, it depends if you're a premillenniest or a postmillenniest. Actually, there are some midmillenniest believers as well," I said, staring at his hands. They were large hands, hairless, his nails perfectly formed, clean and shiny.

"This is all nonsense, isn't it? I mean, the rapture, who ever heard of such a thing? It's fairy-tale stuff," he said, taking a large gulp of his coffee.

He looked so self-satisfied, I felt an old twinge of resentment.

"Well, there's a lot of examples in the Old Testament that are metaphors for an evacuation on earth of the true believers. Look at Noah and the ark – that's a picture of the rapture. God pulls out his chosen followers from his judgment on earth. They were protected from the flood. Lot and his family – they were taken out of Sodom before God rained down fire and–"

I heard myself saying the word *brimstone* and cringed. It was such a biblical word, not a word spoken in the ugly outdated cafeteria of the University of Arkansas Student Union. I looked up at the geometric murals, the stained burlap walls, and wished I could take it back.

But Luke was now genuinely interested in my exposition. "Really? What else? What else in the Old Testament could be construed to predict the end of the world?"

His mouth was open, just a bit. His lower teeth were white and straight. When he stretched out his legs under the booth, his jeans brushed my leg, and I wished desperately for a drink in my hand, candlelight, a conversation of innuendo. Instead we sat in a cafeteria smelling of chicken-fried steak, with merciless dust-ridden light streaming across our faces while we discussed the Bible.

I sighed and slowly told him all I knew. I recited prophecies from the Old Testament that prophesied the birth of Christ. I told him about Daniel and his visions of the Antichrist. I discussed the Revelation for a long, long time. Luke was alternately fascinated, discomfited, and scornful. He asked a lot of questions, stared at the table in front of him, and fidgeted with his unused silverware.

I had all the Bible and the Holy Spirit to win him; the challenge, the conquest, everything was before me, but the whole time I sat across the booth from Luke, I was the one who wanted to be won over; I wanted to be the one seduced.

As graduate students, we taught composition and literature to large classes of freshmen born and raised in Arkansas and poorly prepared for college. We consoled each other over the stacks of papers we had to read and carefully grade. It was a tremendous amount of work if you took it seriously, and almost all of us did. Five of us shared a long, narrow office. We were in the middle of a grading session when Luke walked in. It was the first time I'd seen him since our discussion of the end times over coffee.

"Hey," he said. "Way too much frivolity in here. You're writers, damn it. I bet there's not a self-respecting potential suicide in this room."

Don looked up, cleared his throat.

"Sorry, Don, didn't mean to forget about you," Luke said, settling onto the sagging couch in the corner of our office.

"No offense taken," Don said flatly.

"Julie's student wrote that he loves a fine 'dairy air' on a girl," Sue said. "Two words: D-a-i-r-y A-i-r."

Luke whooped. "God, that's great. I love those dairy airs, too," he said, stretching his hand in my direction. "That gal over there – she's got a great one. Too bad she's so religious. All she wants to talk about is the end of the world. What's it called again, Carolyn?"

"The rapture," I said quietly.

"The what?" Sue asked.

"Jesus, I know about that," Leonard said. "When I was a kid, my parents dragged me to this movie at our church called *I Wish We'd All Been Ready*. It was about the rapture – when all Christians disappear and it's the end of the world."

Luke nodded at me, encouraging me to say something. I didn't want to.

"It scared the shit out of me," Leonard said, laughing nervously. "I knew I was a sinner and my parents were going to be raptured without me. I had nightmares for years afterward."

The shelves of the office were filled with literary journals, student papers, ancient coffee mugs, and brown paper towels from the rest room, our only napkins. Some of us had brought art and prints to hang above our desks. Don displayed a book called *Why Cats Paint*, a Barney poster, and an autographed picture of Heather Whitestone, the first deaf Miss America.

Everyone began asking questions. I turned away from them and let Leonard describe the scenes: the planes suddenly without pilots, the cake mixer whirring into oblivion, the electric razors dropped into the sink, buzzing for days on end. Suddenly Toni, the lawyer-turned-writer, gasped loudly.

"Oh, God," she moaned. "I saw that, too. Jesus Christ, that was a terrorist piece of shit."

I knew they would be fascinated to know that I had watched *I Wish We'd All Been Ready* with no skepticism whatsoever. But I was tired of being the novelty act in the M.F.A. program. Some of my colleagues had never heard of the rapture, and others were incredulous that the film depicted it. I opened my mouth once and closed it. I looked down at my legs, black tights, and stylish shoes. I tried to remember who I was again. I saw the face of Jesus, fleetingly, that face I had loved for so long.

I gathered my things, picked up my backpack, and felt my face burn. I was ashamed of what I had been all of those years.

Then on the heels of that, I was struck with a second and deeper shame: I had just denied something very sacred, something holy. It was my closest moment to hearing the cock crow. I kept picturing the planes that went down in the film. Again and again, they dove toward earth. Explosion and fire, smoke everywhere. I could hardly see a thing.

Anthony Hawking – the writer-in-residence that fall – gave a party in the middle of the semester. The fiction workshop had just finished round one of shopping one another's stories: critiquing, blasting, occasionally praising a fellow student's work. Anthony was mixing cocktails as fast as we could drink them. We were all in various stages of inebriation. I was still not used to drinking and was the first to become sloppy. I joined some of the writers in the darkened dining room.

"You guys should feel the muscle in my calf. It's like rock, it's so hard," I announced.

Leonard smiled broadly and rushed over; next Jack; stoned as usual, moved in slowly; and finally Luke grinned his way over to us.

"Not bad, Carolyn," Leonard said, smiling. He pushed his blond hair back from his forehead. "Not bad at all. In fact, in my expert opinion, you've got the best legs in the program."

Jack reached for my other leg with pincerlike hands, robotic and automated. I didn't like his dead eyes and moved away. Leonard was distracted by a younger woman, Lana, who had come into the room and stretched herself out along the door frame. She wasn't wearing a bra. "I can see her nipples, Carolyn," Leonard had whispered earlier in the evening. "It's such a turn-on. Quite thrilling, actually."

Luke followed me into the deserted hallway.

"I'm more interested in feeling your thighs," he said.

I burst out laughing. So it was true – he was attracted to me.

"No way, Luke. Go ask Lana," I said, downing the rest of my martini.

"You're the head turner, not Lana," he said, reaching for my waist. He kissed me. He just put his cold mouth on mine and kept it there while I laughed, and then he laughed and still our lips were together.

Two days after the party, I was sitting in Dr. Hawking's office for the midterm conference he had scheduled with each one of us. He held my manuscript in front of him. It was a pretty transparent story. Like everyone else in the fiction shop, I wrote about myself. Just changed my name to Ellen and wrote away. In my story, "Deluge", a middle-aged woman considers an affair with a stranger on a plane.

"This woman wants sex ba-a-ad," he drawled. He looked at me candidly. "Boy, does she ever want it."

I shrugged. "Yes, she does. But she wants more than sex. She's searching for a lot more than sex."

Dr. Hawking snorted. "Do you think she can handle the fast track?" he asked, raising his eyebrows.

"Well, I think it's clear from the story that she decides she can't. She doesn't go through with it," I said as professionally as I could.

"Oh, but I think she's changed her mind," he said meaningfully.

I played dumb. "I sure don't see that in the story. I don't know where you're getting that."

He paused and looked at me with the slightest shake of his head. He shook a cigarette out of the pack and put it between his lips, never taking his eyes off me.

"She's going after what she wants," he said shrewdly.

I told him that I had to leave, that I had just a few minutes left on the meter. I stood up, folded the manuscript, and put it in my purse. I smiled sweetly in Anthony Hawking's direction but could not make myself look him in the eye.

Luke called me at home that night. Eric was sitting across the room at the computer, so it was a curious, stilted conversation, but what Luke told me chilled my bones.

"Hawking saw us the other night," he said.

"Shit," I said. Eric looked up from across the room. I turned my face away from him. "I knew it. What did he say?"

"He was into it," Luke said. "He told me to go for it. Have an affair with you."

"What else, Luke? What else did he say? You have to tell me."

Luke hesitated. "He said you'd be savage, that you'd be a hell of a lover."

"Oh, Jeez," I said. "My God."

"Don't let it get to you. Everyone's kind of sick around here. They like other people to act out their fantasies for them," Luke said gently. "They love nothing better than gossip, you know that. Writers are assholes, Carolyn. Everyone knows that."

The dog started barking at the door, and I told Lauren to let him out. Eric asked, "Are you about through? I need to get online."

"Carolyn?" Luke asked.

"Sorry, I gotta go. Things are crazy around here. I'll see you at school," I said, and hung up.

"Who was that?" Eric asked.

"Nobody, just someone who had a question about an assignment," I answered so smoothly that I scared myself.

I kept hearing Hawking's voice: "She's going after what she wants." Yes, I finally decided. I'm going to do it. I'm leaving.

I told Eric that I needed to move out for a while.

"What are you talking about? Move out for a while?"

"Eric, you know what I know. Our marriage is paper thin; there's not much here. You can live with it this way. I can't."

"Then we'll get counseling. You don't just leave."

"Just until the end of term, Eric," I said. "Just let me have these six weeks by myself. I'll spend the weekends with Lauren and I'll start marriage counseling with you, I promise."

"Who are you sleeping with?" he groaned.

"No one," I said, relieved to be telling the truth for once.

He found an apartment for me, insisting that it be in a safe location. He wrote out a check for the deposit and handed it to me. I took it, put it in my purse, and turned back to my packing.

"Carolyn."

I turned toward him; he was sitting on the edge of the bed with tears running down his face. He tried to speak but couldn't.

"I will," he said, bursting into tears, "pine for you until the day I die."

I rushed across the room and held him. We both cried. I watched us in the bedroom mirror. He was crumpled against my chest, his arms around my waist. I thought of Keats's last letter to Fanny Brawne: "I wish I was either in your arms full of faith or that a thunderbolt would strike me." I had spent my days of apostasy listening for thunder, and I would never have welcomed a bolt of lightning more than at that moment. I held him and stroked his hair, murmuring, "I do love you, Eric. It's not that I don't love you. Please understand."

But he couldn't see it, of course. He didn't understand how I could claim to love him and still finish my packing. I could hardly understand it myself.

When I pulled out of the driveway on that last Sunday at home, my car was loaded down with my clothes, sheets, linens, and dishes. Lauren was jumping on the trampoline. She wasn't bothered by my new living arrangements, something we had told the children was just a matter of saving commuting time while I finished a heavy course load that spring. We told no one in the church at all. No accountability, the Elders at Fountain of Joy would have said, and they would have been right.

Lauren didn't particularly like me. She was fourteen, and I had been in school since she was seven years old. She grew into a daddy's girl while I went to class and studied, stayed late for parties. She waved at me and kept jumping. I couldn't look away. She tucked and spun, her arms and legs spread into the March sky. She's up in the air, I told myself. I backed out of the driveway, but I could not stop seeing her arms flung out, her body frozen in midair, her desperate desire for flight. My baby, as anchorless as I. I can't possibly do this. Time to unload the car now. Time to go back into the house. And then I drove away.

At the age of forty, I was on my own. I had an apartment and I lived there *alone*. For the first time in my life, I had a bedroom that belonged only to me. I had walls that were my walls and drawers that were my drawers and a front door that was my front door and a phone number assigned to me and only me. I knew I was letting everyone down: my parents, my children, the church, my husband. More than anything, I was letting down God. I had not persevered in my faith, the final P in TULIP. I had denied all of it now. And I was going to pay for it; that's what I remember thinking the most.

I slept in my new bedroom alone. I pulled down the sheets and covers and slept on my side of the bed out of habit. When I awoke, I reached for Eric.

"This is what you wanted," I whispered to myself. "Don't you dare cry."

Two things kept me going that spring. First was my planned trip to Ireland. I was going to attend graduate school on the west coast of Ireland for six weeks in a sister writing program with the University of Arkansas. I borrowed all the money I could in a student loan and counted the days until I was there. Second was my friendship with Don. Unlike Luke, with whom I shared a kiss or two and not much more after that, Don stuck with me in those months of depression and anxiety. We took late night walks. He told me I was being very brave to make this break and that the best part of my life was still before me.

"You remind me of Edna St. Vincent Millay," he said.

"Why?"

"You're so girl-like, so wistful, but you're damn sexy, too. 'My candle burns at both ends' – she was the one who wrote that, you know. She died after sitting on the stairs all night smoking and rereading *The Aeneid*."

"My God," I breathed. I could see her, the book slipping from her hand.

It began to rain and we ducked into a stairwell. Don leaned against the door and kept talking, wiping the rain out of his eyes with the edge of his thrift shop shirt.

"She lived for poetry," he said. "But she had lovers and she traveled all over the world. That's what you need to do, Carolyn. I'm fucking glad you're going to Ireland."

"I can't wait," I said. "I don't think I ever believed I would actually cross the ocean."

"You'll blossom there, C. You really will. You'll probably go to Yeats's Thoor Ballylee. You have to. God, what an amazing man – he used to get shots of monkey hormones in his balls to keep him young."

The rain paused, and I rushed out of the stairwell ahead of him.

"Look, Don, so many people leave their curtains drawn."

I stared hungrily into the lighted windows of my new neighborhood. I knew this world, the one with lamps and Olan Mills family pictures and the smell of dinner still lingering in the kitchen. Jonquils and irises, tulips along the driveway, a basketball hoop over the garage door. There was still a part of me that wanted to live in a house like that, that wanted to be chauffeuring kids and sitting on committees at the junior high. But it was too late for all that; no one would let me in if I knocked, no one would recognize me anymore. I was outside now, where the sidewalks were buckled and uneven and pools of water stood in the broken places. I stepped around all that I could, but it was dark and I couldn't see well. And then it began raining again.

After six weeks, the school term was over and I moved back in with Eric. We had a brittle peace while I prepared to leave for Ireland. My head was still full of the drama of becoming the next Edna St. Vincent Millay, and it was hard to begin the housewife duties I knew by heart: sprinkle Comet, scrub, wash the pine steps of dog hairs, taxi Lauren to her best friend's house, fix Sunday dinner. I peeled potatoes and thought of the visiting writer dedicating his reading to me: "a beautiful woman just coming into her own." I dusted my oak tables and remembered the frank admiration of my professors, an embrace under a porch light, late night discussions about Chekhov while a flock of crows settled around us, all of us earnest and intellectual and wise about life and love. I nearly swooned in remembering. At the same time, Eric was begging me to get counseling, scolding me about my neglect, worrying about my approaching absence overseas. We attempted to have sex one night, but it was an awkward and ill-timed effort. He hovered over me, his eyes suddenly reminding me of the young boy, the high school boy who had liked my poem so much that he had cut it out of the newspaper. Or even further back, the anxious ten-year-old with a good-size fish, his boyhood picture I had framed and put on our dresser.

"Say it, say you want me," he pleaded.

"I can't," I wept. "I can't say that."

We began to read together instead. Every night we both held our books and stayed on our own sides of the bed. We read late into the night and then we slept. I counted the mornings I had left to wake up next to him. He touched my feet with his and told me it was his only comfort, his only reassurance that he knew me at all.

Sometimes I'd find him in the living room, cradling his guitar. He had begun playing the old songs, the songs we had listened to before our conversion. He sang until his voice cracked, and then he would pull out records, old pagan records he had never been able to part with – America; Loggins & Messina; Crosby, Stills, Nash & Young – and play the scratchy songs on the turntable. What magic did he still think those songs held? What part of his brain still believed in music as a healer? I let him play the songs. I fixed him dinner. I let him touch my feet each night.

IRELAND

That summer my family scattered. Allison was at Stanford with an internship. Joshua had completed his first year of college and bought a car. And Lauren was going to be at summer camp, her grandparents' house in Iowa, and with her best friend's family on vacation. My children had seemed to accept my apartment in Fayetteville as a temporary thing. But they had certainly noticed the steady change in me. I wasn't preaching to them all the time. I was always at the computer, writing poetry or working on a short story. I had started skipping church. I wasn't the mother they remembered. And now I was going to Ireland.

Allison bought me a travel guide for Ireland and told me to take lots of pictures. Joshua kept talking about Guinness. "Watch it, Ma, that stuff will sneak up on you." Lauren just asked me for twenty bucks and didn't say anything about my trip at all.

Eric was still, out of habit, supportive. "I'm happy for you, honey," he said, even during that last week before I left. Oh, I wanted to stop it all then. Stop everything that had happened, take it back, turn away, repent. But I could not slow the momentum. I could not shake the feeling that I was on the verge of true happiness, that I had to be brave and do the hard stuff necessary to get there. I didn't want to think about Eric or my marriage or the church. There would be nothing for me to obsess over in Ireland but literature and history. There would be museums and cathedrals. I had a vague idea of cultivating a polite and distant relationship with the European God. I believed Him to be wise and tolerant, patient for time and history to see His will finally accomplished, not like the fiery Fundamentalist and choleric God of Middle America.

During those six weeks, I went to Christian marriage counseling because I had promised Eric I would. Every week Eric and I drove to the counselor's office, a squat brick building downtown. The counselor was especially revered in Fundamentalist circles. He had saved many marriages that the Enemy had almost destroyed.

This became the pattern. The counselor, a large man with a beefy ex–football player's face who wore Hawaiian shirts, quickly discerned that our marriage was in trouble because of me. I was obviously a wanton woman, and he was going to deal with me.

"Are you sleeping with anyone?" he asked.

"No," I answered quietly, studying his wedding ring on his finger. I could almost see him rolling up his sleeves, rubbing his hands together, and relishing the one-on-one with a sinning woman. We would spend an hour in his office. The counselor divided up the time between Eric and me. I got fifty-five minutes while Eric sat in the waiting room. Then Eric got a five-minute update on the state of his sinning wife from his grieving brother in Christ while I stared at the fish tank. I avoided the periodicals and books on all sides of me: *The Sword of the Lord, Holiness in Marriage, God's Way to Harmony.*

Then the counselor began scheduling sessions for me alone. Sometimes he was almost amused, it seemed. Other times he was horrified at the way I was flagrantly turning my back on God and Eric.

"Do you know what you're doing? You're crucifying Christ all over again. You've been driving the nails through His wrists and ankles. You've become an enemy of the cross," he said dramatically. "That's who you are, woman."

I looked at his shoes. They were expensive: wine-colored loafers with tassels.

"God won't let you get by with any of this," he said, squinting his eyes at me. He straightened the ring on his left hand and cleared his throat. "He is going to crush you."

I nodded, miserably certain he was right. The thought of doom was never very far from my mind. I could not reason this away; no amount of bravado lessened my fear that I was going to suffer judgment from the hand of God.

"Last year, just about this time," the counselor began, "I was at McDonald's eating an Egg McMuffin. About ten o'clock in the morning. I looked across the way and saw a clergyman I recognized. He was the pastor of some liberal church in town, and everybody knew he was having an affair with his secretary."

My mind was racing. Why is he telling me this story?

"Well, God told me to go over there and tell that sorry sinner to repent, to turn away from evil. I didn't want to say anything to him, I admit, I didn't want to. I wanted to eat my breakfast and get out of there," he said, looking at me as though he expected my sympathy. I began to nod encouragingly at him, out of habit, I suppose. I stifled it, though, and stared at his tie instead.

"But I had to obey God. I walked across the restaurant and stood beside him. He looked up at me. I said, 'Brother, God knows what you're doing. Turn away from your sin. Turn away and be healed. If you don't, God's gonna deal with you.' Fella gives me a look and tells me to get the hell out. I left then. I'd done all I could do. Later that day, this same guy loses control of his car out on the Pig Trail. His car goes over the side of the mountain. Dead instantly."

I lifted my chin then and looked him in the eye. I dared him to continue.

"Sister," he said, "I'm eating my Egg McMuffin all over again."

We both sat there for a while afterward and didn't say anything at all. He leaned back in his swivel chair and looked at the ceiling. I crossed my legs and bit my lip. The tissue I had been twisting for the last fifty-five minutes was limp and docile in my hand.

"Well," I finally said.

He checked his watch and nodded. I stood up. He opened the door for me and waved me toward the receptionist. "Make an appointment for next week."

I wrote a check for one hundred dollars and then I left the redbrick office of the Whole Counsel of God. I looked both ways before crossing the street. I wore my seat belt and I obeyed all the traffic laws, but I knew now it was only a matter of time. Judgment was coming, and I could not escape.

I desperately wanted to laugh it all off. I tried to tell myself that the counselor was an idiot, but he was someone I had looked up to for ten years – someone important in the Fundamentalist community. Part of me longed to capitulate, to say I had been wrong, that I had gone way too far. Everyone in the church would be so thrilled, and God would be glorified. I could give my testimony and stop other women from making the same mistakes. I even imagined the counselor and me traveling all over Arkansas as we told my story in churches across the state.

"This woman was deceived, brothers and sisters. She was deceived by the Father of Lies himself. She just about destroyed her family and herself in the process," the counselor would say, and he would be looking at me tenderly this time.

I would weep in repentance as I told my story. Those listening would murmur in compassion for my pain and gratitude to God for rescuing me from myself.

I closed my eyes, imagining the thunderous applause of the righteous. The shouts of praise to God rising to the vaulted ceilings. The light streaming through the stained-glass windows. The presence of the Holy Spirit and arms outstretched toward heaven.

Yes, it was almost real, nearly a possibility.

But in the end, it wasn't real enough. I pulled into my driveway and said aloud, "I am through with this, with everything, I'm done.

"I'm not going back to counseling, Eric," I said as soon as I walked up the stairs to the living room. I threw my keys on the desk and pulled off my high heels.

"What do you mean? You have three sessions left," Eric said, looking up from the book on Christian marriage he was reading. "You promised you'd do this."

"He said God was going to crush me, Eric," I said. "He threatened me, he told me an awful story about some guy, some minister guy, being killed on the Pig Trail because he wouldn't repent of his sin," I said. "I am not going back there." I meant to sound emphatic and strong, but suddenly I could picture my own horrible accident. I could see myself flying through the air as I plunged off one of the dark hillsides outside of town. I took a deep breath, and it caught in the middle of my chest. I didn't want to cry again. One of us was always crying.

Eric closed his book and stood up from the sofa. "He shouldn't have said that to you. I'm sorry." He held his arms open for me.

I couldn't hold it back. I wept in his arms while he patted my back, smoothed my hair, told me how sorry he was again and again. I looked down at the book he had been reading, *What God Hath Put Together*. A man and a woman smiled at each other with perfectly white teeth. They each had a cardigan knotted over their shoulders and Bibles in their hands.

"Is that a good book?" I asked, pulling away from him. I wiped my eyes with the back of my hand and picked up the book and leafed through it.

He looked embarrassed and nodded. "It's all right."

"I should make dinner," I said, handing his book back to him.

"Carolyn, what are we going to do?" he asked.

"I'm going to Ireland," I said. "That's what I'm going to do."

"Damn it, what about this family? What about your children? What about Lauren? She's only fourteen – she needs her family together."

"She'll have a family, Eric, no matter what," I said. "I would never leave my children."

"You're leaving us all! You're going to the other side of the world, leaving us all!"

No, you're the only one I'm leaving. That's what I wanted to say, but I couldn't. He was distraught, red faced, and hopeless as he stood in front of me. The text in the book he had been reading was highlighted and underlined. He had scribbled notes in the margins, waiting for me to come home from Christian counseling to tell him what I had learned. Instead, I had thrown it all back in his face. I could not make him more miserable this day. I would not. I made him a ham-and-cheese sandwich and then I washed the dishes.

The next day I called a lawyer.

When word got out that I was leaving Eric, the church was angry, grieved, and vindictive. I began receiving phone calls, notes in the mail, unannounced visits from the brethren. Dean was very ill, and Violet had all she could do to care for him. My abdication was letting her down, both of them; I knew this and I deeply regretted the additional pain I brought them. She called me from the phone in the hospital lobby and left messages, but I did not call her back.

The brothers and sisters who wrote me notes were no longer praising me for my talent or dramatic skill. No, this time I received long-winded letters full of odd observations and threats: "You're worshiping at the altar of self. You are kneeling in homage to your own flesh. Your children will never ever forgive you for this. You will die alone and forsaken." The pastor-Elder of Mt. Olive Fellowship received the news sadly. He wrote me a letter accepting my resignation of membership and telling me how much he regretted my decision: "I hope you find what it is you are looking for." This, more than any other recrimination, shook me up. He wasn't condemning me for my lack of faith or my outright betrayal. It was the most *human* voice I had ever heard in the church, and I had heard it after the door was shut behind me.

Later, when I was actually flying over the Atlantic, I remembered the counselor's prophecy of my sudden doom, and I looked around me, sorry for the innocent passengers who would perish with me as our 747 fell swiftly from the sky. I imagined what it would be like to drown in the cold salt water of the North Atlantic. I mourned for my children and regretted for their sake that I had done this to myself – put myself square on God's list of the doomed. Then I opened *Dubliners* and became anesthetized by language, my solace, my resting place.

When I stepped onto Irish soil for the first time, I wasn't the girl from Allendale. I wasn't the obedient zealot with the long skirt and braid. I wasn't even the graduate student with her fistful of stories, waved in the face of any takers. I was someone else.

I shared a flat at university with four other students. We each had our own room and bath. Outside our apartment building, the river Corrib ran dark and swift. Swans swam at the edges and anglers waded out to catch trout. Wildflowers, yellow and pink, grew everywhere along the river, and I could see ruins of ancient buildings from my bedroom window. After I unpacked, I was anxious to get out and explore, but my flatmates were resting or dawdling with their unpacking. I stood in front of our apartment to see if any of the other students were going to walk into Galway City, two miles away. I watched the undergrads take off and didn't want to tag along. No one invited me to join them.

If Eric were here, I started to think, and then stopped myself. He wasn't here, and I was perfectly capable of finding my own way to town. I packed my backpack with Irish punts and a camera and a map and took off. I wandered along the river, the tall grasses tickling my legs, while I picked flowers for my room. I bought tea and scones and ate them sitting at an outdoor table alone. Galway Bay stretched blue green, almost tropically hued, in front of me. I shopped in the open market for carrots and potatoes, fresh bread, candles with wildflowers embedded inside. I browsed through shop after shop, choosing linens and jewelry for the girls, my mother, Lisa, and Delia. I found the house where Joyce had lived, a tiny little place on a narrow street. James Joyce, my God.

I went to St. Nicholas often, the church where legend says Christopher Columbus had prayed before he left for the New World. Every step I took, every cobblestone my feet brushed over, excited me. Had Columbus stepped here? Leaned on this wall, surveyed that Christ? I lit candles here and everywhere I traveled throughout Ireland. I dropped my fifty pence into the offering plate and lit my own candle. I knew nothing about lighting candles in churches; it was not a Fundamentalist practice, but I liked the idea. I could never find any words to pray, so I would just watch the flame for a while before moving on.

One day in a bookshop, I found a long, slender card with a picture of George Eliot. Underneath, this quote:

"It's never too late to be what you were meant to be."

Automatically, I assumed it was a platitude meant for my eyes. An omen. A sign. I was awash with hope and optimism.

It wasn't too late, I rejoiced. Not too late for me, after all.

But then something went wrong. My habit of translating life events into profound meanings suddenly faltered, and I knew I wasn't receiving a message from God or anything close to it. I was only reading a mass-produced card marketed to women at midlife. There was no miracle taking place in Kenny's Book Shop. The fat woman near me jostled my arm and looked at me without apology. I could hear a sharp voice in the store-room. Someone pounded a bell at the front of the store; it rang and rang, but no one answered. I was alone in the universe.

My hand trembled as I held the card. I read it again and then placed it back on the shelf. There is no God, I groaned inwardly. There is no God. What am I going to do? I didn't know how to walk out of the store with that knowledge. I imagined waking up morning after morning in a world where there was no God. What a lonely place it was going to be. I wore my sunglasses on that cloudy day in Galway City. I wept for blocks as I walked toward the blue green sea. I did not pray.

A week later I kept a promise I had made to William, an Irishman who had also been an M.F.A. student in Fayetteville. After taking his comprehensive exams, William had packed and sold everything as he prepared to return to Ireland. He had taken me aside at his going-away party and asked me if we could get together when I arrived in Galway, where he lived with his elderly mother. He wanted me to meet his mother and to show me around. I'd look him up, wouldn't I?

He had made it clear many times over the years in Fayette-ville that he found me attractive, but I wasn't interested. He was a drifter, a vagabond, the sort of man who had gotten by on his looks and charm. He was now close to fifty years old, with no wife, children, or real accomplishments. So, whether he was talented or not, and William was talented, I knew better than to get involved with a man like that, no matter how handsome he was. I agreed to stay the weekend with him and his mother. It would be interesting to see how real Irish people lived, and if his mother was going to be there, it would certainly be safe enough.

When William's mother opened the door, her face was radiant with joy.

"Oh, Carolyn!" she exclaimed. "A hundred thousand welcomes. Ye must come in, your room is all ready. William, darling, take her to her room."

And there was William, improbably tanned and healthy looking. His face was as illuminated as his mother's, but shy and modest, eager. A boy's face as he stood beside his red-haired mother. I was charmed. He carried my bags to my bedroom, where pink roses from the garden had been placed on the dresser. The walls were turquoise, the furniture large and imposing, a thick comforter on the bed. I had never been in an Irish home, and the wonder of my whole adventure swept over me again. I smiled at William.

"This is lovely. I don't know how to thank you," I said, pulling off my cardigan.

"You're here, Carolyn. You have no idea how often I pictured you here," he said. He reached out to touch one of the roses. "I picked these for you. Do you like them?'

"They're beautiful," I said, and then I didn't know what else to say.

"You should rest," William said quickly "I'm sorry for standing here. Please. I'll wake you for dinner." He closed the door behind him.

I stripped to my full-length slip and then lay under the comforter. The curtains blocked out almost all of the late afternoon night. When I awoke, it was evening. I reached over to turn on the bedside lamp and then looked at my face in the mirror on the dresser. I reached for my hairbrush and began to brush my hair.

William knocked softly. I looked down at my slip. Why not? It was modest enough. "Come in," I said.

If he was startled to see me in a slip, he didn't let on. He crossed the room and sat in the rose-colored chair in the corner and chatted as I continued to brush my hair. I brushed slower and slower as I felt his eyes trace my back, my bare arms, my long hair. Good God, I thought, I'm in Europe, half-naked with a handsome man in my bedroom. I smiled to myself. I kept smiling when I turned to William and told him I was looking forward to seeing more of Galway City.

The next day we sat at the kitchen table and ate scones with marmalade. I poured tea for William and watched as he added three sugar cubes and a large dollop of milk. William started to tell me how long he had been attracted to me, how much he wanted to be with me. I told him that even though Eric and I would be getting divorced, I wasn't ready for a serious relationship with anyone else.

"I want you to fall in love with me," he said, gripping my shoulders and looking down at me intently. Leonard used to say that William looked like a movie star. He was the closest thing I'd ever seen. He was tall, with wavy gray hair and great cheekbones, gray green eyes that were clear and luminous when he was taking care of himself.

"Not now, William," I said. "I don't know what's going to happen to me when I get back home. You've got stuff to think about, too, don't you? Looking for a job, I mean. You can't keep living on the dole."

"Put your arms around me," he said.

We stood there holding each other in his mother's kitchen, and then he bent down to kiss me. A long, gentle kiss that left me feeling warm and weary, but happy. It felt so good to be kissed. I didn't think I would ever be able to take something like that for granted.

After that weekend in William's home, I had two more

weeks in Ireland. Each day I went to my classes and then met William afterward. He held me in his arms while we watched the sunset at Galway Bay. He rowed us up the river Corrib and tied the boat next to a castle ruin. We lay in the tall grass surrounding the castle and talked. Once in a while, he leaned over and kissed me. My head was spinning as I looked over his shoulder into the rare Irish sun. The walls of the castle were charred and broken, but still they stood. Broken people. Broken places. No God. Take the happiness you can find. All of this running through my mind as he held me and whispered to me and told me I was the most beautiful woman he had ever known, that life with me was his dream, his only hope for the future.

The last day before I left to go back to the States, William and I sat on the spongy green grass on top of the Cliffs of Mohr. I had just told him that I would not sleep with him, not that summer. I didn't want to have sex on the night of my departure and then be guilty, sad, and filled with longing months later. That wasn't the kind of relationship I had waited a lifetime for.

"But I'll write you a letter," he said.

I wanted to laugh. A letter? He wanted to share the most intimate of encounters and then respond with airmail? I shook my head again.

"No, I can't, William. I just can't," I said. I watched a seagull that hesitated in flight nearby. It was so close that I could hear its wings, delicate and forceful.

He was silent, his face turned toward O'Brien's Tower to our left.

"You don't understand what it's like, to be in love with you so long, and now you're leaving," he said quietly. "I've been alone a long time, Carolyn. I don't want to spend the rest of my life alone. I want a life with you more than I've ever wanted anything."

"Then we'll just have to see if it happens. Yes, write to me. Come to Fayetteville at Christmas," I said. "We can see if there's a way for us to be together."

He sighed. "Let's go to dinner, shall we?"

We walked along the lane to Liscanour. It was a misty night, the air was drenched with the fragrance of the wild roses that grew along the stone walls on either side of the road. The sea crashed against the cliffs in the distance. No cars anywhere to be seen. William grew quieter and quieter and didn't speak until midway through our dinner at a dark pub in town.

"I'd be a better friend to you than lover, Carolyn," he said sadly. "I should just give up on the idea and be your friend."

"That's what I've always had for a lover," I said. "A friend."

"You have no idea what true passion is, you know that, don't you?" William asked. "You don't even know what it's like, to be lost in someone, to long for the burning, the intensity never to end, your arms and legs wrapped around each other, calling out in ecstasy. I don't care what kind of religious bullshit you used to believe, making love is the only miracle. It's what I want with you."

"Yeah," I said softly. "You're right. I don't know what that's like." I pushed around the chunks of greasy lamb in my stew. "Do you want some of this?"

He looked deflated, hopeless. "No, I've had enough. We should probably get back."

"Yeah, I'm really tired. No, I mean, I'm really *knackered*," I said, and smiled at him, pleading for peace between us.

He leaned across the table, reaching for my face. He held it in his large hands, just cradled it, and looked into my eyes.

"You're such a beautiful woman," he said. "I'll wait for you. There's nothing else I can do, is there?"

We left the pub and walked through the streets to the bus stop that would take us back to Galway. The next morning, I hugged his mother good-bye, gathered my luggage, and got into the taxi William had called to take us to Shannon Airport. Our taxi driver told us stories during the hour-long drive. William squeezed my hand in the backseat and told his own stories back to the driver. Language and history and Irish exuberance filled the car as we sped in the bright July sun. I didn't know what was going to happen, but I knew that I was living a life that I had never dared hope to have. Uncertainty was not the dread state I had imagined it to be. You were just floating a little bit, that's all, and sometimes it felt as if you were flying.

On the long trip home a sign flashed above our heads in the 747: "Flotation Devices Are Stored Below Your Seat". My God, I thought. I glanced around at the other passengers to see if they were alarmed. No one seemed to have noticed. I took a deep breath and looked out the window to look for fire coming from the engines or leaking fuel. Then I looked down at my finger. I was wearing the Claddaugh ring that William had given me before I left. Two hands held a crowned heart, representing love, faithfulness, and friendship; a traditional wedding ring. I deserved to die and I knew it.

I realized that I should repent, that now was the time to repent, to beg God's mercies before I died and stood before His throne for judgment. I pulled out the card that William had given me: Psyche's First Kiss. Inside he wrote that his life began on July 17, the day he had first kissed me in his mother's kitchen. I remembered William's insistent lips, his arms around me, his words of love. I didn't repent of that. I didn't repent of having my own apartment or of sleeping alone, spread-eagle across the white space. I wasn't sorry that I had let go of a narrow and exacting faith, that parsimonious and capricious dealer of joy. I turned the ring around and around. I opened my pretzels. I watched the movie without putting on the headphones, but I did not repent of anything.

After a long time, the sign went off. Finally, we began to fly over land. A young girl in front of me squealed in excitement.

"Look, I see America!" she said. She was unmistakably Irish. "Mother, I see America!"

At first I could only agree sadly that it was America. I longed for the plane to turn around in midair and take me away again, because I knew Eric was waiting at the airport in Tulsa. His letters had begged me to give our marriage another chance, to forget the divorce, and to consider more counseling. But our marriage was over. I had lit candles in churches all over Ireland, and I had not prayed for us when I'd had the chance.

I had not even prayed for myself. Those flickering flames in the heart of cold stone churches reminded me of what my life had been. Living for God had been consuming and intense, and the paradoxical excitement and security had satisfied me for a good long while. But afterward, when things had grown cold and silent, I was left with only ash. For a long time now, I had tried to stir the fire back again, my white finger drawing through what remained.

"I see Disneyland, Mother! Mickey Mouse!"

I looked at the little girl again, her fingers gripping the edge of the window, her face spilling over with eagerness, and this time I couldn't help smiling back.

If I still believed in signs, I would have thought I was looking at myself. I would have thought, My God. This is what you have finally become. Young.

ACKNOWLEDGMENTS

I owe a great debt to my teachers. Few of them realized how closely I was listening or how fervently I wanted to understand the new world they represented. They were my guides – I trained my eyes on them and followed them out. Thank you, Dr. Hodges, Dr. Jones, Dr. Vervack, Dr. Bennett, Dr. Burris, Dr. Candido, Dr. Guinn, Dr. Montgomery, and Dr. Van Sycoc. Thank you, dear John DuVal. I worshipped and adored my writing teachers: Skip Hays, Bill Harrison, Michael Heffernan, Joanne Meschery, PattiAnn Rogers, Jim Whitehead. Each one gave me renewed vision and courage to be a writer of integrity. I was an ungainly child in graduate school; at times my metamorphosis must have been as painful to others as it was to me. My friend and colleague David Koen was unceasingly patient as I struggled through years of sticky shell.

My children have loved me on both sides of the cross. I am grateful for their constant love and support, their sense of humor and irony, their sharp cynicism that sustains all of us these days. My mother and father have always been and remain near the center of my universe – I thank them for allowing me to give my version of the Allendale years. If grace is defined as unmerited favor, my sister has showered me with such grace. She encouraged me daily in the writing of this book.

I have depended upon Esmond Harmsworth's guidance and editorial advice from the most infant stages of my proposal. He has been everything an agent should be: enthusiastic, steady, available. Also, thanks to Lane Zachary for her input and help. My editor, Colin Dickerman, proved invaluable to me. His questions resulted in content I never anticipated writing. I am truly grateful for the way he shaped my book. Andrea Lynch read this manuscript carefully and commented insightfully.

Finally, thank you to my love, my husband. We were married on the millennium, nearly as long as I had waited for him, *Mon coeur entier,* forever.

Carolyn S. Briggs
Des Moines, Iowa
August 2001

A NOTE ON THE AUTHOR

Carolyn S. Briggs received her B.A. and M.F.A. from the University of Arkansas. Her short story "Incarnate" won the Heartland Short Fiction Prize and was published in *New Letters*. She currently teaches composition and creative writing in Des Moines, Iowa, where she lives with her husband David.

A NOTE ON THE TYPE

The text of this book is set in Linotype Sabon, named after the type founder, Jacques Sabon. It was designed by Jan Tschichold and jointly developed by Linotype, Monotype and Stempel, in response to a need for a typeface to be available in identical form for mechanical hot metal composition and hand composition using foundry type.

Tschichold based his design for Sabon roman on a fount engraved by Garamond, and Sabon italic on a fount by Granjon. It was first used in 1966 and has proved an enduring modern classic.